Entrepreneur
MAGAZINE'S

ULTIMATE
GUIDE TO

YouTube
FOR BUSINESS

- Produce low-cost, high impact videos
- Put your brand, product or service in front of **millions of potential viewers**
- Master the secrets of successful "YouTubers"

Ep
Entrepreneur
PRESS®

JASON R. RICH

Entrepreneur Press, Publisher
Cover Design: Andrew Welyczko
Production and Composition: Eliot House Productions

This publication is designed to provide accurate and authoritative information in regard to the
subject matter covered. It is sold with the understanding that the publisher is not engaged in
rendering legal, accounting or other professional services. If legal advice or other expert assistance is
required, the services of a competent professional person should be sought.

Library of Congress Cataloging-in-Publication Data
Rich, Jason.
      Ultimate guide to YouTube for business : produce low-cost, high-impact videos, put your
brand product or service in front of millions of potential viewers, master the secrets of successful
YouTubers/by Jason R. Rich..
      p.   cm.
      ISBN-13: 978-1-59918-510-1 (alk. paper)
      ISBN-10: 1-59918-510-5 (alk. paper)
      1. Internet marketing. 2. Webcasting. 3. YouTube (Firm) I. Title.
HF5415.1265.R518 2013
658.8'72—dc23   2013013765

Printed in the United States of America

17 16 15 14 13   10 9 8 7 6 5 4 3 2 1

This book is dedicated to my niece Natalie, and to everyone who has ever produced and shared a video on YouTube.

Contents

PART IV
Appendix

Acknowledgments

Thanks to Jillian McTigue and everyone at Entrepreneur Press, as well as Jeff Herman, who worked hard on this project. My gratitude also goes out to all the YouTube and online marketing experts who agreed to be interviewed for this book, and to the folks at YouTube/ Google who have created an extremely powerful and versatile video streaming service.

On YouTube, You or Your Business Is the Star!

So, you're a small-business operator or entrepreneur faced with the challenge of continuously growing your business, finding new customers or clients, retaining your existing customers, keeping costs down and discovering ways to out-maneuver your competition. You're not alone!

Perhaps you've already discovered that the internet can be a powerful and cost-effective sales, marketing, advertising, and promotional tool, and that online social networking services, such as Facebook, Twitter, Google+, Instagram, and LinkedIn, allow you to easily and informally reach existing and potential customers using text, photos, and other multimedia-based content.

There's yet another online resource you can inexpensively utilize: YouTube, the world's leading streaming video service.

Virtually anyone with a video camera or camcorder, webcam, smartphone, or tablet can record, edit, and publish videos online—about any topic whatsoever—and then share them with the world.

Millions of small businesses, entrepreneurs, and organizations have discovered innovative ways to create original YouTube content as a low-cost tool for building their brand, reputation, and image. It's a way to attract new customers, share information, showcase products and services, and share testimonials.

The *Ultimate Guide to YouTube for Business* will introduce you to just some of the ways small businesses are using YouTube as a business tool. And you'll discover proven strategies that can help you promote your company, brand, products, or services using high-definition video without spending a fortune. You'll learn the best approaches to planning, creating, editing, and then sharing your videos with the public, and how to leverage YouTube's tools to help achieve your objectives.

We'll also look at ways to identify your target audience and keep them top-of-mind as you create your videos. You'll learn how to incorporate YouTube with your overall virtual and real-world marketing efforts so that YouTube can complement and enhance what you may already be doing with a website, blog, Facebook page, or Twitter feed.

We'll look at pre-production, production, post-production, and promotional tasks required in order to create successful YouTube videos. And you'll learn from the experiences of successful YouTube and online marketing experts, who share their advice in exclusive interviews in the last section of this book.

YouTube has changed how people worldwide and from all walks of life experience multimedia content. Now, you can begin tapping this vast and ever-expanding audience in order to grow your own business. Don't worry; it's not too late to jump on the YouTube bandwagon!

Even if you're on a shoestring budget, you can quickly begin using YouTube without expensive video production equipment or Hollywood cinematography skills. Beyond what this book offers, what you'll need to be successful is creativity and a strong understanding of your target audience.

But first, let's take a look at what YouTube is, and focus on just some of the ways small businesses, entrepreneurs, and organizations working in virtually any industry are already utilizing YouTube. That's the focus of Chapter 1, "Using YouTube as a Promotional and Marketing Tool."

Part I

Using YouTube to Market and Promote Your Business

These first seven chapters will focus on YouTube basics for business: how to get started; ways to use YouTube as a marketing and promotional platform; how to plan and promote videos and interact with customers, fans and viewers; and how to monetize your videos—especially useful for consultants and freelancers.

Using YouTube as a Promotional and Marketing Tool

IN THIS CHAPTER
- An introduction to YouTube and how businesses can leverage it
- Developing a YouTube strategy and integrating it into your overall online marketing strategy
- Identifying your audience and its needs
- Developing realistic expectations and goals
- What you need to get started

To be competitive, it's virtually mandatory for a business in almost any industry to tap the power of the internet and online social media. YouTube, the popular video-streaming service and world's second most frequently used search engine, can and should be a powerful part of your overall marketing and promotional strategy. It can be implemented using almost any computer or internet-enabled device, from almost anywhere, 24 hours per day, seven days per week, 365 days per year.

In 2011, YouTube videos received more than 1 trillion views, which is equivalent to 140 separate video views for every person living on the planet. More than 72 hours' worth of new and original video content is uploaded every minute of every day, attracting a truly global audience. At least 70 percent of YouTube users are from outside the United States.

Every week, more than 100 million people click on a "Share" button and tell their online friends about a YouTube video via Twitter, Facebook, Google+ and other social media. Every day, the equivalent of more than 500 years' worth of YouTube videos are watched on Facebook alone; every minute, more than 700 individual videos are shared via Twitter.

Businesses utilize YouTube in myriad ways, including simply buying ads—from text-based and display ads that link to websites, to video messages that resemble 10-, 15-, 30-, and 60-second TV commercials. In many instances, paid advertising on YouTube is one of the most affordable and effective advertising options available on the internet.

Many businesses also produce and publish their own YouTube videos as part of their overall online marketing and promotional strategy, either by hiring a video production company or doing it themselves.

As a YouTube content provider, you're encouraged to create and maintain your own YouTube channel, which can give you the opportunity to share in advertising revenue that's generated when optional ads are shown in conjunction with your original video content on your YouTube channel. In fact, many people have actually developed a paying career producing videos for YouTube, which then generate revenue by attracting large audiences of viewers. These people are often referred to as "online personalities" or YouTubers. When it comes to producing YouTube content, take an extremely creative approach in order to set yourself apart from your competition, capture your target audience's attention, and build their loyalty. Using original video to do this is the focus of *Ultimate Guide to YouTube for Business*.

FIRST, LET'S GET ACQUAINTED WITH YOUTUBE

YouTube's launch in early 2005 changed forever how people use the internet. YouTube allows for everyday people, entertainers, business operators, and entrepreneurs from all walks of life to produce, upload, and share original videos, for free, and build a potentially global audience for them. YouTube can also be used effectively to target a regionalized audience.

Now, anyone with even the most basic of video cameras can participate as a content producer. YouTube makes it extremely easy for non-technologically-savvy web surfers to use their computer or most other internet-enabled devices to quickly find and watch videos. Today, YouTube attracts more than 800 million unique users per month. Since 2005, these people have watched more than 4 billion hours' worth of YouTube videos. These days, content you'll find on YouTube is as diverse as the people who create the videos. Virtually every topic imaginable is covered. When people want to find information on the web, they often turn directly to YouTube's search feature, as opposed to a search engine such as Yahoo! or Google, to find exactly what they're looking for.

MAKING YOUTUBE WORK FOR YOUR BUSINESS

As a small-business operator, you have vast opportunities with YouTube, limited by your ingenuity, creativity, the time you invest, and to a much lesser extent, your video production and promotional budget. Later in this book, we'll explore just some of the ways small-business operators are utilizing YouTube as a cost-effective sales, marketing, promotions, and advertising tool. Just about any entrepreneur or business can benefit from utilizing YouTube as a cost-effective way to entertain, inform, educate, or rally your audience/customers (or potential customers) to action. To use this online-based marketing and promotional tool to its utmost potential, however, you need to determine:

- What YouTube is capable of and how it can be used
- Your core message and how YouTube videos can be utilized with your other online marketing and promotional efforts
- Your target audience and what they're interested in
- The best way to use video to present your core message

Exploring YouTube

Before you begin developing, shooting, editing, and uploading videos, however, start by establishing a YouTube account for yourself or your business—it's free. At the same time, you should also begin exploring the service and seeing firsthand what's possible.

When you begin exploring YouTube, seek out videos that are of interest to you and that relate to your business or industry. Beyond just watching free videos, invest the time to become an active part of the YouTube community by "liking" videos, posting comments, and sharing videos with your online friends. Find videos already available on YouTube that cater to your target audience, and then consider ways you can create content that will further benefit your intended audience (your potential or existing customers).

All of the videos published on YouTube are easily searchable using keywords and search phrases. You can also seek out videos by category, the channel on which they're offered, and by using the popularity charts and "trending topics" that YouTube publishes, and that are continuously updated. It's also possible to link your Facebook, Google+, and Twitter accounts to your YouTube account and discover what your online friends are watching on YouTube.

As you begin to consider who your target audience will be for your YouTube videos, consider that traffic on YouTube from mobile device users tripled in 2011. Thus, more than 20 percent of the people who access YouTube to watch videos now do it from some type of wireless mobile device. So when you start producing and sharing your own videos, you'll want to avoid production elements that will be hard to read on a small screen, such as a lot of text. Download the official YouTube app for your tablet and smartphone to experience small-screen viewing.

Then, when you're ready, follow the directions offered within Chapter 4, "How to Start Your Own YouTube Channel," in order to establish a YouTube channel for you or your business. This is the online-based forum you'll use to upload, showcase, and share your own video productions via YouTube.

DEVELOP YOUR STRATEGY

If you're an entrepreneur or business operator, as you explore the YouTube service and check out how your competition is already tapping the power and capabilities of this service, you'll discover it's possible to create, produce, and publish videos that can help to:

- Boost your company's brand awareness and enhance its credibility
- Introduce details about a new product or service
- Advertise an existing product or service
- Share details about your company and what it offers with a local, regional, national or international audience
- Generate new leads for your sales team
- Teach potential customers about the benefits of your product(s) or service(s), and explain how to best use them through demonstrations, thus helping to remove buyer objections
- Share customer endorsements or testimonials with potential customers
- Compare your product/service with what the competition offers
- Tell your company's story—its history, philosophy, and goals
- Provide support for real-world or online-based retail promotions or contests
- Share highlights of a particular event with customers/clients or others who couldn't attend in person
- Increase direct sales for whatever your business sells. Someone could watch a video, click on an embedded link, and then place an order from your ecommerce website or call a toll-free order line, for example.
- Expand and enhance your company's product or customer support
- Enhance your company's internal employee training

As you consider how other businesses like your own are already using YouTube, consider some of the ways you can begin using this service to share original video content with your intended audience. Remember, you'll want to study what's already offered on YouTube carefully, pinpoint a niche, and then figure out who your target audience will be. Only then can you begin writing, producing, and publishing videos that have the potential of going viral and gaining the popularity you'll need to generate the online audience you desire. Later in Part III, you'll read interviews with small-business operators and online marketing experts who discuss how YouTube can be used by all sorts of small businesses and entrepreneurs, whether you're promoting a product, service, company, or an individual.

Develop Your Core Message

With a specific goal or set of goals in mind, the next step is to draft a core message that you want to consistently convey through your videos to your audience. This message should be consistent with the existing marketing and advertising messages that you've already developed for other forms of media.

The message you develop should be carefully crafted for its intended audience, short, memorable, and easily understandable. Now, once you have brainstormed your core message and the goal(s) for your YouTube online presence, start thinking about all of the ways you can present that message, via your individual YouTube videos, again focusing on originality, memorability, and consistency. Depending on the approach you take with your videos, you'll want to keep them short (between one and three minutes in length), and stay on-point with your messaging. YouTube viewers have very short attention spans, so it's important to capture someone's attention quickly and only expect to hold it for a short period of time.

Determine how you want your audience to react as they watch your video(s), or after watching them. For example, do you want people watching your videos to visit your company's website and place an order, or do you want them to share your message with their own online friends? Think about how you'll rally your viewers to do whatever it is you'd like them to do. This will be your call to action.

Always remember, however, that your videos should help to convey your core message, be synergistic with your company's other online activity, and be aimed at achieving your overall goals or objectives.

MAKING YOUTUBE A PART OF YOUR ONLINE MARKETING STRATEGY

When it comes to your online activity as a business operator or entrepreneur, everything you do in cyberspace should be synergistic, focused on the same core message, and be fully integrated. In other words, use your Facebook page and Twitter feed, for example, to promote your YouTube videos, while using your YouTube videos to drive traffic to your website, blog, Facebook page, or Twitter feed. At the same time, your videos should drive home your core message and call to action.

How you approach this online synergy can be blatant and in your face, or you can take an extremely subtle approach, based on your audience makeup and overall objectives. We'll explore this concept in greater detail within Chapter 6, "Promoting Your YouTube Videos."

For now, however, as you learn more about what's possible using YouTube, consider what you're already doing in cyberspace and in the real world, and also figure out what you could be doing using services like Facebook, Google+, Twitter, LinkedIn, Pinterest, Instagram, and others in conjunction with what you plan to do on YouTube. Think synergy!

Synergy also refers to how you communicate your message. Fonts, color schemes, specific wording, music, sound effects, logos, the use of slogans, and other elements that appear within your YouTube videos should also be consistent with what your audience will see on your website, within your blog, on your Facebook page, by reading your Twitter feed, and as they explore your online presence on other social networking services.

Identify with Your Audience and Discover What It Wants or Needs

Using YouTube requires that you take a dual approach when writing, developing, producing, editing, publishing, and then promoting your videos. First, focus on your own wants, needs, and objectives. Figure out how to use your YouTube Channel, your individual videos, and your overall online activity to achieve those objectives.

Then, put yourself in your intended audience's shoes and consider absolutely every aspect of your video productions and the focus of your overall YouTube Channel, as well as your other online activity, from their perspective.

As someone who is a member of your target audience, from their perspective, ask yourself:

- Why should they watch your video(s)?
- What is it within your video(s) that will appeal directly to them?
- What will they get out of watching your videos?
- How will watching your videos address their wants and/or needs?
- How will your videos solve their problems, help them overcome their challenges, save them time, save them money, and/or provide them with information that they deem valuable or important?

- Why should they watch your video, as opposed to one of the countless others on YouTube that cover the same material? How is your approach different and more beneficial to your audience?
- What will inspire the viewer to take whatever call to action you include within your videos?

Only by truly defining your audience and then understanding it can you answer the questions posed in this section. Do your market research. Understand your product/ service. Learn as much as you possibly can about your intended audience, and then use your videos to reach it with what you deem to be the perfect message.

Choose the Best Type of Video Content to Appeal to Your Audience

There are very few limitations when it comes to producing and presenting original video content on YouTube. It's your job to tap your creativity and present your message and call to action in a way that works toward achieving your goals using what's at your disposal. As you brainstorm the concepts for your videos, keep in mind, you can utilize:

- Live-action video (video of people, places, or things)
- Graphic titles (text) that can be stationary on the screen or animated
- Voice-overs (a voice from someone who isn't seen, but who can be heard speaking)
- Music and sound effects
- Animated graphic sequences
- Animated or still charts and graphs
- Visual special effects
- Interactive hyperlinks embedded in videos (called Annotations)

With this in mind, what is the best way to present your message to your intended (target) audience? What approach will they understand and relate to the best? Remember, your YouTube audience's attention span will be short. It's essential that you capture someone's attention very quickly (within the first few seconds of your video), and then present your video and your message in the shortest time possible (within just a few minutes).

In addition to competing with all of the other videos available on YouTube, which for your audience are always just a mouse click or screen tap away, the content and quality of your videos need to meet or exceed your audience's expectations from a production standpoint. Thus, if you're planning to produce your own videos inhouse, but don't have the resources and know-how to produce a slick, animated sequence that you envision including in your videos, don't instead settle and use an amateurish or cheesy-looking animated sequence. Instead, choose an alternative way to communicate your message that will look professional and help you build, protect, and maintain your company's online image and reputation.

There is a wide range of software and online-based tools that can help you create and produce extremely professional-looking graphics, animations, and other production elements that can then be incorporated into your videos. Most of these tools, however, require some level of knowledge and skill to use properly.

You'll learn about just some of these tools, such as Apple's iMovie (www.apple.com/ ilife/imovie), Apple's Final Cut Pro X (www.apple.com/finalcutpro), Microsoft Movie Maker (http://windows.microsoft.com/en-US/windows-live/movie-maker-get-started), Adobe's Creative Suite 6 Production Premium (www.adobe.com/products/creativesuite/ production.html) package and Microsoft PowerPoint (http://office.microsoft.com/ en-us/powerpoint), from Chapter 10, "Filming YouTube Videos," and Chapter 11, "Editing Your YouTube Videos."

However, it's up to you to invest the time needed to learn how to effectively use these and other tools, and not simply clutter your videos with an overload of eye candy or bells and whistles that will wind up distracting or annoying your target audience.

It's very rare that your content will be so compelling or perceived as so important or valuable to your audience that they'll forgive amateurish production quality and sit through a poorly produced video. Instead, they'll simply watch another video or exit out of YouTube altogether and seek out the information they are looking for elsewhere—from your competition's website or Facebook page, for example.

At least initially, as your company begins to develop its online marketing and promotional strategy—especially if you want to include video in that plan—consider hiring an independent video production company that can help you write, produce, edit, and promote YouTube videos that will cater to your intended audience and achieve your goals. Hiring professionals can help you avoid costly and potentially embarrassing mistakes, plus help you generate the desired results much faster and with the least amount of confusion or frustration.

DEVELOPING REALISTIC GOALS AND EXPECTATIONS

Yes, publishing videos on YouTube is free, but it will require a financial investment to produce the videos, whether you do it yourself or hire someone else to do it.

And even if you produce an absolutely amazing video, that's worthy of an Academy Award, simply putting it on YouTube won't guarantee you an audience. If all you do is publish your videos on YouTube and then let them sit there, nobody is going to actually see your productions. It is necessary for you to heavily promote them.

Keep in mind, having your video go viral and be seen by millions of people would be nice, but to realistically achieve your company's online goals, this probably isn't necessary. Instead, if you carefully target your videos to a specific niche audience—your potential or current customers—you can achieve the desired results even if your videos receive just a few hundred or a few thousand views.

With more than 1 billion views as of January 2013, the official *Gangnam Style* music video by Psy is an example of a video that's gone truly viral—with no paid advertising support whatsoever. It's an example of a quirky and original video that has captured the attention of a grass-roots audience. For a video to ultimately go vital, it must begin to get traction online via word-of-mouth, and then somehow pique the interest of a major traditional media outlet so that it gets mainstream attention. This attention then drives more traffic to the video, fueling its popularity until it ultimately skyrockets.

If you have visions of producing videos that go viral or that attract vast audiences, that will require you to make a significant time and financial investment in order to promote your videos and your YouTube Channel on an ongoing basis, after the videos are produced and published online. What you'll soon discover is that videos that have gone viral are often a result of an accident, pure luck, or a fluke, not careful planning.

Realistically, for videos produced and published by mainstream companies, the popularity of these videos is typically driven by extensive promotional efforts by the company itself, using both online and real-world resources. With this fact in mind, it's important to develop very realistic expectations. Whatever time, money, and resources you invest in the production of your videos, this is only the beginning.

In order to gain viewers for your videos and generate a consistently growing audience, you will need to invest time, effort, and potentially money to promote your productions and your YouTube Channel on an ongoing basis. Only if you achieve your objectives within the content of the videos themselves, and then promote them properly and consistently to the right target audience, will you achieve your overall goals related to using YouTube as a marketing and promotional tool for yourself, your company, and/or its products or services.

Figure Out What You'll Need to Get Started

Based on your objectives, it's possible to begin producing quality YouTube videos on a tight budget, and then, over time, upgrade your equipment and tools in order to achieve more professional-quality production results. However, step one is to create a YouTube Channel for your company, customize the look of the channel's page, and then populate the channel with original video content. It all starts by visiting www.YouTube.com, clicking on the "Sign In" button, and then clicking on the "Create An Account" button.

In later chapters, you'll learn how to pinpoint some of the key video production equipment you'll need, which will include a video camera that's capable of shooting

1080p HD resolution video. You'll also need to contend with lighting and sound quality considerations in order to ensure good enough production quality that will satisfy your audience's expectations.

What you'll need to consider during the pre-production (brainstorming and preparation), production (filming), and post production (editing) phases of the process will all be covered within Chapter 10, "Filming YouTube Videos." Once again, the key to success during each of these phases is to stay on message as you cater to the wants, needs, and expectations of your intended audience, while also staying within your budgetary limitations.

Specialized Skills That May Be Required

As you read each chapter of *Ultimate Guide to YouTube for Business*, the focus will be on one or more aspects relating to the pre-production, production, post production, publishing, and promotional phases of creating YouTube videos. While you'll no doubt face many challenges as you embark on this project, you also have the opportunity to be creative and have fun as you discover cutting-edge and innovative ways of growing and/ or promoting your business.

Like so many things, producing semi-professional or professional quality videos requires that you learn a handful of different skills, all of which will ultimately be used together during the pre-production, production, post-production, and publishing phases. For starters, you'll need to become proficient at brainstorming unique ideas for videos, and then figure out how you'll take your raw ideas and transform them into video productions that achieve their goals. To do this, you'll need to master skills such as:

- Storyboarding and scripting (writing the scripts) for your productions
- Video camera operation
- Set design or location scouting
- Lighting
- Sound recording and mixing
- Managing a cast (people who will appear in your videos) and crew (people who will help shoot and edit your videos)
- Dealing with hair, makeup, and wardrobe considerations for your "cast" (the people appearing in your videos), if applicable
- Video editing
- Managing production resources and budgets
- Creating and incorporating special effects and titles into your videos
- Incorporating music and sound effects in your videos during post production

- Using YouTube's tools for uploading and publishing your videos, and then managing your YouTube Channel
- Promoting your videos in the real world and in cyberspace to build an audience for your videos
- Interacting with your audience on an ongoing basis

At least initially, you probably won't have all of the skills, knowledge, and experience needed to juggle all of the responsibilities that will be required of you as a YouTube video producer. Thus, you have several options. First, seek out friends, coworkers, employees, or relatives who might be able to somehow contribute to your productions and lend their expertise. Another option is to hire freelance professionals to help you. You can also utilize the free online tutorials offered by YouTube by clicking on the Help option that's constantly displayed near the bottom of the page when using the YouTube service.

Professional writers, camera operators, production crew, hair stylists, makeup artists, lighting experts, sound engineers, musicians, animators, illustrators, video editors, and people who are experts when it comes to using online social networking sites for marketing and promotional purposes, for example, can all be hired on a freelance, per-hour or per-project basis.

Use Craigslist.org, or a service like Elance.com, to help you find people with the experience and skill set you need to round out your production crew. If you need specialized on-camera or voice-over talent for your productions, you should also contact local talent agencies or modeling agencies, or hold an open casting call by publishing an audition notice on Craigslist.org or another show-business-related website that caters to your geographic area.

Another excellent and low-cost (sometimes free) resource when it comes to putting together a video production crew that has specialized and needed skills is to seek out college interns from a local college or university. College students who are majoring in video production, writing, video editing, computer animation, lighting, sound engineering, fashion, cosmetology or marketing, for example, will jump at the opportunity to intern for your company and get real-world, hands-on experience working on a project that they can later showcase on a resume, within a portfolio, or as part of a demo reel.

What's great about using college interns with specialized majors is that they're typically very familiar with the latest trends, technologies, and tools for producing semi-professional or professional quality videos, and they're willing to work for little or no money. To find college interns, contact the career counselor or internship coordinator at a local college or university and discuss your needs. With permission, you can also post "help wanted" fliers on bulletin boards on college campuses, or publish internship opportunities online (on The Monster Board, http://hiring.monster.com, for example).

To achieve the best results right from the start, don't try to cut corners and just "wing it" when it comes to producing your videos, especially if your productions will represent your company and/or its products/services and will have the ability to enhance or tarnish your company's overall image and reputation. Instead, gather a production crew that together has the skills, knowledge, experience, and creative talent you and your company will need to achieve your overall objectives.

Ten Ways People, Companies, and Organizations Are Successfully Using YouTube

IN THIS CHAPTER

- Learning from popular videos
- What it costs to get started
- Ten ways businesses use YouTube

This chapter offers a general overview of ten ways your business or organization can use YouTube as a sales, marketing, and/or promotional tool. One important concept to understand right from the start is that there are millions upon millions of individual videos already posted on YouTube, with many more being added each and every day. Making your video(s) stand out and get attention will probably be the biggest challenge you face.

Just because you post a video on YouTube, this does not guarantee it will quickly go viral and be seen by millions of viewers. It's important to have realistic expectations, but know that there is a wide range of things you can do, either for free or inexpensively, to promote your videos and build an audience for them. You'll learn about several of these techniques within Chapter 5, "Interacting With Viewers and Subscribers," as well as Chapter 6, "Promoting Your YouTube Videos."

While some YouTubers have established a large audience on YouTube and are able to generate a respectable and ongoing income as a YouTube Partner—by displaying other company's ads in conjunction with their videos—many traditional businesses, entrepreneurs, and online business operators, for example, have discovered other ways to use YouTube as a powerful, low-cost marketing, advertising, and promotional tool that can generate new customers and sales in other direct and indirect ways.

YouTube videos can also be used effectively to demonstrate products, provide how-to or educational information pertaining to a product or service, showcase customer testimonials, and/or to help establish and build a company's brand and online reputation. One way small businesses are able to use YouTube videos very effectively is to "personalize" their business by introducing key personnel, and to tell the company's story in a way that captures the attention of their potential and existing customers.

Regardless of how you decide to use YouTube videos, make sure the videos you create are well produced, short, to the point, and highly engaging. The content needs to be easy to understand and well organized. Consider taking advantage of YouTube Annotations, for example, to add subtitles, links, and other interactive elements to your videos, as appropriate. YouTube Annotations are online tools you can use after uploading a video to incorporate active hyperlinks to lead viewers to your company's website, blog, Facebook page, or to other YouTube videos.

SEE WHAT'S CURRENTLY POPULAR ON YOUTUBE

YouTube constantly monitors what videos people are watching, and maintains ever-changing charts of top videos in various categories. As you prepare to create your own videos for YouTube, invest some time in watching other videos to see what works and what's popular. To view YouTube's current most-watched videos, visit www.youtube.com/charts.

From these charts, you can view what's popular today, this week, or this month, plus see a listing of the all-time most popular videos based on a variety of criteria. You can see charts compiled based on the "Most Viewed" videos (in standard or HD), as well as the "Most Discussed," "Most Liked" or "Most Favorited" videos. It's possible to view charts based on videos from "All Categories," or see popular videos from a particular category, such as "Comedy," "How To & Style," "People & Blogs," "Sports," or "Travel & Events," for example.

Many of the all-time most viewed videos on YouTube are actually music videos from well-known recording artists and bands, such as Justin Bieber, Jennifer Lopez, Eminem, and Lady Gaga. Some of these videos have received more than 776 million views each. However, there are many other types of popular videos that use humor or some type of original content in order to capture the attention of viewers.

Depending on what your goals are for using YouTube and the type(s) of videos you plan to produce, focus on watching similar videos that have already become popular to discover what works well and what YouTube audiences are responding favorably to. In addition to studying the content of other videos, focus on their production quality, use of music or sound, as well as how special effects and YouTube Annotations are being utilized in a positive way.

Simply studying other popular YouTube videos can be highly educational and useful when it comes to creating your own videos. You can also discover how other people, bands, artists, performers, entrepreneurs, traditional business operators, and online business operators, for example, are using YouTube to their advantage, and how they're integrating YouTube videos into their overall online presence and marketing strategy.

As you're brainstorming concepts for your own videos, planning and then producing them, keep in mind your audience's short attention span. Most people do not access YouTube to watch long-form programming. Even if your video is highly entertaining and engaging, keep it short (between 30 seconds and five minutes) and to the point. If you believe your video concept needs to be longer, consider breaking it up into a series of short videos that appear on the same YouTube Channel and that can be linked together using the tools available with YouTube Annotations.

Keep in mind, producing multiple short videos, as opposed to one long one, will also work to your advantage when it comes to search engine rankings and optimization (SEO), because each video will be listed separately when someone uses YouTube's search feature or Google.

Remember, simply producing and publishing a video on your custom YouTube channel is only the first step. If you want your video to achieve its objectives, attract an audience, and be seen by the masses, you'll need to invest considerable time and resources to promote your videos and your YouTube channel. While you'll learn more about promoting your videos later, as you're brainstorming ideas for your videos, consider what your target audience will want and appreciate, and then stay focused.

Also, as you're brainstorming ideas for your own YouTube videos, especially if you're a small-business operator, focus on three primary objectives: entertain, educate, and/or inform.

The YouTube "Trends" blog is written by Google and focuses on what videos are currently trending (the most popular) on the YouTube service. To read this insightful blog, visit http://youtube-trends.blogspot.com.

THE COSTS ASSOCIATED WITH USING YOUTUBE

YouTube itself is a free service, but, depending on the production quality you're striving for, there are costs associated with producing and editing professional quality videos, and there can be costs associated with marketing and promoting your videos—both online and in the real world.

Chapter 6, "Promoting Your YouTube Videos," discusses some of the potential costs you may encounter when promoting your videos and building an audience for them. Chapter 8, "The Equipment You'll Need," and Chapter 9, "Selecting the Right Video Camera," both explore some of the costs associated with producing and editing professional-quality videos.

That being said, plenty of individuals have used nothing more than the camera that's built into their computer or smartphone to film videos that they upload to YouTube, and some of these videos have become as popular, if not more popular, than videos that cost hundreds or even tens of thousands of dollars to produce.

The quality of your videos—both from a content and production quality standpoint—should cater to your target audience's expectations and demands. For example, if your business is using YouTube to promote a product, your audience will expect a professional-quality video that's in focus, shot in HD, and that's well lit and has good quality sound. Achieving these results will mean investing in higher-end equipment and editing tools.

So, while actually using YouTube will cost you nothing, to achieve professional-quality results, you will most likely need to pay for video equipment, lighting, sound equipment, editing tools, props, sets (backgrounds), license music and/or sound effects, and acquire other necessary equipment related to the production and editing of your videos. How to develop a realistic budget, based on your unique needs, will be covered within Chapter 8, "The Equipment You'll Need," and within Chapter 10, "Filming YouTube Videos."

TEN WAYS YOU CAN UTILIZE YOUTUBE TO REACH YOUR INTENDED AUDIENCE

Everyone who uses YouTube to somehow promote themselves, their company, a band, product, service, or organization; to share information; or just provide entertainment to their audience has their own goals. The following is information about ten popular ways YouTube can be used as part of your overall online strategy to achieve your company's particular goals.

Based on your own creativity, as well as the new features and functionality that are constantly being added to YouTube and the ever-more advanced tools available for shooting and editing video, you'll probably come up with many ways YouTube can help you reach your intended audience in a cost-effective way.

Promote Yourself as an Online Personality and Entertain Your Audience

YouTube offers the ultimate platform that allows you to turn a video camera or webcam onto yourself and to say or do just about anything that you believe will capture an audience's attention. While there are a few limits, on YouTube, few topics are taboo. You'll find these limitations by reading the YouTube Community Guidelines (www.youtube.com/t/community_guidelines).

One strategy small businesses use effectively to personalize their brand and build a rapport with the audience is to use YouTube videos to introduce their company's leaders and position these people as spokespeople who appear in the videos.

That being said, millions of people, while sitting in the comfort of their own bedrooms, basements, backyards, or offices, have used YouTube as a platform (a virtual soap box) to communicate with whoever will listen and watch. Out of all the people who post their rants and exploits online, some stand out and ultimately break out as online personalities who wind up with thousands or even millions of dedicated viewers (and subscribers). This is often a result of one or more of their videos somehow going viral.

Without the backing of a TV network, movie studio, record label, publicists, tabloid coverage, or red-carpet appearances, many YouTubers have become vastly popular online celebrities as a result of their videos—and for a few, this has escalated them into mainstream stardom. Meanwhile, some company spokespeople have achieved celebrity status as a result of starring in YouTube videos to promote themselves, their products, and/or their companies.

Whether you have something to say, a song to sing, a poem to recite, a joke to tell, a dance to perform, information to convey, knowledge or wisdom to share, or simply want to rant about absolutely nothing important, YouTube offers a forum, as well as a potential global audience. Often, the people being featured in these types of videos wind up becoming popular not necessarily because of the content of their videos, but because of their personalities. So, if you're a small-business owner with a big personality, consider starring in your own YouTube videos in an effort to help build your company's brand and promote its message.

If your videos are able to capture attention, strike a nerve, inform, or entertain, you have a personality that somehow stands out, and you're not afraid to share it with the world via YouTube, you too can become an online personality. Featuring actual leaders of your company can help to personalize your business and build up its credibility. Your spokesperson can demonstrate products, speak authoritatively, and boost your company's brand recognition and reputation.

For your business, one way you can utilize YouTube to promote your products is to put them in the hands of already popular YouTubers and get them to talk to their established audiences about or showcase your offerings within their videos,. As you research who the popular YouTubers are that cater to the audience you're trying to reach, you'll find their contact information on their respective YouTube channel pages. Be willing to send free product samples to the YouTubers you want to target, and request nicely that they showcase what you send in their future video(s).

You'll discover that the subscribers (fans) who follow well-established YouTubers are extremely loyal to those people. So, when that person raves about your product, their subscribers and viewers will pay attention and consider it a positive endorsement.

In essence, just like a Hollywood celebrity, professional athlete, or major recording artist, an online personality or a company that's featuring itself, its spokespeople, and/or its products on YouTube is doing so to build a recognizable brand that they can cultivate on a grass-roots level using YouTube and other online social networking sites, including Facebook, Twitter, Google+, Tumbler, and Instagram. Gaining online popularity on YouTube ultimately leads to a vast and dedicated base of subscribers.

It's important to understand that while there are many YouTubers (who become YouTube Partners) who earn a respectable income from their exploits online, few are able to cross over and achieve mainstream fame and fortune in the real world's entertainment industry, unless they have a remarkable and highly marketable real world talent.

There are some success stories that involve a YouTuber being "discovered" online and winding up starring on a TV show or in movies, or who land a major record deal, for example, but these successes are few and far between.

On the other hand, YouTube offers the perfect platform to share your talent with your followers and help you build an audience, whether you're an up-and-coming singer, comedian, artist, or dancer, for example.

Many small-business operators have also found success using YouTube to feature themselves within their videos in an effort to tell their story, build their brand, educate and inform people about their products, or to demonstrate their products. When business operators themselves appear within their videos, these people are able to reach out and build a virtual relationship with their customers or potential customers in a way that's never before been possible.

Share Your Knowledge, Commentary, or "How-to" Information

One reason why YouTube has become so popular is that in addition to watching countless hours of entertaining videos, you can quickly find informative and easy-to-understand how-to videos about absolutely any topic imaginable.

If you have questions about how to do something, enter it into the "Search" box while accessing YouTube, and chances are you'll find at least a handful of experts providing free answers that you need, day or night.

In addition to well-known experts sharing their know-how and advice in the form of YouTube videos, you'll find everyday people sharing their own knowledge, expertise, and personal passion about a wide range of topics.

At the same time, you'll discover many people on YouTube sharing their own opinions and commentary about just about anything and everything, from politics to the weather. If you're a business operator, chances are you have expertise that other people could easily benefit from. One way to share this knowledge is to present it in the form of videos on YouTube, and in the process, help to build your own personal brand, as well as your company or product's brand awareness.

YouTube offers an informal, yet powerful way to communicate directly with your customers, in your own words, in a forum that gives you absolute control over the content. Using a bit of creativity, chances are you'll come up with a handful of ideas about how your business could benefit from communicating directly with its customers (or potential customers) using YouTube. For example, you could create a product demonstration or product comparison video. Other options might be to showcase customer testimonials within a video, or to create a how-to video that explains how to operate or use your product/service.

Many companies have dramatically cut costs associated with offering telephone technical support by supplementing printed product manuals and product assembly instructions (which people hate to read and find difficult to understand) with informative how-to videos that are highly engaging. Within Chapter 13, "Learn From Business Owners and Entrepreneurs," you'll read about Big Shot Bikes (www.bigshotbikes.com), which uses YouTube to showcase promotional videos as well as instructional videos related to its bicycles.

Introduce a New Product or Service and Direct People to Your Online Store

Especially if you're operating an online-based business, or there's an online component to your traditional retail business, showcasing products on YouTube is a low-cost, yet highly effective way to demonstrate products to your customers, showcase features, and explain how to best use a product. In addition to showcasing a product's features or functions, you can use YouTube videos to answer commonly asked questions.

If you opt to use YouTube to showcase your products, be sure that the production quality of your videos is professional and that what your (potential) customers see will help to boost your company's brand, credibility, and reputation. Trying to demonstrate a top-quality product using a poorly produced or blurry video with bad lighting and inferior sound is counterproductive and can hurt how a (potential) customer perceives your business and what it offers. As you'll discover later, it's possible to produce professional-quality videos on a low budget that will allow you to best showcase your products in a way that will capture the attention of (potential) customers in a positive way, while enhancing your overall brand.

Keep in mind, people who use YouTube do not want to watch blatant commercials for your products or services. Consumers are already bombarded with advertising in their everyday lives. While your videos can certainly promote a product or service, and build awareness or demand for it, definitely take a soft-sell approach that's entertaining as well as informative.

Especially if you're operating an online store or are able to take orders for your product online, using product demonstration videos on YouTube and on your actual website is a lot more compelling than even the best product photography. Ideally, consider offering a variety of professionally shot product photos on your website, plus a short product demonstration video that offers top-notch production value and an opportunity for your (potential) customers to see the product in action. These videos can be embedded in your website and linked from your YouTube channel (where the videos are hosted for free).

Teach People How to Use a Product or Service

Many businesses have discovered that producing YouTube videos as an instructional tool can help improve customer loyalty, reduce returns, and allow a business to enhance its customer service efforts without putting a strain on resources.

How-to videos for a product offer a different approach than a product demo, yet both approaches can benefit businesses looking to promote and sell products. While a how-to video is designed to teach someone how to do something, a product demo simply showcases a product's features or functions and gives the viewer a chance to see a product in action. Either type of video can be used as part of a business-to-consumer or business-to-business sales and marketing strategy.

Instructional videos can help to reduce incoming customer service and support calls. You can produce instructional videos to teach people how to assemble and/or use a product, for example, plus help customers easily discover the true potential of a product, while eliminating their potential frustration.

Whether someone has already purchased your company's product or they're on the cusp of making that all-important purchase decision, offering informative, insightful, easy-to-understand, and entertaining videos about your products is a viable way to share information, as well as assembly, installation, and/or how-to tips that your customers will perceive as valuable. Your videos can also be used to highlight lesser-known features of or uses for a product that your customers might not otherwise consider.

Many consumers are intimidated by difficult-to-read printed manuals or instruction booklets. Offering free YouTube videos that help people best utilize your product also demonstrates a loyalty to your customers. These videos can be promoted on your company's website, within its blog or Facebook page, using Twitter, on the product's packaging, and/or within the product's manual.

Through your YouTube videos, you can also encourage customers to post comments and interact with each other in order to create a close-knit virtual community comprised of people who use and love your products. Encouraging customers to support each other in a moderated online environment (your branded and customized YouTube channel) can help to reduce incoming customer service and technical support calls, as well as product returns.

Use this type of video as an opportunity to share simple solutions to common problems people have that relate to your product or communicate ways people can avoid pitfalls or problems using what you sell.

Of course, you always want to put positive spin on these videos in terms of the content and the approach you take. For example, instead of "overcoming problems," you want to stress "how to fully utilize" a product or its features.

When posting videos on your YouTube channel, be sure to select the option that allows you, the channel's operator, to approve all viewer comments before they're publicly posted. Then, encourage your customers to share their own ideas and testimonials.

Share Video Footage of Business Presentations You've Given

As a business leader or expert in your field, if you've presented a lecture, workshop, or some type of presentation, consider uploading the video footage of it to YouTube for your customers, clients, and the general public. This will help establish you as an expert or authority, allow you to convey valuable information to potential customers and clients, plus help you build awareness of you and your company.

This information can be supplemented with an animated and narrated digital slide (PowerPoint) presentation that you post on your YouTube channel, and/or include a recorded one-on-one interview with you talking about something in which your (potential) customers or clients would be interested.

Provide Background Information About Your Company and Tell Its Story

Every company has a story to tell, as do the founders or current leaders of that business. By telling your story, chances are you'll be able to enhance your customer loyalty and brand awareness, while also educating the public about what your company does and its core philosophies.

Any type of "behind-the-scenes" videos can also be useful. For example, you can produce and publish a video that focuses on how your product(s) are actually made, provide a tour of your company, plus introduce some of the people who work at your company within the video(s).

Showcase Customer Testimonials

If you have been in business for a while and have earned the respect of many loyal customers or clients, using a YouTube video to showcase some of these people or companies providing real testimonials for your products/service can be a highly effective and low-cost promotional and sales tool.

Present a Call to Action

Because YouTube allows you to speak directly to your audience, you can use your videos as a platform to raise awareness about a particular issue or encourage your viewers to take a specific action after watching your video. A video's call to action is a request that the people watching your videos take an immediate action—such as to visit your website, "Like" the video, subscribe to your YouTube channel, call a toll-free phone number, send someone an email, share the video's link with their friends, make a donation, make a purchase, etc.

One way many companies use the call-to-action approach is to host some type of contest that encourages people to reply to the video or take a specific action in order to participate, with hope of winning some type of prize. Keep in mind, there may be legal guidelines you'll need to adhere to, based on the type of contest you want to host, so do your research first.

For a business selling a product, one potential call to action is to embed a link within your video to a website that offers a money-saving coupon or special offer for what you're selling. This might be 20 percent off the purchase price, free shipping, a buy-one-get-one-free offer, or some other incentive to encourage someone to make an immediate purchase. Make it clear within the video that it's an exclusive offer to people watching the video, and make the "special offer" available immediately at the end of the video.

Incorporating a call to action within a video is one of the key ingredients for producing a successful video when it comes to communicating with your audience and getting them to take action. When using a call-to-action approach within a video, follow these basic strategies:

- Include the call to action multiple times within the video, not just at the end.
- Start by describing the reward, and then tell people exactly what they should do. For example, "To receive $50 off of your first order, visit our website right now by clicking on the link below."
- Make sure your call to action appeals to your target audience and that it's easy to understand. Be specific and succinct.

You can also use YouTube to conduct unofficial focus groups or research. In your video, showcase a product, for example, and then solicit feedback from your (potential) customers by asking specific questions and using a call-to-action approach to encourage viewers to post comments with their honest feedback, criticism, and ideas.

Create Mindless Entertainment, But Utilize Product Placement

Many people turn to YouTube for entertainment, because the service is chock full of funny, whimsical, and absolutely outrageous videos. You or your company can jump on this bandwagon and produce videos that offer mindless entertainment, but at the same time, offer subtle product placements or marketing messages about your company or its products within the videos.

For this type of video, creativity is essential, as what you post needs to be unique, engaging, funny, and entertaining. Again, taking a soft-sell approach is key.

Promote or Share Highlights From an Event

By default, any type of event in the real world that you or your organization participates in is held at some geographic location and will draw crowds from the surrounding area. However, by sharing videos of an up-and-coming or recently held event, you have the opportunity to share it with the world. Showcasing footage from a previous event can also generate interest in and help boost attendance for future events.

Once you publish your videos on YouTube, be sure to take full advantage of the YouTube Analytics tools to help you discover who the audience is for your videos and other useful details about when, how, and by whom your videos are being watched. Use this information to help you better promote your existing videos and improve the focus of the content of future videos.

In Part III, you'll read interviews with small-business operators and online marketing experts, who will discuss real-world examples of how various types of video or approaches within videos can be used successfully. Right now, as you develop ideas for your company's videos, think beyond simply producing a video that replicates a TV commercial or infomercial.

Instead, consider ways you can use video to communicate effectively with your intended audience in order to build and expand your company's online reputation, educate the audience about your products/services, separate yourself from your competition, address the wants and needs of your (potential) customers, share information, or entertain your audience in a way that will help you and your business achieve its goals.

Planning Videos That Will Capture Your Viewers' Attention

IN THIS CHAPTER

- What it takes to create successful YouTube videos
- Keeping your audience in mind
- Why some videos fail
- How to generate ideas for your videos
- Taking your idea into pre-production
- Avoiding copyright woes

Before you start brainstorming, storyboarding, and filming your first YouTube videos, it's essential that you seriously consider your overall goal for your videos as a whole, as well as for your YouTube channel. Chapter 2, "10 Ways People, Companies, and Organizations Are Successfully Using YouTube," outlined just some of the ways YouTube videos can effectively become part of your overall online marketing and promotions strategy. Hopefully, you will now begin kicking around some video ideas in your head, or writing them down so you don't forget them.

Next, clearly define the overall message that you want to convey within your videos, what the video's call to action will be, and who your videos will target. As you engage in these pre-production steps, it's important to really focus on what information about yourself, your company, and/or your products/services you want to convey, and how you ultimately want to share this information.

Once again, it's important that the message(s) and call to action you incorporate into your videos be consistent with your company's overall image and reputation, and that they be synergistic to all of your other branding and online activities (on Facebook, Twitter, Google+, etc.).

A FEW COMMON TRAITS OF SUCCESSFUL YOUTUBE VIDEOS

No perfect formula exists for creating a successful YouTube video. What works for one company in order to reach a specific audience will not necessarily work for another. However, if you analyze other successful videos on YouTube, particularly videos produced by your competitors or that target the same audience as you're striving to reach, you'll probably discover some common elements.

Many popular videos produced by small businesses and entrepreneurs typically have some or all of the following traits and production elements:

- The video is short and to the point. Keep your videos under three minutes in length.
- Within the first few seconds of the video, what the video is about and what it offers are quickly and clearly explained to the viewer.
- The video's call to action is incorporated into the video near the very beginning, and then repeated several times within the video, including near the very end. The call to action begins by stating what reward the viewer receives for following through and completing the call to action.
- The video somehow incorporates contact information for the person or organization that created it. This can be done using voice-overs, statements by the people featured within your video, titles/captions, and/or annotations or links embedded within the video itself.
- The video is targeted to a very specific audience and has a specific goal or objective.
- The content of the video is somehow unique and tries to set itself apart from the other videos on YouTube.
- The video offers information that the viewer perceives as useful, informative, entertaining, highly engaging, educational, or somehow directly relevant to what they're looking for, want, or need.
- In terms of production quality, the video is professional looking and offers good quality sound.
- The video uses some type of background music.

- The video offers clearly defined and easy-to-understand information that the viewer doesn't have to wait too long to receive. The information is not buried in clutter or hidden by eye candy or audio that can be distracting or confusing to the viewer. For example, animated shots or scene transitions are not overused, and the background music is set at a proper level and is appropriate to the content.
- The look and messaging within the video is consistent with the company's brand and reputation.
- The title of the video is appropriate, descriptive, and directly to the point. When someone sees the video's title, they immediately have a good idea what the video is about and what they can expect from it. This is supported by a carefully worded description and accompanied by a carefully selected group of relevant tags and keywords.

With these common traits in mind, as you explore YouTube for yourself, you'll easily discover very popular videos that follow none of these suggestions and that offer a truly unique or vastly different approach. There are no hard-core rules to follow, because video production is a highly creative endeavor. Focus on originality and ways you can communicate your core message as quickly and easily as possible to your intended audience.

Within the last few chapters of this book, you'll hear directly from a handful of experienced YouTube experts who share their own insight into what it takes to produce a successful YouTube video. Even the information these experts offer is based on their own unique experiences and opinions, and may or may not apply directly to what your company's objectives are for using YouTube as a promotional, marketing, advertising, or customer service-related tool.

TAKE ADVANTAGE OF MULTIPLE MULTIMEDIA ELEMENTS IN YOUR VIDEOS

A YouTube video can contain live-action video footage, text (titles), graphics, animations, charts, diagrams, music, sound effects, voice-overs, and other multimedia elements that can be used separately or together in order to effectively communicate with your audience. It's your job to first define your message, and then choose the best way(s) to convey it within your videos.

Sometimes, simply adding appropriate background music and title graphics will give your video better production value, plus make the information you're trying to convey more engaging. Whenever possible, avoid the "talking head" approach, in which all that the viewer sees is a closeup of a person talking for more than 10 to 15 seconds at a time.

When you watch a news program or talk show on TV, for example, you'll notice that the same camera shot is never used for more than a few seconds at a time, and that titles and graphics are often used to add eye candy to a talking head. Use this same strategy in your own videos, if applicable.

In general, you'll add titles, voice-overs, animations, music, sound effects, and other enhancements to your videos post production, during the editing process, after the raw footage has been shot. The post-production phase of creating YouTube videos is covered within Chapter 11, "Editing Your YouTube Videos."

KEEP YOUR AUDIENCE IN MIND

Knowing you have the communication capabilities that live-action video footage, titles, graphics, animations, charts, diagrams, music, sound effects, voice-overs, and other multimedia elements offer in order to communicate with your audience, once you have a goal in mind for each of your videos, the next step is to select the approach you'll take to achieve your objectives.

It's your job as a video producer to research your audience, figure out what types of videos will appeal to them, and then cater specifically to their wants and needs. A video that's designed to introduce pre-teen girls to a new product will need to be produced vastly differently from a video designed to appeal to men between the ages of 18 and 34, for example.

Figure out what types of video your target audience already enjoys watching on YouTube and then incorporate some of these production elements and concepts into your videos. Remember, your approach should be unique to your company and audience. Do not simply steal someone else's idea or try to mimic what your competition is already doing.

Using your own creativity, a YouTube video can adopt one or more approaches to capture your target audience's attention. For example, the video can take on the form of an infomercial, traditional commercial, or an advertorial in order to promote and sell a product or service. However, you can often take that same raw material and package it into a video that takes more of an instructional, product or service demonstration, or a how-to approach, that uses a much more subtle sales message. You may discover that your audience will have a greater interest and appreciation when you adopt a less sales-focused approach in your videos, which can also include customer testimonials, if applicable.

A YouTube video can also be used to tell a story. For example, using your video, you can take viewers behind the scenes at your company or manufacturing facility to show people how your products are made, introduce them to the people who create them, or have the company's founder share his story about how the company was conceived. Storytelling on YouTube can be a very powerful way to communicate with your audience, especially if the person featured in the video (or who's heard speaking) has a compelling, entertaining, and outgoing personality.

A YouTube video can also be used to showcase a presentation, speech, or special event, serve as a video blog (vlog or video diary), or have the goal of simply entertaining people. Keep in mind, video is a visual medium, so use it. Don't just talk to your audience, for example. Actually show them what you're talking about. Instead of just featuring a "talking head," if your video's goal is to showcase a product, for example, be sure to visually show off every aspect of that product within your video.

If you opt to share news, facts, or information with your audience, choose the most visually interesting and entertaining way to convey the information in order to keep your viewers' attention. Creatively using entertainment and/or humor, for example, is an excellent way to make otherwise complicated or boring information palatable in a YouTube video. You can also create and use colorful and animated charts, graphs, tables, and bulleted lists, when applicable.

Within the first few seconds of every video, and in using your YouTube channel as a whole, one of your core objectives should be to quickly build a rapport with your audience, while at the same time building up your credibility. Your viewers should want to hear what you have to say in your videos and also trust what you're saying.

REASONS WHY MOST VIDEOS NEVER BECOME POPULAR

Out of all of the videos uploaded to YouTube every day, a very small percentage generate more than a few hundred views, and only an elite few of those actually manage to go viral and attract thousands, millions, or in a few rare cases, billions of views. Instead of focusing on trying to create viral videos, dedicate your efforts to catering specifically to your target audience when writing, producing, shooting, and editing videos. The results you'll then receive in terms of the percentage of appropriate and interested people watching your videos and following through on your video's call to action will be significantly higher. These days, when it comes to measuring a successful video on YouTube, it is not about the number of views. What's more important is the quality of the engagement the viewer of your video has.

The quality of engagement is measured based in many ways, such as:

- How much of your video someone watches before clicking out of it
- The percentage of people who watch your entire video versus how many people click out of it before it's over
- The number of people who "like" your video versus how many "dislike" it or take no action after watching it

- The number of comments a video receives
- The percentage of people who follow through with the video's call to action

Even if your video has top-notch production value and costs you a fortune to produce, this does not in any way guarantee an audience. Later, in Chapter 6, "Promoting Your YouTube Videos," you'll learn more about how to effectively promote your videos once they're published online. However, you first need to develop ideas for your videos and then produce them, which is the focus of this chapter, as well as Chapter 10, "Filming YouTube Videos."

There are many reasons why videos fail to attract an audience. Some of the more common reasons include:

- They're poorly produced and boring to watch.
- The content of the video is unoriginal, and doesn't stand out from the competition.
- It fails to cater to its target audience.
- The content is not entertaining, informative, or perceived as containing any type of valuable information—it does not address any type of work or need.
- It's too long and fails to hold the viewer's attention.
- The content doesn't properly take advantage of the visual aspect of multimedia, so it fails to keep the viewer's attention. If the viewer wants to just listen to content that doesn't utilize visuals, he/she could download or stream a podcast or audiobook, or simply turn on the radio. Consider ways to make your videos visually compelling.
- The video is given a nondescriptive title and has poorly chosen tags associated with it, which makes it hard or impossible to find using YouTube's Search feature or a search engine.
- The video isn't properly promoted after it's published on YouTube.
- Early on, the video receives "dislikes," low ratings, and negative comments, which indicates to those who stumble upon it later that it's not worth watching.
- The producer or "star" of the video has a negative reputation online, which turns potential viewers off to what the video has to say.

Now that you know some of the more common reasons why many videos published on YouTube fail to attract an audience, you can more easily avoid these pitfalls by taking a different approach when presenting your unique content to your target audience.

Remember, creating videos with top-notch production value and appealing content requires creativity, skill, and experience that you'll probably develop over time. It's not realistic to expect everything to fall into place perfectly as you're creating and producing your first few videos. Right from the start, however, make sure your videos will help establish or boost your company's image or reputation. If you're not able to achieve a good enough production value to showcase a professional image, seek the help of a professional video production company or upgrade your production equipment.

As you publish your first few videos, take advantage of YouTube Analytics and the comments, likes, ratings, and other feedback you receive from your initial viewers. This information can all be extremely useful as you're getting to know your audience and discovering the types of videos and approaches within your videos that work best.

For a video to become successful on YouTube, it has to offer the right content and approach, that's targeted to the right audience, within an appropriate time frame, and then it needs to be promoted properly. Thus, many different pre-production, production, post-production, and promotional elements need to come together.

GET TO THE POINT—FAST

Whatever approach you take with your videos, remember that it's your job to capture your audience's attention very quickly, and then keep the content of your videos succinct, so their running time is kept short.

You're much better off producing a few short three-to-five-minute videos that can be daisy chained together as a YouTube "playlist" than you are trying to hold your audience's attention for 10 to 15 minutes or longer with a single video.

The attention span of most people who use YouTube is extremely short. The moment people get bored with whatever it is they're watching, they'll simply click to the next video. If someone decides that they want to watch your video, and it's just a few minutes in length, chances are they'll watch it as soon as they stumble upon it. Most people aren't too concerned about investing two to five minutes out of their already busy day.

However, if that same person sees that watching your video will require a commitment of five, 10, 15, or 20 minutes, they're going to be much more reserved about clicking the play button. If a viewer notices a video's long play length, that alone can be a huge deterrent, especially if the viewer doesn't know who you are and doesn't already subscribe to your YouTube channel.

There is no optimal length for a YouTube video. How long someone will commit to watching a single video depends on the subject matter, the production quality of the video, how the content is presented, and a wide range of other factors. That being said, the chances of someone choosing to watch your video, and then sticking with it until the end, are much greater if the video is short, engaging, and to the point. On average, most YouTube users prefer videos three minutes or shorter in length, regardless of the topic or content. If the content is of interest to them and presented well, you may be able to keep their attention longer, but don't push your luck.

As you're managing your YouTube channel, you can group videos together as a playlist for your viewers, so one video automatically plays after the next, in the order that you preset. Of course, a viewer can pause or exit out of the playlist at any time, but if one of your videos holds the viewer's attention until the end, having another relevant video then begin automatically is an excellent strategy for retaining viewers as they watch multiple videos. This is ultimately a great way to build your audience and YouTube channel subscriber base.

HOW TO GENERATE IDEAS FOR YOUR VIDEOS

Ideas for new videos can come from anywhere. Look for inspiration in your daily life, and be sure to seek out ideas from friends, coworkers, employees, customers, and clients. You'll also want to invest time to explore YouTube, and watch plenty of different types of videos that other companies and individuals have produced.

The core concepts for videos that you generate should stand out and excite you (as well as your intended audience). They need to be original, creative, interesting, thought-provoking, entertaining, and/or informative, and at the same time, be of direct interest to your intended audience. One way to begin your search for ideas is to determine what your competition is already doing, and then figure out how you can do that better or differently within your videos.

With so much content already available from YouTube, coming up with truly unique ideas is going to be extremely difficult. Instead, focus on ways to set your ideas apart from what's already out there. Don't be afraid to jump on the bandwagon and use currently popular videos as your inspiration, as long as you're able and willing to add a unique, original, or compelling twist to your videos. If you opt to use other videos as inspiration, make sure you're not violating anyone else's copyrights, intellectual properties, or trademarks when you produce your own videos.

Once you have a general idea about what your overall goals are for YouTube, have defined your audience, and have outlined your primary message, it's time to brainstorm ideas for individual videos. Start by determining what you want to say. Then, based on your video production skills, equipment, and capabilities, consider the very best way to present that content.

For each potential idea you come up with, ask yourself these questions:

- Is my idea consistent with what I'm trying to accomplish on YouTube?
- What is the best approach to take with my idea within the video?
- Will my idea and my intended approach appeal to my intended audience?

- Do I have the skill, knowledge, and proper equipment to produce the video I'm envisioning and do it well?
- Can the video be produced within my budget, without compromising production quality?
- How do I want the audience to react to the video? What will be the call to action?
- How do I anticipate the audience will actually react to the video?
- Will watching this video entice the viewer to watch other videos already published on my YouTube channel, to somehow make contact with me or my company, and/or place an order for my product/service, if applicable?
- While someone is watching the video, or immediately after it's over, will they be motivated to click on the "Like" button, give it a good rating, write and post a favorable comment, and/or share the video (or a link to it) with their online friends (via Facebook, Google+, or Twitter, for example)?
- Does the video, its message, its call to action, and its overall approach fit with what I'm already doing for myself or my company elsewhere in cyberspace, using Facebook, Google+, and/or Twitter, for example?

During the entire pre-production phase, and then later when engaged in post production for your videos, go back and ask yourself these questions again and again to make sure you're remaining on target.

As you answer each of these questions, you'll often discover the need to fine-tune or tweak your original ideas in order to transform them into something that's more viable or on-target with your message, call to action, and overall goals. At the same time you're evaluating your ideas, however, think about creative, off-beat, and original ways you can present your content in a fun, unusual, or memorable way.

Then, before investing too much time or money as you move forward in the pre-production phase, perhaps bounce your ideas off of other people who are familiar with you, your company, its products/services, your target audience, and your online goals. Sharing ideas with other creative people whom you trust is always a good strategy, plus it'll help you consider things from different perspectives that could impact how your videos are perceived and/or accepted by your audience.

If your goal is to launch a YouTube channel and populate it with new videos on a regular basis, whether it's daily, weekly, or monthly, during this early phase of idea generation, develop a list that outlines concepts for your first 10 or so videos. Then, as you brainstorm ideas in the future, be sure to write them down so you can later refer back to your ideas.

Make sure that what you intend to do with your YouTube channel is sustainable and consistent with your brand, online business reputation, and overall business model.

For example, you may have great ideas for your first few videos, but what will you do to maintain and build your audience several months or even several years down the road? Keeping YouTube channel content fresh over the long term proves to be a huge challenge for many companies and individuals.

TAKING YOUR IDEA INTO PRE-PRODUCTION

After you develop what you think is a great idea for a YouTube video, before creating the storyboard and writing the script, choose what approach you want to take with the video. For example, will it be how-to related, informational, tell a story, showcase an interview, take on the format of an advertorial or commercial, offer a product demonstration, or focus on entertainment? As you've already discovered, the possibilities are limited mainly by your imagination, skills, production budget, and the capabilities of the video equipment that's at your disposal.

At this point, it's a good strategy to create a storyboard for your video concept. On a sheet of paper, draw a series of boxes, like a cartoon strip, and within each of the boxes, sequentially sketch out what will happen in each scene of your video. Use stick figures, if necessary. The appearance and artistic quality of your storyboards is far less important than the raw ideas your storyboard conveys.

As you do this, below each box, write the scene number and a few words about what multimedia elements will be incorporated into the screen. So, the first box on your storyboard might contain the main title of the video or a sketch of the opening shot, along with a brief description of what will be said in a voice-over or what music will be heard.

Depending on the complexity of your overall video concept, the storyboard for a three-to-five-minute video might be spread out between five and 10 storyboard boxes. Creating a storyboard will help you expand on your video idea and develop it into a graphic and text-based outline for what will ultimately be shot.

Later, as you write the script for your video, if applicable, you can add the script elements under the appropriate frames in your storyboard. Especially if you'll be working with multiple people on your video production team, a detailed storyboard in conjunction with a script will help everyone develop a good understanding of the video's concept and content before you begin shooting.

Sometimes the core concept for a video may seem viable when it's written out in one or two sentences, but once you expand the concept into a rough storyboard, you may discover that everything you want to include within the video either won't take up three to five minutes, or that you'll need way too much time to convey your video's core message to the viewer.

Within your storyboard, you ultimately want to plan out each scene and shot, associate each scene or shot with dialogue, and then determine when and where titles, animations, graphics, music, and sound effects, for example, will be used.

Many art supply stores sell oversize pads that have pre-printed storyboard grids on them. Levenger (www.levenger.com/Special-Request-Storyboard-3-Ring-Ltr-Core-8098. aspx), for example, offers 8.5″ x 11″ storyboard paper with three-ring binder holes, while Moleskine (www.moleskine.com/us/collections/model/product?id=59317#) offers 5″ x 8.25″ hardcover notebooks containing preprinted storyboard grids on each page.

Write a Compelling Script

By focusing in on your video's goal, and then reviewing your storyboard, at this point you should be able to determine the approximate length your video will be and then be in a position to begin drafting a shooting script, which contains exactly what will be said, word for word, within the video and describes who will say each line. Not all videos will require a script. If you deem a script to be unnecessary, it's even more important to create a detailed storyboard for your video idea before you begin shooting.

Assuming your video does require a script, be sure to write it in a style that caters to your intended audience, using language, phrasing, and an approach that viewers will easily relate to and understand. Within your script, make sure your intended message is presented clearly, and that toward the end of the video you present your call to action.

Scriptwriting is a skill in itself that takes years to master. Your best bet as you start out is to focus on what you're most familiar with and knowledgeable about.

In addition to being a skill, scriptwriting is also a creative art form. Even a script for a three-to-five-minute video could take hours, possibly days, to write, rewrite, and fine-tune. You want the wording and approach to be exactly how it needs to be in order to properly present your core message to your audience in a way that's succinct and compelling. It also should sound natural for the people who will be saying the words on camera—whether it's you, an actor, voice-over announcer, or your company's spokesperson.

As you're writing your script, keep that age-old saying, "A picture is worth a thousand words" clear in your mind. When possible, use video images, photos, charts, graphs, or other graphic elements to convey concepts or ideas quickly and visually. Remember, you're creating a video that can include many visual and audible elements simultaneously in order to get your message across. Don't be afraid to use what's at your disposal during the shooting of a video as well as in post production.

For a short video, your script can be written using any word processor. However, if you'll be crafting a more elaborate script and want to format it the way scriptwriters for commercials, TV shows, and movies do, consider acquiring special script-writing software to help you organize and format your script accordingly.

Final Draft 8 (www.finaldraft.com/products/final-draft/), Movie Magic Screenwriter 6 (www.screenplay.com), and the screenwriting software available from Celtx (www.celtx.com) are three examples of specialized software packages for script writing. You'll find details about additional software at http://en.wikipedia.org/wiki/List_of_screenwriting_software. In addition to helping you properly format and print the scripts for your video productions, these software packages offer tools to help you flesh out ideas and assist with the creative process of scriptwriting.

Within your script, be sure to include as much direction and detail as possible related to shooting locations, camera angles, and types of shots. Describe the actions that the performers in the video take and how music and/or sound effects will be used. Indicate when special props, charts, graphics, or other animated or multimedia content beyond live-action video footage will be used.

If your video will include dialogue between two or more people, ensure that the words you're writing in the script sound natural and easily understood when they're said aloud by the people featured in your video. How something reads on a page is very different from how it sounds when spoken, especially if it's a conversation between two or more people.

Develop a Budget

After the idea for a video has been fleshed out and storyboarded and/or scripted, sit down and develop a realistic production budget for it, based on what will actually be involved in producing the video you're envisioning. Every element of the video's production should be considered in advance. Use the "Video Production Budget Worksheet" in Figure 3–1 on page 39 to help you calculate your costs.

Depending on the scale of your video production, you may need to use professional and highly trained crew, such as a director, writer, camera operator, sound engineer, production assistants, and video editor. These people are typically paid a daily rate, which will vary greatly based on their skill level, experience, your geographic region, and whether or not they're in a union.

Using professional versus amateur actors and/or voice-over talent will also have a huge impact on your budget, as will the type of camera and related equipment you'll be using for your productions.

Keep in mind the costs outlined in the budget worksheet relate to pre-production, production, and post-production costs. You will still need to include video promotion costs into your overall budget. It's not uncommon for a promotional budget to be greater than the production budget for a video being published on YouTube by a

Expense Description	Cost Per Day	Total Cost
Actors/Presenters		
Crew—Writer, Director, Camera Person, Sound Engineer, Set Designer, Hairstylist, Makeup Artist, Production Assistants, etc.		
Location / Set-Related Costs		
Wardrobe, Costumes, Makeup, and Props		
Microphones and Sound Equipment		
Lighting Equipment		
Music/Sound Effects Licensing and/or Royalties		
Animation and Graphic Development		
Editing and Post Production		
Camcorder/Camera Equipment Purchase or Rental		
Catering / Food		
Shooting Permits		
Other Special Needs or Considerations		
Total Budget		

FIGURE 3–1. Video Production Budget Worksheet

company or organization. More information about planning the promotional budget for your videos can be found in Chapter 6, "Promoting Your YouTube Videos."

Use the worksheets provided within Figures 3–2 and 3–3 to help you determine exactly what will be needed during a video's production. Create duplicates of each worksheet, as needed, for each performer and set/location to be used within each of your videos.

Set Your Production Schedule

Again, based on the complexity of your video, you may be able to shoot it in one take and have the whole thing wrapped up in an hour. Or, for more elaborate productions, the shooting alone might take several days. Once you have the concept for your video finalized, sit down and figure how much time will be required for pre-production,

Actor / Performer	Cost	Date(s) Needed
Wardrobe		
Hair		
Makeup		
Props		
Transportation		
Other:		

FIGURE 3–2. Actor/Performer-Related Needs

Set	Item Details	Cost	Date(s) Needed
Background			
Furniture			
Accessories / Accents / Décor			
Special Lighting			
Production Crew Members Needed On-Set			

FIGURE 3–3. Set-Related Needs

production, and post production. If multiple people will be involved in various phases of the production, try to calculate how much time will be required of each person and when they'll be needed.

Next, set dates and times for each phase of the video's production, and mark your calendar. Be sure that everyone involved is kept in the loop and that people know exactly when and where they'll be needed. If everyone shows up for filming except one of your actors or one or two key people on your production crew, this can result in costly production delays and frustration.

As you plan your production schedule, allow for last-minute problems, unforeseen issues to arise, and for other types of delays. For example, if you'll be shooting on location, expect that at least one or two people involved in your production will get stuck in traffic, get lost, or have car trouble. Also assume you'll run into some type of problem with your video equipment (which will hopefully be easily solvable), or that as you're shooting, you'll want to take a break to fine-tune your script or rework how a scene is being shot.

To help you save time and avoid frustration during your video shoots, plan on recording each scene a handful of times, and shoot scenes out of order if necessary. If several scenes will take place on the same set or at the same location, shoot those scenes back-to-back. You can always re-order your raw footage post production during the editing phase. Also, make sure there's someone in charge at the shoot—whether it's the producer or director—and then try to keep your cast and production crew streamlined, so it's easily manageable.

YOUTUBE COMMUNITY GUIDELINES AND COPYRIGHT INFRINGEMENT

When producing your videos, make sure that all elements of your video are original, or that you have the proper permission to use content or production elements that you don't own outright, such as music, sound effects, logos, and/or artwork. YouTube uses advanced technology to automatically scan videos as they're being uploaded in an effort to thwart the illegal use of copyrighted material.

YouTube prohibits certain types of material to be published on the service, including any type of pornography. All of the rules pertaining to what is and isn't permissible within a YouTube video can be found within the YouTube community guidelines (www. youtube.com/t/community_guidelines).

As a YouTube channel operator and/or video producer, it is absolutely essential that you read and understand these guidelines before you begin filming your videos and uploading them to YouTube. Violating YouTube's community guidelines could result in your videos being taken offline or your channel being suspended.

For example, in addition to prohibiting pornographic material of any kind on YouTube, any type of child exploitation, animal abuse, or videos portraying drug use or underage drinking or smoking, as well as topics such as how to make a bomb, are also forbidden. You'll also discover that YouTube does not permit graphic or gratuitous violence to be shown within videos.

While YouTube does support freedom of speech, it does not permit videos that attack or demean people based on race, ethnic origin, religion, disability, gender, sexual orientation or age. You're also not allowed to issue threats, invade someone's privacy, stalk, or reveal someone else's private information using a YouTube video.

Another thing that YouTube is strict about is enforcing that video producers and publishers use accurate titles, descriptions, tags, and thumbnails when uploading and listing their videos on the service. In other words, you can't use misleading or inaccurate information with the hope of attracting viewers for your videos who might otherwise have no interest in it if it were listed and titled accurately.

The most common violation of the YouTube community guidelines involves someone incorporating copyrighted music within their production without the proper permission. If you don't know whether or not you're about to violate a copyright by including something in one of your videos, visit YouTube's Copyright Help Center (www.youtube.com/t/howto_copyright) and/or consult with an attorney before publishing the questionable video content online. You can also visit The Library of Congress' Copyright website (www.copyright.gov) for more information about filing your own copyrights and how to avoid violating copyrights owned by others. For a quick and animated primer about copyrights, *Take The Mystery Out Of Copyright,* visit www.loc. gov/teachers/copyrightmystery.

In addition to YouTube's automated tools that seek out videos that violate the service's community guidelines, the YouTube community itself helps to police and monitor the service. Anyone who discovers a video that violates YouTube's community guidelines can flag a video by clicking on the "Report" icon that's displayed below every video window as a video is being streamed/watched. At this point, within 24 hours, someone from YouTube will personally review the video and determine if it violates community guidelines.

Even if a video does not directly violate YouTube's community guidelines, it may be deemed inappropriate for viewers below a certain age, and will then have restrictions and warning labels placed in conjunction with the video that pertains to who can and should watch it.

How to Start Your Own YouTube Channel

When you upload a video to YouTube, there are many ways for your potential viewers to find and enjoy it. Every video has a title, keywords (tags), and a description associated with it. It's also categorized by subject matter and given its own unique URL (website address). Plus, links for the video (or the videos themselves) can be embedded into websites, blogs, Facebook messages, tweets, and/or emails.

If your company publishes multiple videos on YouTube, one of the ways your viewers will be able to find your work is through your own YouTube channel, which you should plan on branding with your company logo and contact information. Establishing a YouTube channel is free, and there are many reasons why it makes sense to do this, especially if you're trying to establish a large audience for your videos.

Establishing a YouTube channel is separate from creating a free Google account, which is used to access the YouTube service. To establish a YouTube channel, however, you first need to set up a Google account, or you can use your existing Google+ account as the YouTube identity for your new channel.

A YouTube channel is a special area of YouTube that's dedicated to you (or your company)—the channel's host. When someone visits your YouTube channel, they will see descriptions and links to all of the videos you've published as part of that channel, as well as information about you (or your company), and other channel-oriented details which we'll focus on shortly.

One of the biggest benefits to hosting your own YouTube channel is that people can subscribe to it. Then, based on how they have their own YouTube account set up, your subscribers can automatically receive an email from YouTube whenever you publish a new video via your channel, or they can be alerted of your new video(s) each time they access the YouTube service. Through a YouTube channel, you have the ability to develop and promote your brand, personalize your channel, and cater its contents to your target audience. Your channel's main page can also offer links to your primary website(s), blog, Facebook page, or an online store.

If you're selling a product, you want someone to find your video on YouTube and watch it, learn about your product, and then click on the link within the video window itself, or on your YouTube channel page, that leads to your online store so that the viewer can immediately purchase the product online. However, research has shown that videos that use a hard-sell approach are not nearly as effective as an informational or product demonstration video, for example, that utilizes a soft-sell message.

While big companies often use videos that are in essence slickly produced commercials or infomercials to promote brand awareness or showcase a product, as a small-business operator who's trying to cater to a niche or targeted audience, spending $10,000 to $100,000 or more for a 30- to 90-second, professionally produced video that looks like a commercial is typically not the most cost-effective strategy.

Every YouTube channel page is fully customizable, allowing you to showcase you or your company's brand, corporate image, or your own personality in order to cater to your intended audience. As you develop your YouTube channel page and ultimately populate it with videos, some of your goals for the channel page should be to:

- Get people who watch one or more of your videos to subscribe to your channel.
- Encourage viewers to "Like" your individual videos.
- Solicit comments about your videos from viewers.
- Persuade your viewers/subscribers to share links to your videos with their online friends (via Facebook, Twitter, Email, Google+, etc.). This serves as free and powerful word-of-mouth advertising for your videos, and is one of the keys to helping a video go viral on the internet.

- Entice your audience to follow the displayed links on your YouTube channel page to your primary website, online store, blog, Facebook page, etc.

More information about how to achieve these goals is covered in Chapter 5, "Interacting With Your Video's Viewers and Subscribers," as well as in Chapter 6, "Promoting Your YouTube Videos." Ultimately, you want traffic from your primary website(s) to visit your YouTube channel page and watch your videos, while you want people who access your videos via your YouTube channel page to visit your other websites, especially if you're trying to sell a product or service.

HOW TO CREATE YOUR OWN YOUTUBE CHANNEL

The process for establishing and then customizing your own YouTube channel takes just a few minutes. You'll then want to customize the channel by adjusting a handful of options, uploading your photo or logo, and linking your channel with your other online social networking accounts, like Facebook, Twitter, and Google+.

First, Create Your Free Google Account

If you are starting a YouTube channel for your business, set up a separate Google/ YouTube account from scratch, using a unique and nonpersonal email address. That way someone else from within your organization can run the channel without you having to give out your personal Google account username and password. Keep in mind, only one YouTube channel can be associated with each Google account.

Currently, there is no such thing as a specialized business account or YouTube channel for businesses. You'll need to customize a standard YouTube channel's settings so that it best caters to your audience and showcases your business, its image/brand, and your videos.

To create a unique Google account, follow these steps:

1. Launch any web browser on your computer that's connected to the internet and visit www.youtube.com.
2. From the YouTube homepage, click on the "Sign In" link that's displayed near the top-right corner of the screen (shown in Figure 4–1, page 46).
3. When the YouTube "Sign In" screen appears (with the Google logo in the upper-left corner), click on the "Create an Account" button that's displayed in the upper-right corner. You'll be prompted to first create a new Google account.
4. At the "Create a New Google Account" screen (shown in Figure 4–2, page 46), fill in the fields. You'll be asked to enter your first and last name. Then, you'll be instructed to choose a unique Google username. Next, create and confirm a

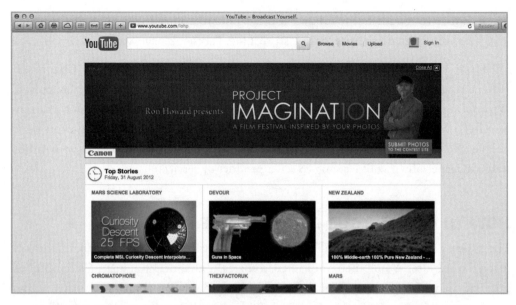

FIGURE 4–1. From YouTube's Main Homepage, Click on the "Sign In" Link That's Displayed Near the Upper-Right Corner of the Screen.

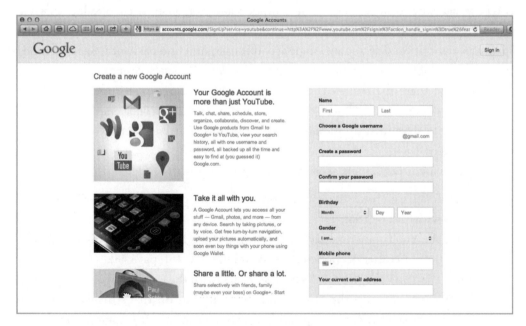

FIGURE 4–2. When the New Google Account Screen Appears, Fill in Each Empty Field with Your Own Information.

password for the account, enter your birthday and gender, as well as your mobile phone number and current email address. If you're creating a YouTube channel for your business or service, for example, do not use a personal email address when prompted for your current email address. Select your location from the pull-down menu, and then agree to the "Terms of Service" that are listed on the screen. Click the "Next Step" button to continue.

The Google username you select will also become your YouTube channel name and a free Google email address (also known as your "Gmail address") will be issued to the account. Use your business name as your username or choose something that's clever, that your intended audience will identify with. The channel name/username should be easy to spell, and something that people will remember. If your YouTube channel will be promoting a product, for example, consider using the name of the product (assuming it is not copyrighted or trademarked by someone other than you or your business) as your username.

Your username can be any combination of letters and numbers, but it cannot include spaces or special characters like punctuation, underscores, or dashes. Also, usernames are not case sensitive, but they can be displayed using upper and lower case letters. For example, as far as YouTube is concerned, the username "JasonRichChannel" and "jasonrichchannel" are the same.

5. Next, you'll need to create your Google Account Profile. This includes uploading an optional Profile Photo (shown in Figure 4–3, page 48). Click on the "Add Profile Photo" button to do this, then click on the "Next Step" button to continue. If you're creating an account for your business or organization, upload a company logo or product photo, as opposed to a personal photo or headshot. This will be a visual identifier for you (or your business) when you're doing anything related to your YouTube channel or associated Google account. If you're using a logo, for example, make sure you own the legal rights to use it online.

6. Once you establish your Google account, click on the "Back to YouTube" button.

7. Within a few minutes, you'll receive two emails from Google. One will ask you to verify your current email address. Simply click on the link provided within the email to do this. The second email you receive will contain details about your new Gmail account. Save the information within this email for later reference.

Transform Your Google Account into a YouTube Channel

Using your Google account (which also serves as your YouTube account for watching videos), you can easily establish and customize your own YouTube channel, and then

FIGURE 4–3. When Prompted, You Can Upload Your Own Photo or a Company Logo as the Profile Photo for Your Account.

populate it with your own videos. Follow these steps to create a free YouTube channel once you have a valid Google account set up.

1. Access www.youtube.com and sign in using your Google account username and password. The main YouTube home screen will be displayed (as shown in Figure 4–4, page 49).

2. Near the upper-right corner of the screen, you'll see your account profile picture. Click on it to reveal the Google Account Menu, which will also be displayed near the top-right corner of the screen.

3. Click on the "My Channel" link (the upper-right portion of the screen is shown in Figure 4–5, page 49). The "Create your YouTube channel" screen will be displayed. From this initial screen, you will see your profile photo, as well as your username and/or first and last name displayed. Click on the "Edit" link that's associated with the "From Your Google Profile" option in order to customize your Google profile, which will be your identity containing public information about you that people will see online. See the "Customizing Your Google Account Profile" section on page 57 for more details.

4. Under the "Activities you'll share on your channel" heading (shown in Figure 4–6, page 50), you'll see four options, labeled "Like a video," "Comment on a video," "Favorite a video" and "Subscribe to a channel." Add a checkmark to

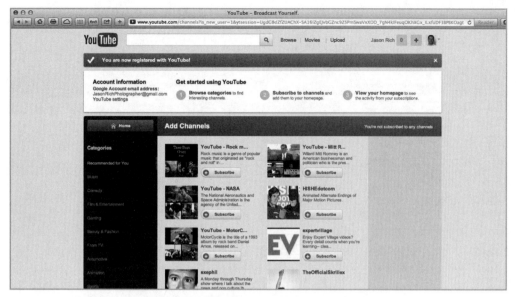

FIGURE 4–4. The Main YouTube Homepage

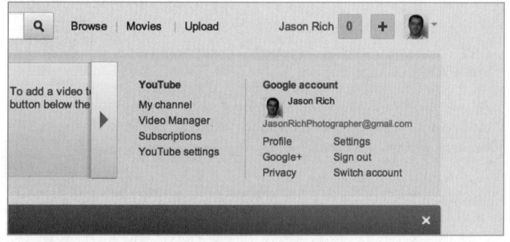

FIGURE 4–5. Click on the "My Channel" Option to Create a YouTube Channel
from Your Google Account.

the checkbox that's associated with each activity you want people who visit your
YouTube channel's page to be able to do.

5. Click on the "OK, I'm Ready to Continue" button. Your YouTube Channel has
now been created. The next step is to customize the channel settings, and then
start populating your channel by uploading videos to it.

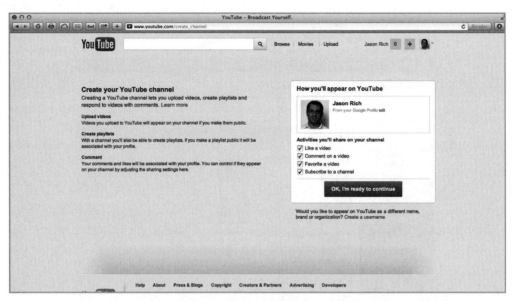

FIGURE 4–6. Decide What Activities Will Be Available to Your Video's Viewers When They Visit Your Channel.

GIVE YOUR SUBSCRIBERS A CHANCE TO INTERACT WITH YOUR CHANNEL

Anytime someone watches a video on YouTube, if the "Like a Video" option is enabled, they can click on the thumbs-up icon to "Like" the video. If a video earns a lot of "Likes," it means that you're doing something right.

Beyond just liking a video, a viewer can also be given the opportunity to "Dislike" a video, as well as comment on a video (if this option is enabled) by composing a text message that is related to the video. As the YouTube Channel operator, you can decide if the comments posted by others will be published online for everyone to see by adjusting the Sharing Settings associated with your YouTube Channel.

Anyone who creates a Google account (with its associated YouTube account) has the ability to create their own personalized collection of favorite videos, which they can refer back to and watch whenever they wish. By activating the "Favorite a Video" option for your channel, people who watch your videos will be able to add them to their own "Favorites" list. By default, when someone then views your video(s), they'll be able to see how many people have added it to their "Favorites" list.

GIVE YOUR SUBSCRIBERS A CHANCE TO INTERACT WITH YOUR CHANNEL, CONTINUED

You, as the YouTube Channel operator, can decide whether to allow other people to subscribe to your channel. If you're creating a YouTube Channel in order to build a large and dedicated following for you, a product, event, service, or your business, you'll want to encourage people to "Like" your videos, add their own comments, "Favorite" your videos, and subscribe to your YouTube Channel. You'll also benefit greatly if you convince your viewers to share your video with their online friends via email, Facebook, or Twitter, for example.

Thus, you'll want to add a checkmark next to each of the checkboxes under the "Activities You'll Share On Your Channel" heading (refer back to Figure 4–6 on page 000).

CUSTOMIZING YOUR YOUTUBE CHANNEL

When you first access your newly established YouTube Channel page (shown in Figure 4–7, page 52), it will look pretty barren. It will display your profile photo, name, and a few details, like your latest activity, date joined, age, and country.

Near the top-left corner of the screen is the "Channel Settings" button. Click on this to begin customizing your YouTube Channel. Then, once it's established and you've populated the channel with one or more videos, you'll want to click on the "Analytics" and "Video Manager" buttons to track your channel's traffic and manage the videos you've uploaded to your channel.

Begin, however, by clicking on the "Channel Settings" button. The "Channel Settings" screen will be displayed (shown in Figure 4–8, page 52). Here, you can fully customize the visual appearance of your channel's page. By default, the "Appearance" tab (near the top-left corner of the screen) has been selected. Click on the "Accept" button to confirm your selection after you're done making your customizations.

Under the "Background" heading, you can upload a digital photo to serve as your channel page's background wallpaper by clicking on the "Choose File" button, or simply choose a solid color background by clicking on the "Choose a Color" option, and then clicking on your desired background color.

If you choose to upload a background wallpaper, the digital image's file size must be less than 1 MB. Using custom wallpaper is a very easy but effective way to give your YouTube Channel page a unique appearance. The custom wallpaper can be a digital photo, or a graphic image you create or edit using Adobe Photoshop or another

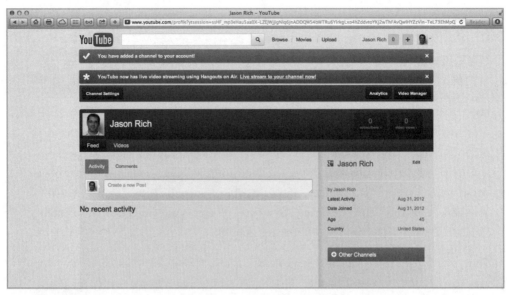

FIGURE 4–7. Click on the "Channel Settings" Button to Begin Customizing Your YouTube Channel's Main Page.

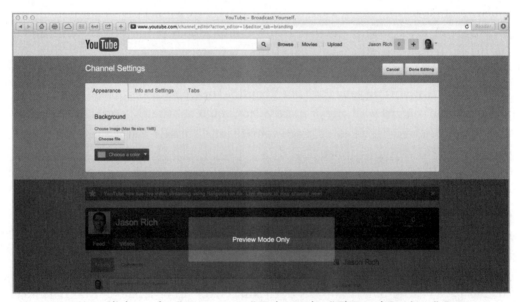

FIGURE 4–8. Click on the "Appearance" Tab on the "Channel Settings" Page to Choose a Background Wallpaper or Background Color.

graphics program. You can also pay a small fee to a graphic artist and have them create a professional-looking wallpaper for you.

When selecting a photo to use as a background, be sure that it's not too busy, or it will distract or confuse your visitors. It's also essential that you own the rights to the image/photo you'll be using. Otherwise, you could get into trouble for copyright violations.

As you're customizing your own YouTube Channel page, it's a good strategy to visit other popular YouTube channels to see firsthand how they're using wallpaper graphics or photos to enhance their channel's page.

Next, click on the "Info and Settings" tab that's displayed under the "Channel Settings" heading (shown in Figure 4–9). In addition to once again giving you the opportunity to edit your Google profile, you'll be given the chance to add a text description of your YouTube Channel in the "Description" field.

Your YouTube channel description should be short and to the point. Explain who you are, the channel's purpose, and provide a preview of your videos so that people will want to visit your channel and watch your videos. YouTube, Google, and other search engines will use this information when it comes to your channel's search engine optimization listings. Once again, be sure everything you include in your channel's description appeals to your intended audience.

Below the "Description" field is the "Tags" field. Here, you should enter a series of keywords or phrases that best describe your YouTube Channel, as well as your product, service, company, or event. Each keyword or phrase should be separated by a comma. When someone performs a search on YouTube or Google, their search terms are automatically

FIGURE 4–9. Edit Your Google Account Profile Information, Plus Add a Description, Tags, and Custom URL to Your YouTube Channel.

compared to the description and tags you've created for your YouTube Channel. If Google discovers a match or matches, your channel will be listed in the user's search results. This is a powerful tool for attracting traffic to your channel and increasing your views.

Google offers online tools for helping YouTube Channel operators develop a list of keywords and search phrases that will help generate more traffic to a video or channel. To find this tool, access www.googlekeywordtool.com.

Below the "Tags" field is the "Channel URL" link. This is a unique URL for your YouTube Channel. Right now, the link is fully functional, but it's comprised of a long list of random numbers and letters. Click on the "Edit" button to create a much easier and customized URL for your channel.

When the "Create Custom Channel URL" screen appears, use letters or numbers to create a URL that's easier to remember and identify. It can be your full name, the name of your company, or something short and clever.

Click on the "Create Channel URL" button to establish your custom YouTube Channel URL, which will take on this format: http://www.youtube.com/[your custom channel name]. After confirming your unique, custom URL, an "Overview" screen will be displayed. From here, you can edit your username and password, plus adjust a handful of other account settings, as well as turn on or off the YouTube functionality that allows you to display ads from other companies on your channel page and within your videos so that you can potentially earn revenue.

As you customize your YouTube Channel page, click on the "Tabs" option that's displayed under the "Channel Settings" heading to customize what options will be available to people who visit your channel's page. Click on the "Done Editing" button to continue.

If you're establishing a YouTube Channel for a business or organization, from the "Account Settings" page, be sure to customize the channel title, profile image, channel description, and channel tags so they're associated with your business/organization, not yourself or an individual.

For example, the channel title should include your company's name. While you cannot change your Google account username once it's set up, or the YouTube channel's custom URL (once you set it initially), you can modify the channel title at any time. The channel's description should include details about your business or organization, and the channel's tags should relate directly to your company or whatever the channel itself is being set up to promote.

To edit the channel title, access your YouTube channel and click on "Channel Settings" button. Next, click on the "Info and Settings" tab. Click on the "Edit" option that's associated with the "Profile" option. Near the top-left corner of the screen, click on your current username or channel title.

When the pop-up window for your username appears, click on the option that says "More Options." In the "Nickname" field, enter your company name or the new channel title. Then from the "Display My Name As" pull-down menu, select the new nickname (your channel title/company name). Click on the "Save" button to store your changes.

Depending on your goals for your YouTube Channel, you may or may not want to display ads from other companies on your channel page and within your videos. But if you're creating a YouTube Channel for a business, you don't want ads from other businesses or organizations displayed. You can choose whether or not ads will be displayed from the "Account Settings" tab.

You're now ready to start populating your YouTube channel with videos, and then promoting your channel to the public in order to solicit viewers and subscribers.

Once you begin publishing videos on your YouTube channel, you can embed those videos directly within your website, blog, or Facebook page. If you want the ability to do this, be sure to turn on the "Embed" option when you upload and publish a video

ADD YOUR WEBSITE, SOCIAL MEDIA PROFILES, AND OTHER LINKS TO YOUR YOUTUBE CHANNEL PAGE

Your YouTube channel page can also help drive traffic to your website, blog, online store, Facebook page, or Twitter feed. Be sure to add links to these online destinations as part of your YouTube channel page.

To do this, revisit your page and look to the right side of the screen (shown in Figure 4–10, page 56). To the right of your username (channel name) and channel description is an "Edit" option. Click on it.

Scroll down to the "Add a New Link" option. One at a time, enter the title and URL for each website, blog, and/or online social networking service account that you want to promote on your YouTube channel page (shown in Figure 4–11 on page 56).

To add additional websites or URLs, click on the "Add" button. Then, as you scroll down along the right side of the screen, you can decide whether or not to display your latest activity, when you joined, your age, your city, and/or your country. Click on the "Apply" button when you're done to save your changes. On the right side of your YouTube channel page, your links will now be displayed and active (shown in Figure 4–12, page 57).

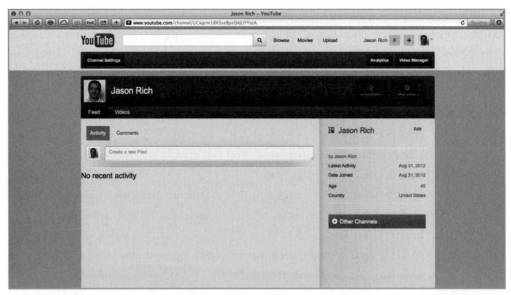

FIGURE 4–10. Click on the "Edit" Option Next to Your Username to Add Links to Your YouTube Channel Page.

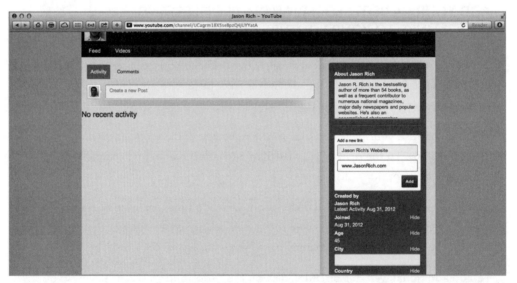

FIGURE 4–11. One at a Time, Add the Name/Title and URL for Your Main Website, Blog, Online Store, Facebook Page, Twitter Feed, etc., to Your YouTube Channel Page.

to your YouTube channel. You'll learn more about uploading and embedding YouTube videos in Chapter 12, "Uploading Your Videos to YouTube."

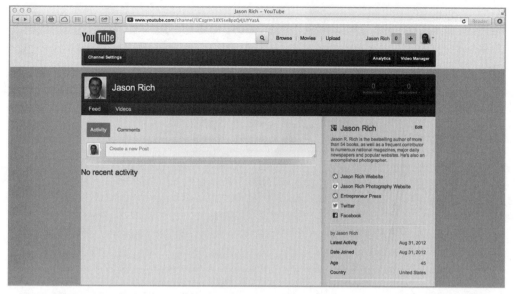

FIGURE 4–12. Ultimately, Your YouTube Channel Page Can Drive Traffic to Your Other Websites or Online Social Networking Accounts, While You Use Your Website(s), Blog, Facebook Page, and Twitter Profile, for Example, to Also Drive Traffic to Your YouTube Channel Page.

Once your videos are online, you can access real-time details about viewers for free, using the online (and free) YouTube Analytics tools.

CUSTOMIZING YOUR GOOGLE ACCOUNT PROFILE

Your Google account is used to manage your YouTube Channel account. By default, it also establishes your online identity on YouTube, and on all of Google's other online services, including Google+. Every Google account has a profile that contains your full name and/or a nickname (which can be your company name), and your username (which is unique and something you create when you set up the account).

Your Google account can also display your profile picture (a photo of you or your organization's logo), as well as additional details about you or your company. To edit your Google account profile, log into your Google account and click on your profile picture that's displayed in the upper-right corner. Next, click on the "Profile" option.

When your "Profile" page is displayed (shown in Figure 4–13, page 58), click on the "Edit Profile" button that's displayed near the center of the screen, to the right of your name, and to the left of your profile photo. You'll now discover dozens of fields into which you can add information about you (or your company) that will become publicly viewable (shown in Figure 4–14 on page 58).

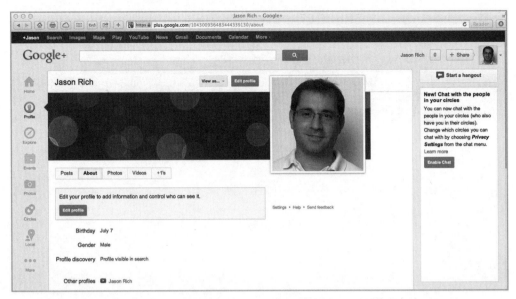

FIGURE 4–13. Initially Your Google Account "Profile" Page Will Be Almost Empty. It's Up to You to Populate it with as Much Information as You're Willing to Reveal to the Public.

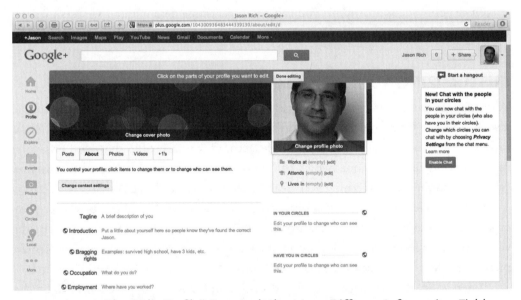

FIGURE 4–14. The "Edit Profile" Page Includes Many Different Information Fields for You to Fill in to Create Your Profile. Anything You Put in Your Profile Becomes Public and Searchable.

Only enter information into fields that allow you to convey information that you want to share with the public and your audience.

You can and should add a tagline (which is a short description of yourself or your company), an introduction (where you can include additional details), and other information to explain who you are and how to contact you. Your YouTube channel page, your account profile and each of your videos should contain your contact information. Always make it as easy as possible for your potential and existing customers/clients to find and contact you.

Click on the "Done Editing" button to save your changes and publish them online.

Before promoting your YouTube channel to the public and uploading videos to it, make sure you've customized all available aspects of the channel's page so it appeals to your intended audience and displays appropriate and relevant information, as well as links to your website, blog, Facebook page, and/or Twitter feed.

Once your YouTube channel page becomes popular, you can display the number of subscribers your channel has, as well as the number of "Video Views" your channel has received.

As soon as you establish a YouTube channel, it automatically becomes searchable via YouTube and Google, for example. Thus, depending on how good your channel name, description, and tags are, your target audience will be able to find you. It's essential that everything on your YouTube channel page, as well as within your videos, use consistent branding and messaging with whatever is used in your company's other online and real-world endeavors.

The logo, color scheme, slogans, product descriptions, company information, and other content that you showcase on YouTube should all work toward building and promoting your overall brand while simultaneously helping to enhance your company's online reputation. To accomplish this successfully, consistency and synergy is essential. Remember, having an attractive or eye-catching YouTube channel page is essential. It sets the tone for your videos and the online brand or image you're trying to convey. However, what's even more important is your ability to populate the channel with videos that will appeal to your target audience.

When designing your YouTube channel page, always focus on your target audience and what will be of interest to them. This includes thinking about your target audience when designing your page's wallpaper graphic, as well as when writing your channel's description, compiling a list of tags, deciding what links will be displayed on the YouTube Channel page, and choosing what interactive elements you'll allow your viewers to have when they're viewing your page and/or videos.

USE YOUTUBE ONE CHANNEL TO BRAND YOUR YOUTUBE CHANNEL AND MAKE IT UNIQUE

YouTube is continuously evolving, and each time the service launches new functionality, businesses like yours discover how to best utilize the latest tools in order to achieve their online goals. Built on the concept that branding a business in cyberspace is extremely important, and that more and more people are using mobile devices to access YouTube, the service has introduced what it calls YouTube One Channel.

Using this online-based set of tools, a business can fully customize its YouTube Channel page using its own logos, photos, and artwork, plus ensure that their branded page looks consistent on any computer or device. In other words, YouTube One Channel page design becomes cross-platform compatible, regardless of whether it's being seen on a computer monitor, smartphone, tablet, or HD television screen.

One of the features of YouTube One Channel is that when someone new visits your channel page, they'll automatically see a special trailer video that you produce. This video is only shown to first-time visitors. Return visitors directly access your main YouTube Channel page. Use this trailer video to quickly introduce people to your business and your channel.

Another feature offered by the YouTube One Channel toolset is the ability to manually arrange the order of the videos on your YouTube Channel page. They no longer need to be displayed in reverse-chronological order. This makes it easier to group together related videos and to put together custom playlists for your visitors. This tool can also be used to introduce or reintroduce your subscribers to older videos that they might have missed.

Now, it's possible to select how videos are displayed on your YouTube Channel page in terms of on-screen formatting, based on the customized layout and design you implement. This functionality allows you to create a visually one-of-a-kind YouTube Channel page that caters specifically to your intended audience and that best promotes your business.

Of course, the specialized tools related to YouTube One Channel are offered free of charge. To learn more, visit www.youtube.com/onechannel. Free videos to help you create and customize your YouTube One Channel page can be viewed at www.youtube.com/user/youtubehelp.

Interacting with Viewers and Subscribers

IN THIS CHAPTER

- How to build an ongoing rapport with your viewers, fans, and channel subscribers
- Ways to interact with your fans
- Strategies for expanding your online following
- Safety and privacy considerations

According to Pixability (https://app.pixability.com/radar), as of January 2013, the top 100 global brands host more than 1,272 YouTube channels, which are populated by more than 150,249 separate videos. More than 7,000 new videos are being added to these channels every month, and they have thus far attracted more than 4.7 billion views.

Companies like Disney, Google, Samsung, Sony, Intel, Coca-Cola, Honda, Toyota, Nike, Nintendo, and Nokia have each discovered how useful YouTube marketing can be, and a growing number of these companies have managed to cost-effectively reach more than 100 million views on their respective channels. As a small-business operator, even if you reach 500 to 1,000 potential new customers in a year, for virtually no cost using YouTube, that could provide a tremendous boost to your company's growth.

In this chapter we'll look at ways to solidify your YouTube marketing strategy by developing interesting, effective, and unique ways to interact with your audience.

To continuously build your subscriber base and cater to your channel's viewers, you'll need to develop efficient ways to interact with your fans in a manner that seems highly personal—but without you investing the time and resources to communicate directly with each individual (which is obviously a time-consuming and ultimately costly endeavor).

When you publish a video on YouTube, it's a one-way communication. People simply watch your videos. Encouraging people to post comments, like and/or rate your videos, and give feedback directly on your YouTube Channel, however, this creates an informal and interactive online community, based around your video content.

You can opt to make comments on your videos public or private via the "Advanced Settings" menu shown in Figure 5–1 on page 63. It's also possible to choose whether you'll have the opportunity to first read and approve all comments before they're published on your YouTube channel page; this is a feature that you should definitely take advantage of. You also have the option to allow users to vote on comments, view each video's ratings, and/or allow for video responses. A video response is when an individual publishes their own video in response to yours, and then links their response video to yours so viewers can watch both videos together.

As a small-business operator, you can use video responses as a way for your customers to solicit feedback and/or provide you and your YouTube channel audience (and subscribers) with testimonials about your products or services.

The more active you become on YouTube, the more important it is that you integrate your YouTube channel with all of your other online activity, including your company webpage, blog, Facebook page, Twitter feed, and/or Google+ account. These other online services offer much more robust toolsets for interacting with people, and all can be cross-promoted through your YouTube channel and your individual videos.

Also, be sure to encourage people to share links to your videos with their online friends through these online social networking platforms. When someone clicks on the "Share" button of your videos, this helps you build up your audience through virtual word-of-mouth advertising, which is highly effective and free. The easiest way to do this is to display "Share" buttons in conjunction with your YouTube videos.

CONSIDER YOUR TARGET AUDIENCE

Just as you did when planning your YouTube channel, before interacting with your audience on an ongoing basis, you need to understand their wants, expectations, and needs by having a good understanding of your audience's demographics.

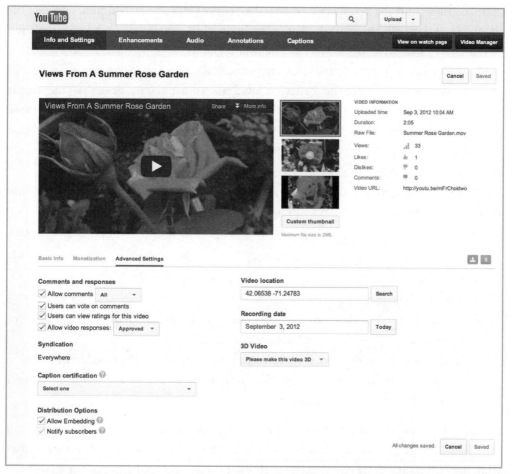

FIGURE 5–1. By Allowing Comments, Votes, and Ratings as People Watch Your Videos You Can Indirectly Interact with Your Viewers.

The demographics of your audience can be categorized by their age, sex, geographic location, income, education level, race, religion, political party affiliation, interests, hobbies, career, employment status, sexual orientation, what computer or technology they use, what type of car they drive, what shows they watch on TV, their favorite books or magazines, or by a wide range of other factors that you determine to be important. By figuring out how you can best describe your target demographic, you can then determine the best approaches to take on YouTube and in your videos to best cater to the wants and needs of that audience.

For example, you may determine that your target audience is comprised of single men, between the ages of 18 and 24, who are currently in college, or graduate school, and who enjoy playing or watching football. Alternatively, you may determine that your ideal customer and the people you want to target on YouTube are women, between the ages of 24 and 49, who are college graduates, live within a major city, who are employed full time, and who have an annual income over $45,000.

You can use any combination of the previously mentioned criteria or traits, or develop your own list that you believe allows you to accurately describe your target audience. The more you ultimately get to know about your audience, and the more clearly you can define this group of people, the easier it will be to produce videos that will appeal to this audience and then promote your video in a way that reaches these people in a cost-effective way.

In addition to determining your audience's basic demographics, for example, think about exactly who comprises your intended YouTube audience:

- Are they technologically savvy?
- What computer equipment do they use?
- When and where do they watch my videos?
- Why do they watch my videos?
- Are they active on Facebook, Twitter, Google+, LinkedIn, or another popular (or up-and-coming) online social networking site?
- What are some of the best ways to communicate with them outside YouTube?
- Is real-time or direct communication important to them? How could I benefit from real-time communication?

Once your videos are published online and available for the public to watch, you can then determine exactly who is watching them—and how to better target that audience—by using YouTube Analytics tools. In addition to helping you plan your next videos, the information helps you more efficiently interact with fans, subscribers, or viewers. It can also tell you if your fans' demographics are slightly different than you had anticipated and if you need to adapt your video planning and communication strategies.

HOW TO DEVELOP AN ONGOING RAPPORT WITH YOUR VIEWERS, FANS, AND SUBSCRIBERS

Once you get people to watch just one of your videos, make it easy for them to watch your other videos as well. This can be done within the videos themselves, on your YouTube channel's page, via email announcements of new videos, and announcements on Facebook, Twitter, and other social media.

Remember, within every video you produce, it should contain some type of call to action—a request that your viewers immediately do something. This call to action should be accompanied by a reward. For example, say something like, "To save $50 off of your first order, click here to visit our website."

You can add a direct call to action within a video in a handful of ways:

- Add a message inviting people to watch your other videos.
- Embed easy-to-find links to your other videos within each of your videos and on your channel's page.
- Encourage your viewers to like and rate your videos.
- Make it easy for people to share your videos via online social networking or email by enabling the "Share" function.
- Ask viewers for ideas for future video topics, so they feel like they're part of the creative process.
- Pose specific questions and encourage viewers to post their video responses. You can also ask survey questions or solicit feedback. For example, if you're using a YouTube video to demonstrate a new product, ask people to post their thoughts about the product itself, or their own ideas about how they'd use it.
- Ask fans, customers, potential customers, or subscribers to send you questions via email, Facebook, or Twitter, and answer the most common questions in future videos. When you do this, be sure to credit the questioner. For example, begin with, "Bob Smith from White Plains, New York, asks . . ."
- Encourage people to visit your webpage, read your blog, visit your Facebook page, and follow you or your company on Twitter.

If you're using YouTube video to communicate with your potential or existing customers, it's essential that you publish your contact information in conjunction with your videos. However, only do this within your videos and/or on your YouTube channel's page if you intend to actually respond quickly and, potentially, personally. Otherwise, simply ask your viewers, fans, and subscribers to post comments related to your videos through YouTube and make it clear that you read them all.

When it comes to your overall online presence, think synergy. Promote your YouTube videos and channel via your webpage, Facebook page, Twitter feed, etc., and at the same time, provide links and mentions of your other online activities within your videos and on your YouTube channel's page, as well as within your videos. You'll probably discover, however, that it's easier and more efficient to interact with your audience through a Facebook page or Twitter feed.

One thing to avoid when interacting with your YouTube audience is engaging "haters" or "trolls"—people who continuously post negative or hateful comments related to you, your company, or your videos. Responding to these people in either a public or private forum often leads to escalation of their behavior. If you determine someone is simply trying to be a nuisance by posting negative information, delete their comments and do not respond to them.

Obviously, if one of your viewers, customers, or potential customers has a legitimate gripe, address that on a one-on-one basis by phone or email. But be aware that there are many "haters" on YouTube that simply make a habit of posting negative and potentially reputation-damaging comments on the service for no good reason whatsoever. Later in this book, you'll read interviews with YouTube and online marketing experts who explain in greater detail how to best handle these people.

Determine Who in Your Audience Has Influence

Using tools available online, such as a service called Klout (www.klout.com), or simply by reviewing the number of friends your viewers, fans, or subscribers have in conjunction with their own Facebook, Google+, Twitter, and/or LinkedIn accounts, you can see firsthand how much influence each person has over others in cyberspace.

As you're working to promote your videos and YouTube Channel, analyze your audience, figure out who the influencers are, and try to cater to them, through direct contact. At the same time, figure out who is producing videos that are similar in focus or content to yours, as well as YouTube channels that are catering to the same target audience, even if their content is vastly different from what you're offering.

In addition to reviewing the video content, production quality, and approach, pay attention to how they're being promoted, what keywords are being used, and who is their intended audience.

You can find similar videos using a keyword search on YouTube itself, or you can use a service like Pixability (https://app.pixability.com/radar) to help you find videos that are somehow related to yours, or that have a similar target audience.

HOW TO CONTINUOUSLY EXPAND YOUR ONLINE FOLLOWING

In addition to the steps you take to actively promote your videos, there are also many subtle ways of generating more video views and for increasing viewer loyalty.

Include Accurate and Relevant Keywords in Your Video's Title, Description, and Tags

As you're uploading and publishing each new video, compose a creative, well-thought-out, informative, and captivating title for each video and a detailed description that's short, direct, and enticing. Equally important are the tags you associate with your videos.

Every word in a video's title, description, or tag(s) becomes keyword searchable—not just on YouTube, but through search engines like Google. Ideally, if someone is interested in a topic that's related to one or more of your videos, they should be able to discover your video easily by entering appropriate keywords or a relevant search phrase into the YouTube search field.

You'll be pleasantly surprised by the number of views you can achieve simply as a result of random people using a keyword search. So it's essential that you incorporate as many keywords as possible within a video's title and description, and that you also associate relevant keywords as tags. This is all done when you upload your video, but can be updated at any time via your YouTube channel's "Video Manager" menu, by clicking on the "Info and Settings" tab, and then entering the basic information that's requested for the title, description, and tags. Even after a video is published, you can add or revise a video's title, description, and/or tags in an effort to reach a broader audience.

Use Twitter to Solicit YouTube Video Views and Interact with Your Audience

Twitter is an extremely powerful tool for developing an audience. This service allows you to communicate with all of your followers regularly, informally, and simultaneously. As you do this, be sure to incorporate topic and keyword hashtags into your tweets. Doing this makes it easier for Twitter users who are not following you to still find and read your tweets, via a keyword search.

Anytime you're posting a tweet announcing that you've published a new video on YouTube, in addition to providing a direct link, include a brief, detailed preview of what people can expect and include several hashtag topics (#topic) at the end of the tweet. You also have the option of setting up your YouTube account to automatically publish details about your newly uploaded videos via your Twitter feed. However, when this automatic process works, you don't control the exact outgoing message or which hashtag topics are included.

For example, the tweet could say:

> Discover tips for growing roses in Main Street Florist's new video. Visit www.
> [video URL].com #roses #garden #flowers #plants

Anyone using Twitter and searching for *roses, garden, flowers,* or *plants* will quickly find your tweet and see a link to your video. Then, you can encourage people to tweet their gardening questions to you and you can publicly answer those questions by directing people to your videos.

Tips for Building Your Twitter Following

If all of the videos on your YouTube channel relate to the same core topic, perform your own search on Twitter using keywords or search phrases that relate to your channel's content. You'll be able to view all of the tweets from other users that include those terms.

You can then follow those people, which will encourage them to follow your Twitter feed. It's also possible to contact each directly via Twitter, by addressing them personally. They will then see your tweets that promote your videos and have the opportunity to view them.

For example, if you notice a Twitter user with the username @flowergrower is actively discussing her interest in rose gardening on Twitter, you can post a message that says something like:

> @flowergrower Please check out Main Street Florist's latest video about how to
> grow roses. [Insert Link].

When you interact with strangers directly (in an unsolicited manner) via Twitter, Facebook, or via email, make sure your solicitations are not perceived as blatant advertisements or spam. This could result in your account getting locked.

You can take this strategy a step further and use specialized Windows or Mac OS-based software, called TweetAdder (www.tweetadder.com), to find followers based on keywords that are relevant to what you're trying to promote. As you can see from Figure 5–2 on page 69, the TweetAdder software offers an easy way to build and manage your Twitter account, expand your following, and interact with your followers using an automated process.

TweetAdder requires a short learning curve, but once you get it up and running, you can use one or more of its features to more effectively interact with your existing Twitter following, while at the same time constantly work toward expanding the number of followers you have. To make the best use of this software, plan on running its automated functions for about 30 minutes per day while you're doing other work on your computer.

Using the TweetAdder software, which is priced between $55 and $188 (depending on how many Twitter accounts you want it to support), you can easily add dozens or even hundreds of new Twitter followers every day. There is no recurring fee for using TweetAdder. Then, use the tweets you post to promote your YouTube videos.

Among other things, TweetAdder can also be used to compose and send automated responses to new followers, as well as to Twitter users who send you direct messages using the service. Thus, you can appear to be interacting directly and personally with your Twitter followers.

Part of your online marketing strategy that includes producing, publishing, and promoting YouTube videos should include using Twitter to promote those videos and your YouTube channel, as well as to more directly interact with your viewers, fans, and subscribers. An ongoing flow of new tweets (on Twitter) and updates on your company's

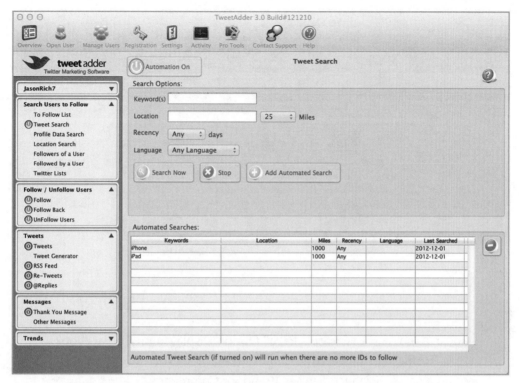

FIGURE 5–2. The TweetAdder Software Is Shown Here Running on a Mac.
A Windows Version Is also Available.

Facebook page, for example, are excellent vehicles for interacting and communicating with your audience between new video YouTube posts.

Build an Audience for Your Videos on Facebook

A Facebook page for your business allows you to share content that you create with the service's more than 1 billion users worldwide. Once your Facebook page is created, it's easy to promote YouTube videos by embedding them directly on your Facebook page and/or by including links to the videos in your Facebook status updates. You can also publish stills from your videos in Facebook's online photo albums and include detailed captions and tags.

To create a Facebook page for your company, product, group, or organization, go to www.Facebook.com, and click on the "Create a Page" link that's displayed along the bottom of the screen. From the "Create a Page" menu (shown in Figure 5–3 on page 70), choose the type of page you want to create in order to better communicate with your audience or customers. Your options include:

FIGURE 5–3. Use the "Create a Page" Option Displayed on the Facebook Homepage to Create an Online Presence for Your Business, Product, Service, Brand, or Community.

- Local business or place
- Company, organization, or institution
- Brand or product
- Artist, band, or public figure
- Entertainment
- Cause or community

Once you choose the type of Facebook page you want to establish by clicking on it (based on what type of business or organization you're trying to promote), use the displayed pull-down menus and fields to define the purpose of your page, its subject matter, and, if applicable, its location. Each category offers a different selection of relevant pull-down menus and fields to fill in. Next, click on the "Get Started" button (shown in Figure 5-4, page 71). For a small business, you'd probably want to choose the "Local Business or Place," or the "Company, Organization or Institution" type of Facebook page. However, if the page you're creating is specifically to promote a product or brand, select the "Brand or Product" option. Choose the option that's most relevant based on who you are trying to establish yourself as in terms of an online entity and what you're trying to accomplish.

FIGURE 5–4. Based on the Type of Facebook Page You Choose to Create, Use the Displayed Pull-Down Menus and Data Fields to Define the Purpose of Your Facebook Page, Then Click on the "Get Started" Button.

When prompted, create a Facebook account by providing your email address, an account password, your date of birth, and other requested information. Or, if you already have a Facebook account, click on the "I Already Have A Facebook Account" option. Follow the on-screen prompts to establish a Facebook page. Next, as you begin posting content to the page, you can embed your individual YouTube videos as posts. This can be done from Facebook (as you're managing your Facebook page) or while managing your YouTube Channel account.

Based on how you set up your Facebook page, not only can you promote your online presence yourself, but Facebook users will be able to find your page based on keywords and tags you incorporate into the title, description, and other relevant fields when creating the page. Then, in addition to serving as a platform for showcasing your videos, you can use the Facebook page to further promote your company, product, or service. It can also be used to directly communicate with your fans, followers, subscribers, and/or viewers.

Post Comments about Videos Produced by Others

Yet another way to promote your videos is to find the most influential people who are also targeting your intended audience and become active on their respective YouTube Channels, Facebook pages, and Twitter feeds. This can be done by posting your own comments to their videos, and by engaging in online conversations. Comments you post to other videos and channels can help boost your online popularity, assuming the comments you post are constructive and insightful.

Another powerful tool YouTube offers for promoting your channel is to create and publish video responses to popular videos on other channels. Doing this essentially allows you to ride on the coattails of an already popular and relevant video, and potentially reach a broader audience. However, be careful. If your video responses appear too promotional, they could be labeled as spam, which will result in your account being blocked. So, if you plan to use video responses, be creative, subtle, and not overly aggressive.

If you have a budget to promote your videos, consider using keyword advertising on Facebook. These ads are inexpensive, highly targeted, flexible, and easy to create and launch. You can begin advertising on Facebook for as little as $50, and begin reaching potential viewers in just minutes. You'll learn more about advertising on Facebook (and other online services, like Google and Yahoo!) to promote your videos in Chapter 6, "Promoting Your YouTube Videos."

HOST REAL-TIME VIDEO CHATS

Another way to interact with your fans, viewers, and subscribers is to occasionally host live video chats or video conferences, and invite your target YouTube audience to participate. YouTube does not currently offer this capability, but Google+ (www.google.com/+), YouNow (www.younow.com), U Stream (www.ustream.tv), LiveStream (http://new.livestream.com), and GoToMeeting (www.gotomeeting.com) allow you to host free or low-cost, live video conferences or to broadcast live with participants—from a handful of people to thousands. You can then publish recordings of the live conference or chat on your YouTube Channel so people can access them on an on-demand basis.

Keep in mind, Google owns both YouTube and the Google+ service. Thus, the company has made it easy to host a live Google+ Hangout (live conference) and then quickly record and publish it on your YouTube Channel.

A live video broadcast gives your fans, viewers, and subscribers a chance to interact with you in a real-time, safe online environment. Many businesses and successful YouTube personalities host weekly or monthly live broadcasts as a way to interact more directly with people who share an interest in them, their company, or their products or services. Later in this book, you'll read an interview with several YouTube and online marketing experts who use this strategy very successfully.

Hosting live video broadcasts requires a slightly different skill set than recording, editing, publishing, and promoting YouTube videos, because there is no delay, and no chance to edit your content. When you host a live video, it's essentially public speaking, because you're communicating with a live audience. Thus, while you probably won't want to script your broadcast/stream word-for-word, you will want to prepare a detailed outline of what you'll discover or cover within your "program," and then rehearse your presentation before going live.

SAFETY AND PRIVACY CONSIDERATIONS

Online popularity, even if you're a company that develops videos that ultimately become popular on YouTube, can become a double-edged sword. Thus, for the company spokespeople appearing in your videos, it may become important to maintain some level of privacy in their lives. Remember, total strangers from all over the world will potentially have access to your videos. Over time, your audience will feel as if they're getting to know you or your spokespeople—which can be a really good thing.

However, as an online personality or the spokesperson for a business, you'll definitely want to separate your online popularity from real life, or you could wind up with some of your more motivated viewers turning into unwanted stalkers. When it comes to maintaining your online safely and privacy, use common sense. Here are a few strategies you might want to incorporate right from the start:

- Never disclose your exact home address. You can simply refer to home as being within the closest major city to where you actually live.
- Don't disclose too much detail about your family, especially your kids. If you're a business operator, be careful about how much personal information you share about your coworkers or employees.
- Avoid revealing anything that could help unwanted stalkers discover where you live.

■ Create a separate email address that you can share online with your audience. Keep it separate from your personal or work email. Set up a free Gmail email account (http://mail.google.com).

If you want to give out a mailing address, rent a P.O. box from your local U.S. Post Office branch. This can be done online (www.usps.com/manage/get-a-po-box.htm), or at any U.S. Post Office for an annual fee. Be aware, however, that a P.O. box will only accept U.S. mail deliveries, not packages sent through other couriers, such as UPS or FedEx.

Another option that can be beneficial to small-business operators, homebased business operators, or entrepreneurs, for example, is to rent a mailbox from a company like The UPS Store (www.theupsstore.com). Packages from all carriers will also be accepted, and you can arrange for mail forwarding.

Once you disclose information online, it's out there in cyberspace forever, even if you attempt to delete it later. Be very careful about what personal information you disclose in your videos, as well as in your video descriptions and when communicating with your audience via YouTube or other online social networking services.

Promoting Your YouTube Videos

IN THIS CHAPTER

- Hallmarks of video success
- Video promotional opportunities available through YouTube
- Tracking your progress
- Other online approaches for increasing video views
- Utilizing the online social networking sites
- Hiring a YouTube video marketing expert
- 12 proven video promotion strategies

A YouTube video's success is measured in several ways, including:

- The number of people who place an online or telephone order for your product or service after watching your video(s)
- How many views it receives
- The number of subscribers the video attracts to your YouTube channel
- The quality of interaction as someone watches the video (i.e.: Do they watch the entire video or click out of it before it's over?)
- The number of positive (or negative) comments it receives on the YouTube service

- How many people like the video, versus how many people dislike the video, compared to those who watch it and don't click on either the "Like" (thumb up) or "Dislike" (thumb down) icon
- The number of people who favorite a video
- The number of people who share a video (or a link to the video) with their online friends via Facebook, Twitter, Google+, etc.
- The number of people who respond to your video's call to action
- The number of people who watch your video on YouTube and then utilize one of the links offered within the video or on your YouTube channel's page to access your company's website, blog, Facebook page, etc.

Receiving between 100 to 500 video views that ultimately result in additional sales of your product or service may be deemed a huge success by your company. However, if you're looking to extend your brand awareness across a targeted demographic, throughout a region, or an entire country, your goal may be to achieve thousands or tens of thousands of views for each of your YouTube videos.

Whether you're trying to attract 100, 1,000, 10,000, 100,000 or 1 million views for each of your YouTube videos, or your YouTube channel as a whole, you'll need a well-thought-out, ongoing, multifaceted, and creative plan to promote your videos—both online and in the real world—that's specifically targeted to the audience you're attempting to reach. Even if you create an awesome video that perfectly targets your audience, if you don't properly promote it, people are not going to see it. You can't simply rely on people stumbling across your video as a result of a YouTube or Google Search.

This chapter focuses on the promotional aspect of building an audience for your YouTube videos, and includes a handful of no-cost or low-cost strategies you can either implement yourself or pursue using third parties.

Before you begin, define your overall objectives, such as:

- Who you want to see your videos
- How many views you'd like to attract
- What's your objective once people watch your video
- How you'll measure the success of your YouTube efforts
- How much time, money, and other resources are at your disposal to promote both individual videos and your company's YouTube channel

Promoting individual YouTube videos or a YouTube channel requires an ongoing commitment of time and human resources, and potentially some money as well. It's the only way to build and sustain an audience. However, once you develop a dedicated audience for your first few videos and those people become subscribers to your channel, getting them to watch future videos will be much easier. When you reach this point, your goals then include retaining your existing subscribers while continuously seeking out new subscribers.

Most of your promotional efforts will take time to work. Be patient! Don't expect to publish your first video and generate hundreds or thousands of views in the first few days. Have realistic expectations; it takes time to build an audience.

Once you have defined your objectives, consider using at least several of the strategies outlined in this chapter to achieve them. In other words, take a multifaceted approach to these activities. Your promotional/advertising effort should take into account the following three components:

1. *It should be highly targeted.* Figure out how to best reach your intended audience, online and in the real world. If you want a specific demographic to watch your videos, you need to reach those people and inform them of the video's existence, as well as how and where to find and view it.
2. *It should be ongoing.* If you want to maintain a steady flow of viewers, you need to continuously promote your videos and channel.
3. *It should be multifaceted.* Don't just rely on one promotional or advertising activity to build and maintain an audience for your videos, even if you notice a single approach is initially working. Over the long term, you're much better off simultaneously pursuing at least three or more different promotional and/or advertising opportunities to drive a steady flow of viewers.

Be sure to track the results as carefully as possible so you can determine what's working, what's not working, and what efforts need to be fine-tuned to achieve better results. Ultimately, your goal when it comes to promoting/advertising your YouTube videos should be to dedicate as little time, money, and resources as possible to generate the desired results, and to make sure you're generating the best results possible based on your actions.

TRACK YOUR PROGRESS: BE SURE TO UTILIZE YOUTUBE ANALYTICS

In conjunction with your YouTube channel, a free, online toolset called YouTube Analytics is available. These tools can help you track, in real time, information about who is watching your videos. Additional, and in some cases, more powerful traffic and viewership tracking tools are offered by third parties for a fee, or are provided when you take advantage of online paid advertising to promote your videos.

To learn more about YouTube Analytics and how to use these free tools to analyze the audience for your videos, visit www.youtube.com/yt/advertise/youtube-analytics. html. The data provided by YouTube Analytics can help you plan and execute successful video marketing strategies. Google and Yahoo! are constantly upgrading these free tools and adding new functionality. For example, in addition to quickly determining who is watching your videos, where they're from, and how they're engaging with your videos, you can now track their quality of engagement and see if people are clicking out of your videos before they're over, and if so, exactly when. Knowing this, you can go back and fine-tune your videos in order to prevent people from exiting out of them early.

To access YouTube Analytics, you must first create a YouTube channel (refer back to Chapter 4, "How to Start Your Own YouTube Channel") and populate it with at least one video. Once you've logged into your YouTube account, click on the "Video Manager" button (or select the "Video Manager" menu option). Next, click on the "Analytics" tab that's displayed near the top-center of the screen.

Initially, you'll see the "Analytics Overview Report," which displays information about traffic pertaining to your YouTube channel page over the past 30 days. At the same time, the display shows information about your channel's top 10 most viewed videos and provides basic demographic information about your audience in terms of where they accessed YouTube from. From the "Overview Report," you'll also discover how people found your video(s).

This information is useful for tracking the effectiveness of ads, search engine listings, publicity generated about your videos, and other promotional activities. You can also download YouTube Analytics data in a spreadsheet format by clicking on a button that's located near the top-right corner of any "Analytics" screen.

To see specific Analytics information about a particular video on your YouTube channel page, use the "Content" field that's displayed near the top of the "Overview" page. More detailed information about where your viewers are coming from can be obtained by clicking on the "Geography" field, to the right of the "Content" field. By clicking on the "Date" field, you can view data based on a specific date range that you select.

From the "Overview Report," and from subsequent screens within YouTube Analytics, you can click on any data to display more detailed or specific information. For example, while viewing the "Overview Report," try clicking on any of the "Performance," "Engagement," "Top 10 Videos," "Demographics," or "Discovery" data boxes, as well as the "Content," "Geography," and "Date Range" fields.

Under the "Overview" heading that's displayed along the left margin of the screen, you'll see a handful of menu commands that can be clicked on to view additional reports, data, and information pertaining to the views and traffic associated with your YouTube channel page and/or individual videos.

If you don't want to invest further time tracking your efforts and figuring out what worked and what didn't, there are companies you can hire to assist with these tasks. For example, a service called BrandSights from TubeMogul (www.tubemogul.com/

solutions/playtime/brandsights) offers fee-based tools that go beyond what YouTube Analytics offers and help you measure things like brand awareness, message recall, favorability, and purchase intent.

START PROMOTING ON YOUTUBE AND WORK YOUR WAY AROUND CYBERSPACE

It's important to properly title your video, add an accurate description, and then associate highly relevant keywords and tags with it. It's this information that will

EMBEDDING YOUR VIDEO ON YOUR WEBSITE AND DRIVING TRAFFIC

In addition to utilizing the tools available on YouTube, you have the ability to feature your videos on your company's website, Facebook page, within a blog, and through other online social networking services. If you've built up an opt-in email list of your customers, clients, or other individuals, be sure to share a link to your latest videos with those people via direct email. However, you want to avoid using spam (unsolicited email) as a promotional tool.

If you opt to feature your videos on your own company's website or blog, for example, allow YouTube to host them and simply embed the videos using the HTML coding that's supplied by YouTube. While it will be obvious the video is linked to YouTube, every view it receives from your website or blog will help boost your YouTube traffic statistics. The other benefit to allowing YouTube to host the videos that you showcase on your website or blog is that all of the storage space and bandwidth needed is provided by YouTube for free.

To embed one of your YouTube videos within a website, visit the "Video Manager" area of YouTube after logging in to your YouTube Channel. Select the video you want to embed, and then click on the "Share" option, followed by the "Embed" option. Within a window, the HTML code needed to embed the video into your website will automatically be created and displayed. Copy the HTML code exactly as it appears and paste it into the appropriate place within the HTML code for your website. Information about how to do this can be found online at: http://support.google.com/youtube/bin/answer.py?hl=en&answer=171780.

allow people who access YouTube to more easily find your videos, even if they don't have the direct link to the video or details about your YouTube channel's page. This information is also shared (usually very quickly) with the Google search engine. Thus, potential viewers will be able to find your video by entering relevant keywords into the "Search" field of YouTube or Google, as well as other search engines you get the video's link listed on. Keywords and tags are covered in Chapter 12, "Uploading Your Videos To YouTube."

In addition to encouraging your viewers to like your videos, post comments, rate, and share your videos, you should also allow (and even encourage) your videos to be embedded within other websites and blogs, for example, because this will help boost their exposure and accessibility.

One of your responsibilities as you evaluate your audience data is to listen. Pay attention to what your viewers are saying in their comments and video responses. Also pay attention to the number of likes and positive ratings your video receives. These are indicators for how it's being received by your audience that you can use to fine-tune your message and create future videos to reach a broader audience. You can also go back and re-edit or rework your existing videos to increase their effectiveness and appeal based on your audience-related data.

Also, while you can encourage comments and/or video responses, initially keep comments private—viewable only by you. You want to be sure that the general consensus among your targeted audience is positive. Your initial efforts will involve a bit of a learning curve as you get to know how to fully utilize YouTube and become acquainted with your target audience's viewing habits. Keep in mind that negative comments, poor ratings, and "dislikes" will tarnish your online reputation and make it difficult for your subsequent videos to gain traction and popularity.

Team Up with Other YouTube Personalities and Video Producers

In addition to producing and potentially starring in your own videos, in order to promote yourself, your company, and/or your products/services on YouTube, when applicable, try to team up with other well-established YouTube personalities and video producers. You could also team up with other small businesses or entrepreneurs that are not in direct competition with you, but who are targeting the same audience. The variety of ways you can work together in a mutually beneficial way include:

- Pinpoint one or more "famous" online personalities that cater to your target audience, and provide them with free samples of your product so they can feature them within their videos. This is a quick and inexpensive way to reach many thousands of people using someone else's YouTube popularity.

- Hire a well-known YouTube personality to star in one or more of your videos, and at the same time promote your company and products/services as a paid spokesperson. An established online personality might already have tens of thousands or hundreds of thousands of dedicated subscribers whom you can reach through some type of collaboration. This works very much like hiring a paid celebrity endorser or spokesperson, but YouTube personalities tend to cost much less and allow you to reach a YouTube audience.

- Find companies that are effectively using YouTube that cater to the same target audience as you, but that are not in direct competition, and propose either collaborating on a video or cross-promoting each other's videos through your respective YouTube channels, websites, blogs, Facebook pages, and Twitter feeds. The goal is for both companies to benefit from reaching a broader audience in a way that looks like the company you're collaborating with is endorsing you and you're endorsing them.

TAKE ADVANTAGE OF SEARCH ENGINE OPTIMIZATION TO PROMOTE YOUR VIDEOS

Because many web surfers decide what websites they'll visit or which YouTube videos they'll watch based on results given to them by their favorite search engine (such as Google or Yahoo!), one way to promote your videos is to get them listed on the popular search engines and then utilize search engine optimization (SEO) techniques to help ensure a link to your video is one of the first search results someone sees when performing a keyword search using a popular search engine.

Using search engine optimization is a specialized skill unto itself. It requires that you stay up to date on how all of the popular search engines work. When you publish a new video on YouTube, it becomes searchable via Google rather quickly. How effective your Google listing is at attracting viewers will depend on several factors, including the title, description, and keywords that are associated with the video itself. Thus, if you have 10 or more separate videos on your YouTube channel, and each is listed on Google using the same or related keywords and tags, for example, this dramatically increases your company's ability to be found on Google by your potential customers. Instead of having just one listing on Google for your company's main website, you'll now have multiple Google listings, which will improve your SEO rankings. Then, from your YouTube channel, you can link videos together as a playlist, or through links, so your audience will be able to watch all of your videos easily once they've accessed your channel.

Beyond the traditional search engines, like Google, Yahoo!, and Bing, there are a handful of search engines that specialize only in videos, such as Blinkx (www.blinkx.com)

and AOL On (http://on.aol.com). Be sure to list your videos on these services as well, plus upload them to YouTube competitor sites, such as Vimeo (www.vimeo.com).

While you can learn to implement SEO strategies yourself, it requires a considerable learning curve. You may be much better off hiring a legitimate company or independent consultant who specializes in SEO. The investment could increase your chances of success, plus speed up the time it takes for your highly ranked search engine listings to appear.

To learn more about SEO and how it works, and also how it can be used to help you promote YouTube videos or a YouTube channel, download and read the *Google Search Engine Optimization Starter Guide*. You can find this document easily by entering the title into the Google Search engine.

ADVERTISE YOUR VIDEOS: IT COSTS MONEY, BUT WORKS FAST

If you have the budget, seriously consider using paid search advertising (also referred to as keyword advertising) to promote your YouTube videos.

For example, when you use Google AdWords or Google AdWords for Video, or similar services offered by Yahoo!, Bing, and Facebook, you can create short ads that include a direct link to one of your videos or your YouTube channel page. These paid advertising opportunities are inexpensive and highly targeted, ensuring that your ad(s) will be seen at the exact moment someone is searching for content based on a keyword or search phrase that matches specific keywords associated with your video content.

These services work on a pay-per-click (PPC) basis, which means you only pay when someone actually clicks on the link featured within your ad. While thousands of people may see the ad, if only 100 of those people actually click on the link, you only pay for those 100 clicks, not the thousands of views. For you, the advertiser, this is a very economical and risk-free way to promote your videos.

How much you wind up paying per click will vary greatly, based on the popularity of keywords you select to associate with your ad, along with a handful of other factors. How much you pay per click is referred to as the cost-per-click. Another benefit to this type of advertising is that you can set your budget in advance.

For example, if you know the cost per click is 50 cents, and you have a $100 per week budget, you know that in your best-case scenario, your ad will generate 200 new views. You also know that the people watching your videos are well-qualified and part of your target demographic. This method works best when your cost per click is very low, but the click-through rate (the number of people who click on the link in your ad versus the number of people who see the ad) is very high.

A Google AdWords ad, for example, includes a short headline, a web link (URL), and two short lines of text. When you advertise on Facebook, you're also allowed to incorporate a logo or thumbnail graphic into your ad. A Google AdWords for Video ad includes a short video that you produce (that could link to your website or your YouTube channel) that will ultimately be seen before someone watches someone else's video that features related content.

What's not seen by the people viewing your ad, but that you as the advertiser need to create, is a list of highly specific keywords or tags related to whatever it is you're promoting. It's these keywords (along with the content within your ad), combined with a few other factors, that will determine who sees your ad, where it's seen, and how often it's seen. The keywords you select are as important as the content of the ad itself.

Every character, word, and line within a Google AdWords ad, for example, should have a purpose and impact, plus convey a message. The ad's goal is to attract attention and get someone to click on the link in order to immediately access your video, YouTube channel page, or your website that has your YouTube video embedded in it.

All of the major search engines offer keyword advertising opportunities, as does Facebook. To learn more about these opportunities, visit:

- Google AdWords—www.google.com/adwords
- Yahoo! Search Advertising—http://advertising.yahoo.com/article/search-advertising.html
- Bing Ads—http://advertise.bingads.microsoft.com
- Facebook Ads—www.facebook.com/ads/create

All have a very low startup cost but offer the ability to ensure that your ads are seen exclusively by your target demographic within the time frame you select. One of the great things about using these advertising services is that you have the opportunity to target your ad's viewers. Plus, you can create, launch, and see the results from your ads within hours of launching a new campaign. It's also possible to easily run and track multiple campaigns simultaneously that utilize a different ad message or a different assortment of keywords.

Keyword or search-based advertising is one of the most cost-effective ways small businesses can promote their company, product, service, or YouTube videos online. Because Google AdWords is so closely related to YouTube, this is probably the best service to begin advertising with. However, getting back to the multifaceted approach content, ultimately you may want to run ad campaigns using two or more of these services simultaneously in order to reach web surfers when and where they're actually looking for your product or service (or content that's related to your videos).

On the YouTube service itself, one fee-based method for promoting one or more of your videos at a time is to utilize the AdWords for Video program (which was formerly known as The Promoted Videos program). Like the text-based Google AdWords,

AdWords for Video allows you to promote your YouTube videos in a way that's highly targeted, yet it's offered on a pay-per-click and easily affordable basis. One difference between AdWords and AdWords for Video is that the latter includes a thumbnail video image within the ad.

Keyword advertising can help you quickly build an audience for your videos, because you can create and launch an ad campaign within an hour or two and immediately track its results in real time. Based on your budget, consider running multiple ad campaigns, with different wording or keywords associated with each, simultaneously on a single service or across several services in order to more efficiently build an audience for your videos. Use advertising in conjunction with the free promotional opportunities you have available by actively participating on Facebook, Google+, Twitter, and LinkedIn.

Reach a Local Audience in a Specific Geographic Area with Google AdWords Express

If your goal is to reach a local geographic audience, Google has developed AdWords Express (www.google.com/adwords/express), which allows small businesses to reach potential customers within a local geographic radius. This service takes advantage of the latest wireless mobile technologies to help you reach your audience at precisely the right moment, based on their location. Using AdWords Express, all you need to do is select a business category, write a two-line ad, and set your budget. Unlike traditional AdWords ads, there are no keywords to choose. AdWords Express ads also appear in conjunction with Google Maps and other map-related apps used with smartphones and tablets.

When you run ads with AdWords Express to promote a video, for example, only people who do a search in your geographic area for a relevant topic will see your ad(s). AdWords Express ads can lead people directly to a video's URL, your company's website, or a Google+ page, which is provided for free. Like AdWords, when you use AdWords Express, you only pay for clicks, you can start and end a campaign at any time, you control your spending, and you're given access to tracking and reporting tools for measuring an ad's results.

SEEK OUT THIRD-PARTY HELP

There's an entire industry of YouTube video marketing companies selling their services to promote and create audiences for YouTube videos. Some even have video production expertise and can serve as a turnkey solution to creating high-quality videos, targeting a specific audience, and promoting the videos to that audience. The cost can range from several hundred dollars to tens of thousands of dollars per month.

One way to find low-cost help from YouTube video marketing experts is to seek out experienced freelancers using a service like eLance.com (www.elance.com). When you take this route, however, make sure you review each person's resume, evaluate their experience and ask to see samples of their successes and references from their past clients to ensure they have the expertise and experience you're looking for.

There are also many companies that simply sell video views at a specific cost. Be very careful before hiring one of these services, because some of them use fake YouTube accounts and other tools to generate artificial views for a video. While the view counter associated with your video goes up, in reality a human, much less someone from your target audience, never actually sees the video. And if you get caught generating fake views for your videos by YouTube, your video may be taken offline and your YouTube channel could be suspended. In addition, the majority of these services will not help to improve your overall quality of engagement scores, which is now how YouTube gauges the quality, popularity, and success of a video.

Chances are you're being offered some type of scam if a service is selling a specific number of YouTube video views for a specific price. You're much better off hiring a company that will guarantee that the viewers they drive to your video will actually be human, fall into your target demographic, and will actually watch your video. This can only be done by using proven video marketing and promotional techniques that you could do yourself, if you have the wherewithal, knowledge, and time to handle it. To hire a company to handle your YouTube video marketing, and do it well, you'll pay a premium, but you're more apt to see better results faster than doing it yourself if you're inexperienced at managing YouTube video promotions.

Among the companies that are offering legitimate service for helping to boost the popularity of a YouTube video are: YouTubeBuzz.com, Virool (www.virool.com), and Viewbox (www.viewbox.com).

MAKE SURE YOUR EXPECTATIONS ARE REALISTIC

If you have dreams of your YouTube videos going viral, so that they're seen by millions or even billions of people, keep in mind that this is more often than not a fluke, not because of a planned marketing and promotion strategy or the result of spending a fortune to spread the word about a particular video.

Most of the YouTube videos that go viral are either produced by a well-known celebrity who already has a significant following or by an ordinary person, on a shoestring budget, who happens to catch the attention of online influencers who ultimately help spread the word about a video. These videos are truly unique, quirky, funny, outrageous, controversial, or somehow stand out.

Many videos that go viral also receive help by receiving mainstream media coverage—on TV, in newspapers, in magazines, as well as on websites and blogs.

12 PROVEN STRATEGIES FOR PROMOTING YOUTUBE VIDEOS

When it comes to marketing and promoting your YouTube videos, follow these 12 basic strategies:

1. Start by using the tools available directly through YouTube. For example, provide a detailed and accurate title and description to each of your videos, and associate tags (keywords) that are directly relevant.

2. Use a call to action within your videos to encourage people to like, rate, comment on, and share your videos.

3. Begin by promoting your videos to the people you know, including your real-life friends, relatives, customers, and clients. Ask these people to watch your video(s) and share them with their online friends.

4. Take advantage of the power and capabilities of the online social networking sites to promote your videos. As a spokesperson for your company, for example, become active on Facebook, Google+, and Twitter, as well as other relevant services. Be sure to create an online presence for your business on Facebook and/or Google+, and then use that presence to promote your videos.

5. Incorporate your videos into your own company's website and blog.

6. Share links to your videos with your existing customers or clients via opt-in email.

7. Use public relations techniques, such as using press releases to contact bloggers, editors, reporters, and producers in order to generate free media coverage for your videos in mainstream media, as well as in blogs that cater to your target audience.

8. Get your videos (and your YouTube Channel page) listed with the major search engines, including Google, Yahoo!, and Bing, and then focus on SEO strategies to get the best possible listing placements.

9. Try to collaborate on videos with other companies that are already utilizing YouTube effectively, that are targeting the same audience, but that are not in direct competition with you. This will allow you to capture the attention of your collaborator's viewers and subscribers.

12 PROVEN STRATEGIES FOR PROMOTING YOUTUBE VIDEOS, CONTINUED

10. Start promoting your YouTube channel within your company's printed catalogs, brochures, sales materials, as well as within its existing traditional advertising.

11. Consider paying for keyword advertising on Google, Yahoo!, Bing, and Facebook. Google AdWords for Video is also a very cost-effective and powerful tool for promoting YouTube videos.

12. If you have the budget, hire a YouTube video marketing company to help you plan and implement an online promotional campaign for your videos.

The video gets people talking about it and wanting to share it. There are no proven strategies or steps.

The majority of videos that are backed by massive PR, advertising, and marketing campaigns, created and launched by pros, don't wind up going truly viral, although they may generate a lot of views. So, if your budget and resources are more modest than a Fortune 500 company, make sure your expectations for how your video will perform on YouTube are in line with the promotions and advertising you do for it.

Monetizing YouTube: Getting Paid for Your Video Views

IN THIS CHAPTER
- An introduction to the YouTube Partner Program
- How to sign up for the YouTube Partner program
- Generating the most revenue possible from YouTube
- Other ways to earn money from your videos

Online advertising is a big business, which is something that the folks at Google and YouTube understand extremely well. In an effort to encourage video producers like you to display online ads in conjunction with their videos, YouTube has not only made accepting and displaying ads an easy and automated process, but also a potentially lucrative one for its participating YouTube Channel operators.

If you're setting up a YouTube Channel for your own business and branding it accordingly, you probably do not want to display ads from other companies. Based on your video tags and descriptions, if you agree to participate in the YouTube Partner Program, Google matches up ad content with video content, so you could wind up displaying ads from your direct competitors.

Thus, becoming a YouTube Partner for the purpose of displaying ads in conjunction with your company's videos is probably not advantageous. However, you can use Google AdWords and Google AdWords for Video to run online ads in an effort to promote your own videos and YouTube channel. In this case, instead of becoming a paid YouTube Partner, you'd become a paying YouTube advertiser. Refer back to Chapter 6, "Promoting Your YouTube Videos," for more information about using online ads to promote your videos.

WHEN BECOMING A YOUTUBE PARTNER CAN BE ADVANTAGEOUS

The concept behind the YouTube Partner program is simple. You create and publish videos on your YouTube Channel, and then do what's necessary to build an audience for them. Each time someone views one of your videos, either a banner display ad (called an "Overlay InVideo" ad) is displayed within the video window (shown in Figure 7–1), or a short TV commercial-style ad is played prior to your video playing. Plus, banner ads are automatically displayed on your YouTube channel page.

Each time someone views, clicks on, or watches a video-based ad on your YouTube Channel, you earn a little bit of revenue. How much you earn depends on a variety of criteria, including the type of ad that's seen or responded to by the viewer. So, if you want

FIGURE 7–1. An Example of an Overlay InVideo Ad that Can Be Displayed while Someone Watches Your Video.

to earn significant and ongoing revenues from YouTube (as a YouTube Partner), you'll need to consistently generate thousands, or better yet, tens of thousands (or more) video views, each and every month.

Millions of individual people (online personalities/YouTubers) and independent business professionals—freelancers, experts in their field who are not representing a specific employer, or consultants—who operate their own YouTube Channel have actually launched their own YouTube-based career, as a full-time or part-time endeavor, and manage to generate a respectable income from it.

However, achieving this objective not only takes a lot of creativity in order to produce videos that are popular, but you also need to work hard to promote your videos and YouTube channel in order to generate ongoing video views, plus cater to your channel's subscribers.

Becoming a YouTube Partner costs nothing and is totally optional. Prior to April 2012, it was necessary to apply in order to become a YouTube Partner, and not everyone was accepted. You needed to pre-establish a large online following and significant video views before getting accepted into the program. However, this is no longer the case.

Today, anyone who creates and operates their own YouTube Channel can sign up to become a YouTube Partner and potentially begin generating revenues from their videos. At the same time you apply to become a YouTube Partner (so that you can display online ads in conjunction with your videos), you'll also need to set up a Google AdSense account (which is also free), so that you can get paid. This requires linking your Google AdSense account (which gets tied to your Google Account) with your bank account. You'll discover how to do this shortly.

One of the biggest benefits to becoming a YouTube Partner is that Google handles all of the advertising placement, revenue collections, and your payments. Once you become part of the program, Google matches up your videos with advertisers, decides what ads will appear, and keeps track of all traffic (views), as well as ad responses. YouTube then pays you accordingly for your participation in the YouTube Partner program. There is no need for you to find, solicit, or manage the advertisers. This becomes an automated process.

Once you become a YouTube Partner, you can only earn revenue from videos that contain all original content and that adhere to YouTube's Terms of Service and Community Guidelines. Videos that violate copyrights, for example, do not quality for this program. It is possible to become a YouTube Partner and then enable or disable advertising for each individual video added to your YouTube channel. So, as long as you have at least one video published on your channel that has advertising enabled (after you join the YouTube Partner program), you're good to go.

HOW TO JOIN AND PARTICIPATE IN THE YOUTUBE PARTNER PROGRAM

If you ultimately want to generate money from your videos, first establish and customize your YouTube channel. Then populate the channel with original videos. When you're ready, turn on the YouTube Partner functionality for your account using the directions offered later in this chapter, and make sure at least one of your videos has advertising enabled.

Next, set up a Google AdSense account using the same Google Account you used to set up your YouTube Channel. Upon doing this, you will need to provide the bank account details and tax information that is requested. (Yes, you will need to pay taxes on the revenue you earn from YouTube/Google AdSense.)

Remember, your AdSense account must be associated with your YouTube account in order for you to ultimately get paid. It's also essential that you set all of this up before your video(s) are heavily promoted and/or go viral, which results in their popularity. The content of your videos must also be "advertiser friendly."

After you join the YouTube Partner program, remember that only videos that contain original content can display ads that ultimately allow you to earn revenue. For example, if your video contains copyrighted music that you do not own, or visual content that does not belong to you, the video is not eligible.

You are allowed to use content, however, that is royalty-free, or Creative Commons content, as long as the license agreement specifically grants you the right to use that material commercially. YouTube/Google will automatically analyze each video you make part of the YouTube Partner program, determine what type of content it contains, as well as its subject matter (based on the video's title, description, tags/keywords, and category), and then match up ads that will appeal to that same audience. As a YouTube Partner, you ultimately have no say in terms of what types of ads are displayed, nor can you choose which advertisers can have ads displayed in conjunction with your content.

So, if you sign up for the YouTube Partner program in order to generate revenue from people viewing your videos, you could wind up having your competitors advertise in conjunction with your video content. This, obviously, can be detrimental.

However, if you're an online performer, independent consultant, freelancer, or an expert in your field who is not affiliated with a specific employer, becoming a YouTube Partner can help to supplement your income, as long as you are not concerned about competing companies advertising on your YouTube channel or in conjunction with your videos.

Whether or not the revenue generation business model offered by becoming a YouTube Partner works for you is a matter of personal preference, based on your overall goals. That being said, many small businesses have discovered tremendous success by becoming a Google AdWords and/or Google AdWords for Video advertiser and paying to have their YouTube channel, individual videos, and/or their company, product, or service promoted through paid online advertising that gets displayed in conjunction with other YouTube videos.

HOW TO SIGN UP FOR THE YOUTUBE PARTNER PROGRAM

Registering to be a YouTube Partner is something you need to do just once—after your YouTube channel has been established. To add YouTube Partner functionality to your YouTube channel, access YouTube, and sign in using the same Google account information that was used to create the YouTube channel account. Then, follow these steps:

1. Near the upper-right corner of the screen, click on your username or profile picture.
2. When the YouTube menu appears, also near the top-right corner of the screen, click on the YouTube "Settings" option.
3. When the YouTube "Account Settings" screen is displayed (shown in Figure 7–2), click on the "Monetization" option. It can be found on the left side of the screen, under the "Channel Settings" option.
4. From the "Monetization" screen (shown in Figure 7–3, page 94), click on the blue and white "Enable My Account" button.

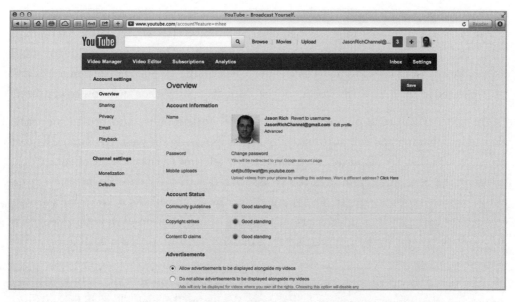

FIGURE 7–2. Click on the "Monetization" Option from the YouTube "Account Settings" Screen.

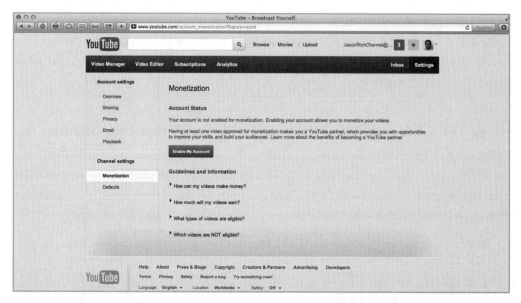

FIGURE 7–3. Click on the "Enable My Account" Button to Activate YouTube Partner Functionality.

5. A pop-up window that displays the YouTube "Monetization Agreement" will be displayed. Near the bottom-left corner of this window, add a checkmark to the three checkboxes indicating that you agree to the terms of the agreement. Click on the "I Accept" button to continue.

6. Another pop-up window will appear. This one is labeled "Monetize My Videos." It offers three options, each associated with a checkbox (shown in Figure 7–4 on page 95). These options include: "Overlay In-Video Ads," "TrueView In-Stream Ads," "Videos Contain a Product Placement." Click on the "Monetize" button that's displayed in the lower-right corner of the "Monetize My Videos" window to continue.

As soon as you turn on the YouTube Partner functionality and opt to monetize your videos, banner ads will automatically begin appearing on your YouTube Channel page. The ads that are displayed are often directly relevant to the content of your video, based on the description and tags you've associated with the video file. In some cases, public service announcements (PSAs) are shown or displayed. As a YouTube Partner, you cannot control which advertisers' ads appear in conjunction with your videos, nor do you have any say over the advertisers' ad message or content. This is all done at the discretion of Google.

The next pop-up window that appears offers a brief introduction to how you can monetize each of the videos you upload to your YouTube Channel. This will be explained shortly. For now, click on the "Got It" button to continue.

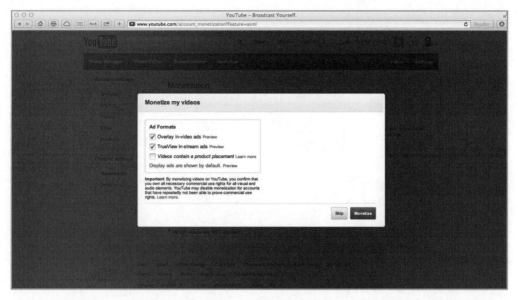

FIGURE 7–4. Select What Types of Ad You Will Allow to Be Displayed within Your Videos.

Your YouTube channel is now set up, and you've been registered with the YouTube Partner program. Again, this only needs to be done once. The next step is to turn on the ad features for each of your qualifying videos. This needs to be done for each video. Then, link your Google account (YouTube channel account) to a Google AdSense account, another process that needs to be done just once.

Be Sure to Activate the Ad Features for Your Individual Videos

Once you turn on the YouTube Partner functionality, then you return to the "Video Manager" page and look at the listing of your uploaded and published videos. To the right of each video title and thumbnail will now be three, not two icons (shown in Figure 7–5 on page 96). The new green and white "$" icon is the "Monetize" icon. Click on it to adjust the monetization settings for each qualifying video.

The "Info and Settings" screen for the video listing you selected will be displayed. Scroll down on the screen to where you see three command tabs, labeled "Basic Info," "Monetization," and "Advanced Settings." The "Monetization" tab should be pre-selected. If not, click on it.

To begin displaying ads in conjunction with the video, make sure a checkmark appears within the checkbox that says "Monetize My Video" (shown in Figure 7–6 on page 96). Next, within the "Ad Formats" box, click on which ad formats you want displayed. To generate the most revenue possible, make sure that both the "Overlay

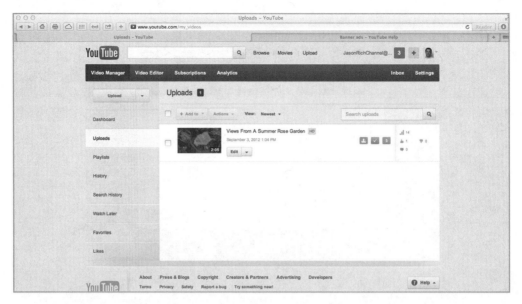

FIGURE 7–5. From a Video's Listing, Click on the "$" Icon to Monetize that
Particular Video, Providing It Is Eligible and Contains No Copyrighted
Material (Unless You Own that Material Outright
or Are Licensed to Use It).

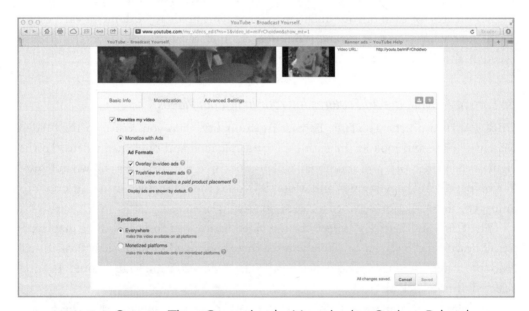

FIGURE 7–6. One at a Time, Customize the Monetization Options Related to
Each Video You Upload to Your YouTube Channel.

In-Video Ads" and "TrueView In-Stream Ads" options are selected and have a checkmark added to their respective checkboxes.

Then, under the "Syndication" heading, select the "Everywhere" option to ensure that the video will be available on all platforms. You can choose the "Monetized Platforms" option, but this will limit who will be able to view your actual videos.

By default, as soon as you make any changes to this page, the new settings will be saved. In the lower-right corner of the window, you should see a message that says "All Changes Saved," and the Saved button should be inactive. However, before leaving this page, if the Save button is active, click on it to manually save your changes.

At this point, whenever someone visits your YouTube channel page or somehow views your video(s), the types of ads you've selected will be displayed. Figure 7–7 shows a TrueView In-Stream ad being played before a video, as well as a banner ad displayed on the right side of the YouTube channel page. While the ad is playing, after about five seconds, in the lower-right corner of the video window will be a message that says "Skip Ad." A viewer can click on this to end the ad and immediately begin watching your video. The length of the ad is displayed near the lower-left corner of the video window. It can be anywhere from a few seconds to several minutes long.

Figure 7–8 on page 98 is an example of an Overlay InVideo ad that appears at around the 15-second mark as someone is watching the video. To make the ad disappear (and

FIGURE 7–7. Shown Here Is a TrueView In-Stream Ad Being Shown Before the Actual YouTube Video Is Played for the Viewer.

FIGURE 7–8. Here You Can See Another Example of an Overlay InVideo Ad, Which Looks Like a Banner Displayed Near the Bottom-Center of the Video Window While Your Video Is Playing.

see the whole video window as your video is playing), viewers will need to manually click on the "X" icon. Notice a banner ad is also displayed on the right side of the YouTube channel page.

If you opt to monetize your videos and permit Overlay InVideo ads, plan the filming of your videos accordingly. Do not have anything too important (such as captions or links) displayed in the lower area of the screen at or after the 15-second mark, or you run the risk of that information being covered by the overlaid ad.

SET UP A GOOGLE ADSENSE ACCOUNT

Once your YouTube Channel is set up and populated with videos, you've activated the YouTube Partner Program for the channel, and you begin seeing ads displayed in conjunction with your videos, the final step is to set up a Google AdSense account and link your bank account information to it, so you can be paid monthly by Google.

All money you earn as a result of being a YouTube Partner is managed through a Google AdSense account. To set up this account, log into your Google account, select the "YouTube Settings" option, and then under the "Channel Settings" heading that's displayed on the left side of the screen, click on "Monetization."

When the "Monetization" window appears (shown in Figure 7–9 on page 100), select either the "Create a New AdSense Account" or "Use an Existing AdSense Account"

OVERVIEW OF THE DIFFERENT AD FORMATS ON YOUTUBE

Google gives its paid advertisers a handful of different formats on the YouTube service. As a YouTube Partner, you can choose which type(s) of ad will appear within your videos and/or on your YouTube channel page, although you can not choose specific advertisers or ad content.

As an advertiser trying to promote your company, product, service, YouTube channel, or individual videos, you can pay to use these different types of ad formats to your utmost advantage.

These ad formats include:

- *Overlay InVideo Ads*. These are transparent banner overlays that appear in the lower portion of the video window while your video is playing. (The ad usually appears about 15 seconds after the video begins playing.) These are static display ads. The person viewing your video will need to click on the "X" icon within the ad to make it disappear from the video window, or they can click on the ad itself to be transferred to the website that's linked to the ad. According to Google, "InVideo ads generate significantly more revenue for partners."

- *TrueView In-Stream Ads*. These are TV–commercial style video ads that will run immediately before your YouTube video plays. After watching the ad for five seconds, the viewer can opt to skip the ad and proceed to watching your video. However, as a YouTube Partner, you only get paid if the viewer watches at least 30 seconds of the ad or the entire ad (whichever is shorter).

- *Banner Ads*. Banner ads measure 300 x 250 pixels and can appear in various locations on your YouTube channel page. Each banner ad includes a link to that advertiser's website.

- *Product Placement Ads*. As long as you follow YouTube's ad policies, you are allowed to include paid product placements within your actual videos. If your videos contain paid product placements, you need to notify YouTube by adding a checkmark to the appropriate checkbox under the "Advertising Options" section, which can be found when you click on the "Edit Video Settings" option when using the Video Manager.

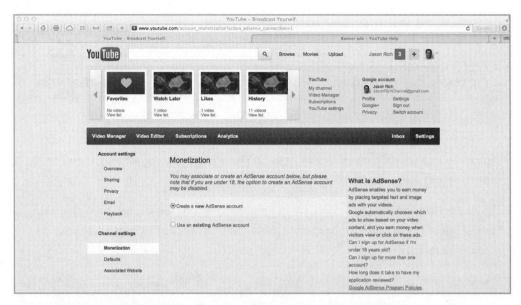

FIGURE 7-9. You Can Either Set Up a New AdSense Account from Scratch, or Link Your YouTube Channel Account to an Existing AdSense Account.

option. For this example, we'll set up a new account by selecting the "Create a New AdSense Account" option. Click on the "Next" button to continue.

The "Create an AdSense Account" screen will be displayed (shown in Figure 7-10 on page 101). Fill in all of the empty fields. Begin by selecting your "Account Type" and "Country or Territory" from the pull-down menus.

Next, under the "Contact Information" part of the on-screen form, fill in your full name and complete mailing address. The full or company name that you enter here must match the name on your bank account. Scroll down on the form and enter your phone number next.

Under the "Policies" section of the online form, you'll need to add a checkmark next to all seven of the checkboxes, and then click on the "Submit Information" button that's displayed near the bottom of the window.

Review the information that's displayed next, and make sure all of your contact information was entered correctly. Click on the "Continue" button to proceed. The Google "AdSense Online Standard Terms and Conditions" screen gets displayed next. Scroll down to the bottom of this screen (after you've reviewed its contents), and add a checkmark to the appropriate checkbox to indicate you agree to the described terms. Click on the "I Accept" button to continue.

Your Google AdSense account will now be enabled and linked to the Google account, and by default, it will be linked to your YouTube channel as well. Within a week, you will

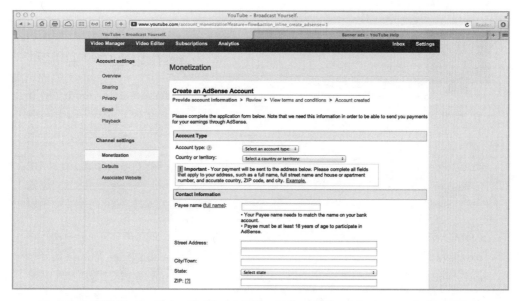

FIGURE 7–10. Fill in all of the Fields with Your Personal or Company Information as You're Prompted for It In Order to Set Up an AdSense Account.

receive an email announcing that your application has been approved. Follow the link within the email to enter your bank account and tax information, when it's requested.

If you create an AdSense account and link it to the Google account used to manage your YouTube channel, be sure you keep the login information private. Anyone within your company or organization whom you assign to manage your YouTube channel could easily gain access to the AdSense account, so be sure to limit access.

TRACK YOUR EARNINGS IN REAL TIME WITH YOUTUBE ANALYTICS

Once everything is set up correctly, at any time, you can visit your YouTube channel's analytics page and see detailed information about your videos and determine the number of views, Likes, Dislikes, and Comments it's received. You can also see how many people have shared and/or favorited each of your videos, and how many people have subscribed to your YouTube channel.

To access your YouTube channel's analytics page, log into your YouTube account, access the menu near the top-right corner of the screen by clicking on your username or profile photo, then click on the "My Channel" option. Near the top-right corner of the page, click on the "Analytics" button.

From this same YouTube "Analytics" screen (shown in Figure 7-11, page 102), you can view your "Total Estimated Earnings" thus far, as well as view the demographics of

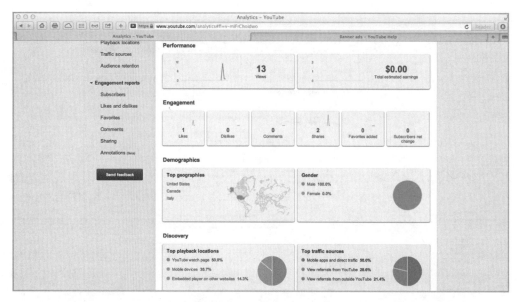

FIGURE 7–11. At any Time, You Can See How Much You've Earned from Your YouTube Channel as a YouTube Partner by Accessing the YouTube "Analytics" Page that's Associated with Your Channel.

the people who have watched your videos, and obtain other relevant information that will help you determine who, when, and how people are accessing your videos.

From the main YouTube "Analytics" screen for your account, click on the "Estimated Earnings" option that's displayed on the left side of the screen to determine how much money you've earned during the current period. Click on the "Ad Performance" option to see more detailed information about how much you're being paid, based on the types of ads being displayed.

Google pays its YouTube Partners on a monthly basis. However, you need to earn a specific amount of money each month in order to actually receive payment. Otherwise, your earnings keep getting rolled over to the following month, until the preset earning threshold is reached. The information reported through Google Analytics is displayed in real time and is constantly updated.

HOW TO MONETIZE YOUR INDIVIDUAL VIDEOS

As you're filming your videos, you can opt to accept money and/or products from companies and then highlight those products within your video in exchange for a paid endorsement. This is considered a paid product placement and is yet another way you can earn money with your YouTube videos.

As a business operator, however, you can also pay other YouTubers and YouTube Channel operators to incorporate your product placements into their videos and somehow showcase or talk about your products. Some YouTubers will do this for free, in exchange for free product samples. Others will seek financial compensation, but you wind up with an endorsement by an online personality who potentially has a vast and very dedicated following.

According to Google, "Paid product placements are defined as pieces of content that are created specifically for a sponsor and where that sponsor's brand, message, or product is integrated directly into the content. A typical example of a paid product placement is one in which a marketer pays a partner to specifically mention their product or brand in what would normally be the editorial part of the content."

To incorporate paid product placements into your videos, you must be a YouTube Partner in good standing, and you must notify YouTube when you upload this type of video. You are also responsible for working directly with the company paying to sponsor your videos to determine the terms of the arrangement and then to collect your own fees. How much you charge is also negotiated directly between you and the company placing products with you to be featured within your videos.

To inform YouTube that a video contains a paid product placement, access the "Video Manager" screen of your YouTube channel and then click on the "Monetize" icon that's associated with the video containing the paid product placement. Add a checkmark next to the checkbox that says "This Video Contains a Paid Product Placement." Promoting your own products or services within your videos isn't considered a paid product placement.

Take Advantage of Annotations within Your YouTube Videos to Make Them Interactive

You can easily incorporate active links into your videos, after they're uploaded to YouTube, by taking advantage of the "Annotations" feature. This allows you to link people directly to your own website, blog, ecommerce site, or Facebook page, for example. From these links, viewers can potentially access more information about your products and/or order them online from you or one of your vendors.

Annotations can also be used to cross-promote multiple videos on your channel. For example, if you have ten different but related videos on YouTube, at the end of each video, you can include links (annotations) to cross-promote other videos, but give people a choice about which video to watch next. Within a video, you could say something like, "To view more information about our products, click here, or to see actual testimonials from our customers raving about our product, click here." Each link would then lead to a different video, allowing your viewer to determine what content they access next.

You can and should also prominently display links to your website and/or online store on your YouTube channel page as part of its branding and customization, and promote your products or website within the description of your YouTube channel page and within the descriptions for each of your videos.

Other Options for Generating Revenue in Conjunction with Your Videos

Many YouTubers, performers, bands, clubs, organizations, charities, and some types of small businesses are also able to earn additional income by designing and selling T-shirts, hoodies, hats, wristband, posters, mouse pads, mugs, digital downloads, and other merchandise with their name, YouTube channel name, likeness, and/or logo. This business model works well if you begin to establish a large and dedicated following through your YouTube channel.

In 2012, YouTube launched a "Merch Store" option and began inviting some of its YouTube Partners to participate. However, you can create and sell merchandise on your own, or by using a third-party company that handles merchandise sales for YouTube channel operators.

There are many companies that allow you to design and sell custom products that the company then manufactures and drop ships to your customers. Thus, you have no upfront or inventory costs. In exchange, the company you hire to handle your merchandise takes a percentage of the sales.

FOCUS ON YOUR OBJECTIVES

Before you commit to displaying ads from other companies in conjunction with your videos and on your YouTube channel page, think carefully about what your objectives are for using YouTube and creating videos, and determine if displaying ads is truly beneficial to your overall goals. Also, make sure you realize that unless you have a significant number of viewers seeing your videos (and the related ads), you won't generate a lot of money.

Beyond allowing you to generate revenue by displaying ads in conjunction with your videos, becoming a YouTube Partner unlocks a variety of other features and tools that you can use to produce and promote your own videos. For example, YouTube Partners are allowed to publish videos longer than 15 minutes in length and qualify to receive free support from YouTube when it comes to promoting your videos and channel.

Google has also created detailed how-to guides for its YouTube Partners to help them produce the best possible videos and use all of the tools at their disposal to promote them and build an audience. You can download and read these free guides by visiting www.youtube.com/yt/creators.

Throughout the United States and in a handful of other countries, Google also supports Creator Clubs, which are groups of YouTube video producers and channel hosts that get together to share their knowledge and experiences. These gatherings also sometimes lead to successful video collaborations and other partnerships. To find a Creator Club in your area, visit www.youtube.com/yt/creators/creator-clubs.html.

To learn about some of the other benefits offered to YouTube Partners, visit http://support.google.com/youtube/bin/answer.py?hl=en&answer=72855#US.

Producing Your
Own Videos

an't bear to let someone else interpret your vision—or you simply don't have the budget for it? These next five chapters focus on what you need to know to produce your own videos, from the equipment you'll need, to filming and lighting techniques, editing advice, and finally, publishing your final product on YouTube.

The Equipment You'll Need

IN THIS CHAPTER
- The equipment you'll need to produce, edit, and publish videos
- Other video accessories, tools, and essentials you may need
- Strategies for saving money on your equipment

Just a few years ago, it would have cost you thousands of dollars and required a significant level of video production expertise in order to shoot, produce, and edit professional-quality videos with good-quality lighting and sound. All that has changed, however.

Today, many smartphones, as well as low-cost point-and-shoot digital cameras, are equipped with a video recording function that's capable of shooting HD-quality video. There are also many low-cost dedicated video cameras available that offer close to broadcast quality. However, if your goal is to produce truly broadcast-quality videos, there are also a plethora of options available when it comes to acquiring the right equipment.

This chapter focuses on the video production equipment you'll probably need to shoot, edit, and publish videos for YouTube. The first step, however, is to carefully define your needs and determine what you're trying to accomplish. A few basic questions to consider are:

- What types of videos will you be shooting?

- Where and when will you be shooting?
- Will you be shooting indoors or outdoors?
- Will you want to shoot your videos in 1080p HD, or is a lower-quality resolution acceptable? If your intended audience is people who will be viewing your videos exclusively on smartphones with small screens, or if you're striving to capture a "grass-roots" or "homemade" look to your videos, using a lower-quality resolution may be acceptable.
- What are your set, lighting, and audio needs?
- Do you require a special camera to shoot action sequences that you (as the photographer) are participating in?

SAVE MONEY BY BUYING USED EQUIPMENT

You can always start with low-end, inexpensive equipment and as you become successful and gain experience producing videos for YouTube, upgrade your equipment over time. You can also save a fortune by purchasing used equipment, such as a used video camera, lights, a tripod, and microphone. You'll find used, consumer-quality video production equipment for sale on eBay and Craigslist, for example.

To find and purchase higher-end used equipment, visit websites like:

- Adorama (www.adorama.com/catalog.tpl?op=category&cat1=Used)
- OneQuality.com (www.onequality.com)
- Full Compass (www.fullcompass.com)
- NewPro Video (http://newprovideo.com)
- B&H Photo-Video (www.bhphotovideo.com)
- UsedAV.com (www.usedav.com)

These are just a few of the countless companies on the internet that sell used equipment.

Before purchasing used equipment from a company you're not familiar with, pay careful attention to the seller's online ratings and the comments posted by previous customers to make sure they're reputable. Also, do your research so you know exactly what equipment you want and need. Make sure you know exact make and model numbers, for example, so that you wind up acquiring exactly what you need.

- Will you be shooting mainly people in your videos, or will you be demonstrating products that require detailed closeups?
- Will your videos require special effects, animated titles, or other graphics?

Next, consider your budget. Do you need to produce the highest-quality videos possible with a low-end camera and no special lighting or sound equipment, or can you afford to invest in basic video production equipment that, if used correctly, will greatly improve the overall quality of your productions?

WHAT YOU SHOULD KNOW ABOUT VIDEO RESOLUTION

When it comes to shooting video and choosing the right equipment, you'll hear a lot about resolution. This relates to the size of the video picture and how many individual pixels are used to make up each frame of the video. A standard definition TV set (SDTV) offers a resolution of 640 by 480 pixels. When video is shot in standard definition (SD), it can be shown on any standard definition TV set, regardless of its screen size. Thus, an SD video will look the same on a 15-inch screen and on a 32-inch screen, for example.

The world has progressed well beyond standard definition, however. In most homes these days, you'll find high-definition TV sets (HDTVs). When it comes to shooting HD video, there are three industry-standard resolutions—720p, 1080i, and 1080p.

Video shot in 720p HD utilizes a 720 by 1280 pixel resolution. Both 1080i and 1080p utilize a resolution that's comprised of 1080 by 1920 pixels. In addition to SD and HD video utilizing a different number of pixels, the aspect ratio of the video is also different.

An SD video, for example, has an aspect ratio of 4:3, meaning that the width of the picture is 4/3 the height. However, an HD video has an aspect ratio of 16:9, meaning that the width of the picture is 16/9 the height.

Shooting videos in HD resolution results in much more detailed, sharper, and vibrant pictures. It's always advisable to shoot in the highest resolution possible. As you're editing your newly shot video and preparing to publish it online, you can always downgrade the resolution with a few clicks of the mouse. However, you cannot easily upgrade an SD video to HD, for example.

Some TV sets connect directly to the internet, or have a set-top box that does so. This grants the viewer the ability to stream and watch YouTube videos on their big-screen HDTVs. However, most people watch YouTube videos on their computer, tablet, or smartphone's screen.

YouTube is compatible with many different video resolutions. As a YouTube channel operator, you can opt to upload and offer HD videos that can be viewed in high definition on any TV set or device, or you can produce and upload your videos in a lower resolution. You should also note that YouTube now supports what's called 4K video resolution, which provides about six times better resolution than 1080i or 1080p HD resolution.

The decision about what resolution to shoot your videos in will depend on a variety of factors, including your budget, your target audience, and what type of equipment you anticipate your audience will typically use to stream your videos—an HDTV set, computer screen, tablet screen (such as the Apple iPad or Microsoft Surface), smartphone (such as the Apple iPhone or Samsung Galaxy S III), or an internet-enabled handheld digital music/video player, such as the Apple iPod Touch.

To keep up with the latest technologies, seriously consider shooting and uploading your videos in 720p or 1080p HD resolution. This will allow people to experience an excellent picture quality, regardless of what internet-enabled device they're using. You'll discover that when watching YouTube videos on a typical computer screen, there's little visible quality difference between 720p vs. 1080p HD videos.

Even low-end digital video camcorders, as well as the video capabilities of point-and-shoot cameras, higher-end digital SLR cameras, and the cameras built into smartphones and/or tablets are all capable to recording in either 720p or 1080p HD resolution.

After you shoot your video and transfer the footage to your computer, tablet, or Smartphone to edit and ultimately upload it to YouTube, it becomes a digital video file. The higher the resolution the video is shot in, the larger the video file will be. Editing HD video that's more than a few minutes in length will require a significant amount of storage space on your computer's hard drive, as well as a fast microprocessor and a lot of RAM within your computer. But because most YouTube videos are less than 10 minutes long, a typical home computer works well.

Video File Formats

Beyond just choosing a resolution and aspect ratio when shooting your videos, you'll also need to choose a file format that utilizes compression. Raw digital video footage utilizes a tremendous amount of data and results in massive digital video files. However, when you transfer your video footage to your computer for editing, you can save it in a specific, industry-standard video format, and later upload your videos to YouTube in a compatible video format that utilizes file compression to make the file sizes more manageable.

Each video file format has a different method of data compression, and the latest video compression technologies allow for video resolution to stay extremely high but for file sizes to be shrunk down dramatically.

When a file is compressed, the compression rate is measured in kilobytes per second (KBps). The more KBps used for the compression, the better the quality of the compressed video. As you begin using specialized video editing software and then uploading your videos to YouTube, you'll discover that many different file formats and compression rates exist. Some of the most common video file formats include: MPEG-4 (.mpg or .mp4), QuickTime, RealVideo, and Windows Media Video (WMV).

You'll learn more about choosing an appropriate video format for YouTube from Chapters 9 and 11. For now, however, you need to understand that there are a variety of popular video formats, and that you'll need camera and editing equipment that's compatible with these various formats.

YouTube accepts a wide range of popular formats. However, the MPEG-4, MPEG-2, or H.264 file formats are the most common, with a resolution of 720p or 1080p. You'll also want to choose an aspect ratio of 16:9, and make sure that the overall file size of your video is 2 GB or less. To achieve this, the video's length will need to be less than 12 to 15 minutes. If given the choice, also select a frame rate of 30 frames per second and the MP3 audio format when creating videos for YouTube.

Using video editing software or the online tools available from YouTube, it's easy to take digital video files that have been saved in almost any format and convert them into a file format that offers better compression and/or that works better with YouTube. You can also use specialized video conversion software for a PC or Mac.

For example, Movavi (www.movavi.com/videoconverter) offers powerful video conversion software for both the PC and Mac. You'll find a handful of other commercially available software packages that can be purchased and downloaded at CNET's Download.com website (http://download.cnet.com/windows/video-converters).

If you don't want to buy video conversion software, there are plenty of freeware applications available for the PC and Mac, such as the Free Video Converter from Freemake.com (www.freemake.com/free_video_converter). It supports more than 200 video input formats and outputs to AVI, MP4, MKV, FLV, 3GP, and HTML 5, among other popular formats.

GETTING THE RIGHT EQUIPMENT

Beyond choosing the right camera, you'll also need equipment to achieve semi-professional or professional production quality. You'll need to think about your set or background, lighting, and sound. You'll also need a computer for editing, viewing, uploading, and managing your videos. Your computer needs a large internal hard drive or a high-capacity external hard drive, a decent microprocessor, plenty of RAM (for processing video) and have specialized video editing software installed. Choosing video editing software is the focus of Chapter 11, "Editing Your YouTube Videos."

The computer or device used to edit your videos will need access to a high-speed internet connection so that you can upload the videos to YouTube. A broadband, DSL, 4G (wireless), or 4G LTE (wireless) internet connection should be more than adequate.

The following is a summary of the core video production equipment you'll need to produce semi-professional or professional-quality videos for YouTube. If you're first starting out, you can easily get away with using low-end equipment. However, if your videos will be representing your company, product, or service, and the quality of the videos is important to maintain your business's image and reputation, and to meet the expectations of your audience, investing in higher-end equipment will be necessary.

Because everyone's video contents and production needs will be different, from an equipment standpoint, here's a rundown of what you'll probably need:

- Digital video camcorder or camera that's capable of shooting 720p or 1080p HD video.
- Tripod or Steadicam®, to hold the camera steady while shooting.
- Lighting to eliminate shadows and create effect.
- Background. Typically, a seamless, solid-color wall, or a cloth, paper, or another type of simple backdrop works best.
- External microphone. The microphones that are built into low-end cameras tend to offer low-quality audio recording quality. An external microphone can be placed on or near the audio source or the person you're filming and can dramatically improve the quality of the audio being recorded, while cutting out the ancillary background noise.
- Computer for editing and managing your videos and then uploading them to YouTube.
- Specialized video editing software. Depending on your needs, you may require additional software for incorporating special effects or graphics into your videos, such as animated titles, scene transitions, and/or computer-generated backgrounds.
- Teleprompter to display your shooting script. It's very hard for some people to memorize scripts. Instead, using a teleprompter allows you to read your script as you're shooting. A professional teleprompter can be expensive, so try using a low-cost app and a tablet to function as a full-featured teleprompter.

Choosing the Right Tripod

You'll quickly discover that all tripods are not alike. The price can vary from around $40 to well over $1,500, depending on what it's made from and what it's designed to do. The main function of a tripod is to hold your camera very steady while shooting, as well as to allow for smooth pans and zooms.

It's almost impossible to hold a video camera absolutely still in your hands as you're shooting. Any movement, and your videos will shake. Without a tripod, it's also very difficult to execute smooth pans and zooms as you're shooting. Choose a tripod designed for your camera's size and weight plus any equipment attached to the camera, such as a light or a microphone.

Most inexpensive tripods are sold as a single unit. However, mid- to high-end tripods have three components—legs, feet, and a detachable (and selectable) head. The tripod head is located at the top of the tripod; it attaches to your camera. There are two main types of tripod heads—a ball head and a pan-tilt head. The type of tripod head you use determines how you can rotate and position the camera at various angles, as well as pan or tilt the camera up and down or from side to side.

In some cases, the tripod and head are one piece. It is also common for them to be offered as two detachable pieces that are sold together. Some manufacturers, however, sell tripod legs and heads separately, allowing you to customize the equipment as needed.

The legs hold the tripod itself steady. On some tripods, the legs can be expended to be different lengths so you can adjust the height at which the camera is positioned. Others allow for the legs to be positioned at various angles. The feet of some tripods are also changeable or adjustable, and should be selected based on the type of surface it's being placed on. For example, rubber feet will keep the tripod from sliding on a flat, smooth floor, while spiked feet will prevent movement if the tripod is placed on grass or dirt.

Other options include an easy-on/easy-off mount, so you don't have to screw the camera on and off of the tripod each time you need to attach or remove it. An easy-on/easy-off mount simply clicks into place, allowing you to attach or remove the camera from the tripod quickly, without compromising stability.

Another useful tripod feature is a level gauge. Accidentally positioning the camera at even the slightest angle could result in your video looking strange or crooked.

The size and weight of the tripod are a consideration if you need to carry equipment to many locations. Some tripods are made from very lightweight aluminum or titanium, yet are strong enough to hold heavy and large cameras. The component materials as well as the features it offers will determine the tripod's cost.

Tripods are available from consumer electronics stores, photo, and video specialty stores, as well as online. Some mid- to high-end tripod manufacturers include:

- Gitzo—www.gitzo.com
- Joby—www.joby.com
- Libec—www.libecsales.com
- Manfrotto—www.manfrotto.us

- Slik—www.thkphoto.com/products/slik
- Sunpak—www.sunpak.jp/english/
- Vanguard—www.vanguardworld.com

Another option is a handheld image stabilization system, such as the Merlin 2 Steadicam from Tiffen Company (www.tiffen.com), or the Slidecam from International Supplies (www.internationalsupplies.com). These devices allow the camera operator to move the camera slowly and steadily as he's shooting. Similar products are available from:

- Glidecam Industries—www.glidecam.com
- JAG35—www.jag35.com
- Manfrotto—www.manfrotto.us
- Redrock Micro—http://store.redrockmicro.com

Choosing the Lighting

Just as with still photography, proper lighting is an extremely important component when it comes to shooting video. Your worst enemy will be shadows. Ideally, you want your primary light source—whether it's the sun or artificial lighting—to be positioned in front of your subject and behind the person holding the camera.

The primary light source should not be shining directly or indirectly into the video camera's lens while you're shooting. This will cause glare, silhouettes, or overexposed footage. When shooting indoors, the "natural lighting" will seldom be suitable for shooting decent-quality video, so you'll need to use additional lighting.

Many video cameras have either a built-in or attachable light, but they can present problems. They can cause shadows, depending on how the camera is positioned. If the light's too bright, it can wash out your subject; if you're too far away, the subject will be underexposed or engulfed in shadows. It can also limit the cameraperson's mobility.

So consider investing in a studio lighting kit that includes two, three, or four lights that can be positioned independently and evenly light your subject when shooting indoors.

Make sure that the lighting kit will provide continuous lighting at an intensity that's suitable for the situation in which you'll be shooting. The type of light bulbs will also affect how colors appear within your videos. Working with incandescent bulbs, fluorescent bulbs, or LED bulbs, for example, each offers pros and cons.

You may need to adjust the white balance feature within your video camera to compensate for lighting warmth or coolness. Unless you plan to shoot broadcast-quality videos, you can probably get away with initially investing in a basic three-light system that will cost between $300 and $400. There are also less expensive options.

B&H Photo-Video (www.bhphotovideo.com) and Adorama (www.adorama.com) both offer many types of lighting kits, as well as individual lights and stands that can be mixed and matched to meet your needs in any indoor situation. Other companies worth checking out for more versatile lighting kits include:

- Gekko Technology—www.gekkolite.com
- K 5600 Lighting—www.k5600.com
- Kino Flo Lighting Systems—www.kinoflo.com
- Lowel—www.lowel.com
- PhotoLite—www.photolite.com
- Studio 1 Productions—www.studio1productions.com

PhotoBasics (http://fjwestcott.com), a division of Westcott, which makes professional video lighting equipment and related products, offers a handful of lower-end lighting systems for amateur and semi-professional videographers. Photo Basics offers several two- and three-light kits that utilize fluorescent or tungsten light bulb options, starting at just under $300.

For shooting outdoors on a sunny day, consider using a silver or gold reflector and a stand to bounce sunlight onto your subject. Some reflectors are large enough so you can redirect sunlight evenly onto multiple subjects at once. They're available from photo and video specialty stores and online. Prices range from under $30 to several hundred dollars. Photo Basics, for one, offers many reflector and backdrop options that are versatile, affordable, and that can yield professional-quality results while using semi-professional level equipment.

Choosing Your Background

Any location, indoors or outdoors, can be used for shooting your videos. However, using random locations poses a handful of challenges when it comes to lighting and audio. And you never want to use a background that's too busy or will distract your audience.

Using lights and specialized microphones, any location can be made optimal for shooting video. However, it's much easier to choose or create a location that allows you to control the shooting conditions. One way to do this is to set up a solid background.

A backdrop can be made from seamless paper, vinyl, or cloth. They're available in a wide range of sizes and in virtually any color from photo and video specialty stores, including B&H Photo-Video and Adorama. There are also companies, like Backdrop Source (www.backdropsource.com) and Backdrop Outlet (www.backdropoutlet.com), that offer hundreds of different backdrop options that can be ordered online.

These backgrounds are created using materials and dyes designed to work perfectly with lighting kits. In some cases, these backdrops can help to absorb the lighting and dramatically reduce shadows. They also make it easy to evenly light your subjects, while creating a visually simple, nondistracting background.

For a good-quality backdrop made from paper, vinyl, or cloth (these are referred to as "muslins"), plan on spending between $50 and $300, depending on the size. Common sizes are 5' x 7', 5' x 9', 10' x 10', 10' x 20', or 20' x 20'. If you're using paper or a cloth backdrop, keep them crease and wrinkle free.

Using an External Microphone

When was the last time you tried to hold a conversation on a cell phone while you or the other person were in a noisy area? Could you hear everything that was being said? Probably not. The microphone built into the cell phone picked up the ambient noise and drowned out the person speaking.

If you don't use proper microphones when shooting your video, you'll wind up recording audio that's as bad as the worst cell phone connection. When you rely on your camera's built-in microphone, the end result will almost always be poor audio quality. That tiny microphone is designed to pick up all of the audio in the immediate area, and the quality of the microphone typically isn't too good to begin with. If the microphone is on the camera, but the speaker is on the opposite side of the room, the video camera often won't adequately pick up the person's voice, and the sound will be hollow.

Most video cameras can connect one or more external microphones, corded or wireless. When you use an external microphone, you can:

- Pick the type of microphone you use
- Choose the quality of the microphone
- Select the position of the microphone
- Control audio input levels while shooting

External microphones can cost hundreds or even thousands of dollars. Before investing any money, determine the situations in which you'll be shooting video and what your audio recording needs will be. Then, consult with an expert at an audio/video store who can help you select a microphone that's best suited to your needs.

In most cases, a handheld microphone, or a lavaliere microphone that attaches to someone's lapel, will work well as you're shooting video. The appropriate microphone can also eliminate unwanted background noise and ambient noise.

Keep in mind, some types of microphone are designed to only pick up and record what's directly in front of it, while other microphones will pick up all audio that surrounds it.

Plan on spending between $100 and $300 for a good quality external microphone that connects to your video camera.

When choosing a microphone, try to select one that can also connect to your computer via an adapter, so that when you're editing your video, you can use it to record any voice-overs. For less than $200, you can also purchase a separate studio-quality microphone that connects directly to a computer via its USB port. One example is the Snowball microphone from Blue Microphones (www.bluemic.com/snowball).

Choosing a Teleprompter

A standalone teleprompter or one that connects to a video camera can cost anywhere from several hundred to several thousand dollars. There are a handful of online retailers, including B&H Photo-Video (www.bhphotovideo.com), Adorama (www.adorama.com), and Prompter People (www.prompterpeople.com) that specialize in this type of equipment and offer teleprompters from various manufacturers.

A far simpler and lower-cost solution is to create oversized cue cards using poster board and markers, or download and use a teleprompter app on your tablet. Search for the phrase "teleprompter" in the Apple App Store and you'll discover at least 45 different iPad apps, from free to around $15. You can then use a stand to position the tablet at eye-level near the video camera as you're shooting. Among available stands are the SpiderArm Stand for iPad ($49.99, www.spiderarm.com) or the HoverBar stand ($79.99, http://twelvesouth.com/products/hoverbar).

Other Video Production Essentials

- *Set and props.* Based on what type of video you'll be recording and where, you may decide you need a set and props. A set can be a table or desk positioned in front of your backdrop, or it can be something elaborate that you design and construct from scratch.
- *Wardrobe, hair, and makeup considerations.* If you'll be featuring people in your videos and shooting in HD, the appearance of the people in your video is important. You'll need to choose what they'll wear, how they'll style their hair, and make sure they wear appropriate makeup that looks natural in the lighting conditions in which you're shooting.
- *Background music and sound effects.* You can record your own music and/or sound effects, however, you'll probably find it much easier to license or acquire royalty-free production music and/or sound effects that you can incorporate into your productions. Appropriate music and sound effects can add a tremendous amount of production value to your videos. These production elements are typically added during the video editing (post production) phase.

Adding Music and Sound Effects

When you're editing your video and adding post-production elements, you'll probably want to add sound effects and music. These audio elements, if used properly, will add tremendous production value to your videos. However, there are a few things to consider.

First, the music and sound effects you use should be appropriate to the production. Music and sound effects can add excitement or anticipation to a video production, or simply make it more pleasant to watch. If used incorrectly, music and sound effects can be distracting or annoying.

Second, the music and sound effects incorporated into your video should be properly mixed so the audio levels are just right. Your video editing software will offer controls for adding and controlling the music and sound effect levels.

Third, you need permission from the copyright holder to use the song or music, and the recording itself. YouTube has very strict rules for using music and sound effects in videos, based on who owns the copyright. If you violate these rules, your videos could be blocked or YouTube could remove all of the audio from them automatically.

If you discover that YouTube has removed the audio track from your video, it's probably because you've violated a copyright. Refer to this page on YouTube's website for more information on how to avoid this situation, and to learn about your options if it happens: http://support.google.com/youtube/bin/answer.py?hl=en&answer=171159.

Potentially infringing content includes TV shows, music videos, movies and movie trailers, videos of live concerts—even if you captured the video yourself—commercials, and slide shows that include photos or images owned by somebody else, according to YouTube.

To learn more about what production music and sound effects you can and can't legally use within your own YouTube video productions, participate in the free, online YouTube Copyright Workshop (https://support.google.com/youtube/bin/answer.py?hl=en&answer=167314&topic=25065&parent=25903&rd=1). This is particularly important if you're a business operator who is planning to use your videos for promotional or marketing purposes.

If you're having trouble finding music and sound effects that you're allowed to use, refer to YouTube's own library of pre-approved audio tracks. Visit http://support.google.com/youtube/bin/answer.py?hl=en&answer=94316.

You can purchase, license, or acquire royalty-free production music in some cases for a flat, one-time fee. Using any internet search engine, enter the search phrase "royalty-free production music" to find links to vast libraries of music. For example, there's StockMusic.net (www.stockmusic.net) that has a library containing thousands of available music tracks that can be acquired on a royalty-free basis for between $14.95 and $39.95 per track. Other sources include:

- Getty Images Music—www.gettyimages.com/music
- Killer Tracks—www.killertracks.com
- Music for Productions—www.musicforproductions.com
- Premium Beat—www.premiumbeat.com/production-music
- Reserve Music—www.reservemusic.com

Adding Professional Voice-Overs

Off-screen voice-overs can be used at the beginning of videos, in conjunction with a graphic title, to narrate content, and/or to emphasize key points.

Many (but not all) video editing software packages will allow you to add voice-over content to your footage by connecting a microphone to your computer. Another option is to hire a professional announcer to record your script digitally, which you can then import into your video.

Many radio announcers and actors do voice-overs on a freelance basis. There are also production houses that specialize in recording voice-overs based on customers' scripts. The cost will vary greatly based on the length of the script and how much production work is involved.

Radio Voice Imaging (www.radiovoiceimaging.com) is one of thousands of voice-over production companies you can hire by uploading your script to their service and then offering some basic direction. The company will then use their announcers to record your script. The 60-second production will be emailed to you within a few business days. It can then be imported into your video production using your video editing software.

Before hiring any voice-over actor, always listen to their demo to determine if their voice is suitable for your production.

To find voice-over announcers and production studios, enter "voice-over production" into any internet search engine. You'll find hundreds of options, including:

- Agent 99 Voice Talent—www.agent99voicetalent.com
- Amazing Voice Talent—http://amazingvoicetalent.com
- Internet Jock—www.internetjock.com
- Muzak—www.muzak.com/sprints/voice_over
- Voice Talent—www.voicetalent.com
- Voice Talent Now—http://store.voicetalentnow.com

PUTTING THE PIECES TOGETHER

Having the right equipment to create your videos is only one of the key steps in a video's production. However, it's essential that you choose equipment that's suitable based on your budget, experience level, what you're trying to accomplish, and what your videos' content will include.

When you're first learning about video production and producing your initial YouTube videos, keep things as simple as possible. Don't spend money on equipment you don't need and don't know how to use properly, unless you also plan to spend time learning how to use it.

As you gain more experience and enhance your skills, you can always incorporate more advanced video production techniques, upgrade your equipment, add special effects, and work toward enhancing the quality of your videos.

Selecting the Right Video Camera

IN THIS CHAPTER
- Using your webcam, mobile phone, or tablet camera to shoot video
- Using the video mode of your point-and-shoot or digital SLR camera
- Choosing a camera to meet your needs and budget

In Chapter 10, "Filming YouTube Videos," we'll explore the pre- and post-production steps that go into the creation of a video. However, before you can start actually filming, you'll need one key piece of equipment—the video camera or camcorder.

If you want your video to be viewable on any computer screen, HDTV set, tablet, or smartphone, you'll want a camera capable of shooting in HD 1080p resolution. There are many options, starting with the camera that's built into your computer (or an external webcam), mobile phone, or tablet. The latest models of the Apple iPhones and iPads, for example, can shoot HD video, as can some popular Android and Windows smartphones and tablets. Likewise, all of the latest iMac and MacBook models have cameras capable of shooting HD video.

If you've already invested in a good-quality point-and-shoot digital camera or a higher-end digital SLR camera, chances are it, too, has a video recording mode, as well as some basic video recording features, such as zoom capabilities. And many of the digital SLR cameras released within the past few years, from companies like Nikon and Canon, can not only shoot HD-quality video, but they also offer the ability to attach external microphones and lighting equipment.

Assuming your sole purpose for the camera is to shoot HD-quality video, a stand alone camcorder offers the most flexibility and video recording features. These are available from many different manufacturers, and can be purchased from consumer electronics stores, photo/video specialty stores, or online.

Low-end but decent-quality video cameras capable of shooting HD-quality video start in price at around $200. However, if you're looking for professional-quality equipment and features, you can easily spend thousands of dollars for a high-end camcorder. Regardless of your budget, it's essential that you use a video camera that allows you to attach external corded and wireless microphones so that you can record good-quality audio in conjunction with your video. This chapter explores your many options when it comes to finding and purchasing a camcorder or video camera that will meet your needs.

Keep in mind, your video camera/camcorder is a key component needed for your video production, but you'll need other equipment as well, including microphones, lighting, video editing software, and equipment, so don't spend your entire production budget on just a good-quality video camera or camcorder.

RENTING EQUIPMENT

If you plan to film only a handful of videos within a short time period, you may want to consider renting high-end equipment from a photo/video specialty store. Typically, you can rent a camera on a daily or weekly basis.

Using any internet search engine, such as Google or Yahoo!, enter the search phrase "video camera rental" or "camcorder rental" to find companies that rent mid-to-high-end video cameras and related video production equipment. Some of the companies you'll find include:

- Borrow Lenses—www.borrowlenses.com/category/Video
- HD Rental—www.hdrental.com
- Radiant Images—www.radiantimages.com
- Rule—www.rule.com
- ATS Rentals—www.atsrentals.com

THE PROS AND CONS OF SHOOTING WITH A WEBCAM

The benefit of using a webcam to record your videos is that the raw video footage is stored directly on your computer, where you can edit, view, and then publish it. This type of camera works best if you're sitting at a desk, for example, and want to record yourself talking into the camera. For this, the microphone that's built into your computer may provide adequate sound quality, although most computers also have a microphone jack or USB port through which you can attach a higher-quality external microphone for better audio quality—a recommended move.

The drawback is that you'll have limited movement options and no optical zoom capabilities. If you plan to record yourself facing your computer and talking directly to your audience by looking into the camera, your audience may get very bored looking at "talking-head" footage for more than a few minutes at a time. Keep your talking-head videos very short, or intersperse other types of footage or content in your edited videos.

If your computer doesn't have an HD-quality video camera or webcam, you can purchase an external webcam that will connect to your computer via its USB port. Several companies, including Logitech (www.logitech.com), offer webcam accessories that are sold online or through consumer electronics stores such as Best Buy.

The Logitech HD Pro Webcam C920, as well as a handful of slightly less expensive webcam models, allows you to record video directly onto your computer at HD 1080p resolution. Microsoft, HP, Tely Labs, Creative Labs, and Brother also make HD-quality webcams that are priced between $50 and $100. These webcams work with Windows as well as Mac operating systems.

The software you use to record videos using your computer's webcam will offer a variety of effects that can be added as you're recording, in addition to the effects that can be added using video editing software during the post-production phase of your video production.

SHOOTING VIDEO USING THE CAMERA BUILT INTO YOUR SMARTPHONE OR TABLET

Many of the latest smartphones and tablets have one or more cameras that are capable of recording HD-quality video. Some also offer the ability to attach an external microphone, and have apps available that offer a variety of options—such as a digital zoom, or the ability to add special effects—while you're shooting.

Videos shot using a smartphone or tablet can then be edited, viewed, and shared using apps on the mobile devices themselves, or the raw footage can easily be transferred to a desktop or notebook computer where you can use full-featured video editing software to polish your video.

Unlike your computer's webcam, a mobile-device camera offers greater mobility, which makes it easier to pan and tilt the camera as you're shooting, adjust the shooting angle, and take advantage of the digital zoom. Assuming the camera that's built into your wireless mobile device offers the resolution you need, this is certainly a viable option for shooting videos on a budget.

However, at best, you can expect to achieve amateur to semi-professional quality, even if you have optimal lighting and use an external microphone to capture the best possible audio.

USING THE VIDEO MODE OF YOUR DIGITAL CAMERA TO SHOOT HD VIDEO

Many point-and-shoot digital cameras and higher-end digital SLR cameras also have a video shooting mode that can also be used for shooting YouTube videos. But the cameras' primary function is to shoot still images, and shooting video will drain a point-and-shoot's battery much faster than when you take still photos, plus you'll need higher capacity memory cards for storing your video footage. Also, you can only use the camera's low-quality built-in microphone to record audio. It's typically not possible to connect an external microphone as you're recording, although during post production, you can replace the audio track with voice-overs, music, sound effects, or an original audio track.

The higher-end digital SLR cameras, from Canon and Nike, on the other hand, have video recording modes that allow you to capture near professional-quality HD video using a wider range of video recording features, including the ability to attach an external microphone and interchangeable lenses. A mid-to-high-end digital SLR camera with a good quality video mode will cost anywhere from $1,000 to $6,000, plus the price of optional lenses, microphones, and other accessories.

The video recording quality of some mid- to high-end digital SLR cameras is often good enough to create broadcast-quality HD video, though the resulting digital video files are massive; and any video longer that 15 minutes may be too big for most personal computers. You'll need a high-end computer or digital video editing workstation to properly edit your videos, even using the latest data compression.

SHOOTING HD VIDEO USING A STAND-ALONE CONSUMER-QUALITY CAMCORDER

Camcorders are designed for one purpose—to record video. Most consumer and semi-professional models are compact, and all are battery-powered. All also offer built-in screens that often serve as viewfinders and/or allow you to play back your video directly from the camera.

If possible, select a camcorder that offers both a traditional viewfinder that you can look through as you're shooting and a large display screen. Using a traditional viewfinder will require much less battery power than a display screen, but having the option to use a large display screen as your viewfinder, as well as to play back your footage, is always nice.

Pay attention to its zoom capabilities. Ideally, choose a camcorder that offers at least a 10x optical zoom lens, as well as stronger digital zoom capabilities. Optical zoom is the physical lens's zoom capability. Digital zoom uses technology to digitally create a simulated zoom. While it often allows for stronger magnification, it's not always as crystal clear as an optical zoom.

All cameras have a built-in microphone, but their quality is typically very poor, and they pick up ambient noise, as well as many camera movement-related noises. You'll want the option of attaching a corded or wireless microphone to the camera for the best audio quality. Be sure to select an optional microphone that's designed for the specific type of audio you're recording, or specific recording conditions.

Camcorders that shoot in HD are more expensive than standard video models. Different HD cameras also use different compression technologies, so it's important that the camcorder you choose is compatible with your video editing software in terms of the digital file format and data compression technology that it utilizes.

The battery life a camcorder offers is an important consideration, so buy at least one or two extra rechargeable batteries and keep them fully charged. Brand-name replacement batteries can cost between $50 and $100 each. For generic batteries at a fraction of the cost, visit a price comparison website, such as Nextag (www.nextag.com), and search for replacement batteries for the exact make and model of your camcorder.

The Video Footage Storage Options Offered by Camcorders

Camcorders come in a wide range of shapes and sizes, and each model offers different options. Many manufacturers offer consumer and semi-professional quality camcorders that are capable of shooting in HD resolution.

One consideration when choosing a camcorder is what type of media will be used to store your footage as it's being shot. Your options include digital video (DV) tapes, mini DVDs, flash memory cards, or an internal hard drive or flash drive. The latest mid- to high-end camcorders feature internal flash drives for storing video footage as it's shot, and many have both an internal flash drive and a memory card slot.

Digital Videotapes

Digital videotapes are quickly becoming outdated. They work very much like cassette tapes in terms of how footage is stored. DV tapes are easy to store and archive, and they come in predefined recording lengths. But they do degrade over time, and you'll need to keep buying new tapes or record over old ones. If you're on a tight budget, however, you're more likely to find a good deal on a new or used camcorder that uses this storage technology.

It is very easy to transfer your video footage from a digital videotape on your camera to your computer, and then transform that footage into a purely digital file that can be edited, viewed, and shared.

Mini DVD

Just like full-size recordable DVDs, mini DVDs fit into the camcorder itself, and the video is stored as it's being shot. The video quality is top notch, and the mini DVD can be played directly on any DVD player that accommodates the mini DVDs. But they are somewhat fragile and can be scratched or damaged easily. They're also more expensive than DV tapes, and are quickly becoming outdated and hard to find.

Camcorders with Flash Memory Cards, Internal Flash Drive, or Hard Drive

The majority of the camcorders rely on an internal flash drive or hard drive for storing video. If you have a choice between a camcorder with an internal flash drive or internal hard drive, choose the flash drive. It's more reliable and durable, especially if you'll be shooting in extreme weather conditions, at high altitude, or trying to capture high action.

The amount of internal hard drive storage space that a camcorder has is measured in gigabytes (GB). Look for a camcorder with a 100 GB or larger capacity hard drive or flash drive, even if you'll typically be shooting shorter videos that will then be transferred to a computer. Camcorders with flash drives often have smaller storage capacities, but enough storage to hold between two and four hours of raw footage.

Other camcorders use interchangeable flash memory cards. When a memory card gets filled up, you transfer your files to your computer and then erase and reuse the memory card. What's great about this technology is that your footage is stored as a data file that can be easily transferred from your camcorder or its memory card to your computer.

One benefit of using a camcorder with a flash memory card is that you can choose the capacity and read/write speed of the memory card you use. The storage capacity will dictate how much video you can store per card. A 64-GB memory card can hold approximately five hours of 1080 HD video. You can find memory cards with very large capacities; the higher the capacity and the faster its read/write speed, the more you'll pay. Choose the highest capacity memory card with the fastest read/write speed you can afford.

MORE ON MEMORY CARDS

With the exception of camcorders manufactured by Sony (which has its own proprietary memory card format), all camcorders that utilize flash memory cards currently use Secure Digital (SD), Secure Digital High Capacity (SDHC), or Secure Digital Extended Capacity (SDXC) memory cards. These memory cards are manufactured by a handful of different companies, including Sandisk (www.sandisk.com/products/memory-cards).

SDHC or SDXC memory cards come in a much wider range of capacities, ranging from 2 GB to 2 TB. The greater the card's capacity, the more video footage it'll be able to store. For example, a 2-GB SDHC card will store approximately 10 minutes of HD 1080p quality video, while a 128-GB SDHC memory card (which will be considerably more expensive) will hold approximately 640 minutes (approximately 10 hours) of HD 1080p quality video.

Many consumer-quality camcorders will accept either SD or SDHC memory cards, although if you're shooting in HD 1080p quality video, you'll definitely want to use SDHC cards. Keep in mind that low-end camcorders may only accept memory cards up to a specific capacity, such as 16 GB or 32 GB. Thus, if you're recording longer videos, you'll need to use multiple memory cards.

Especially if you'll be recording HD 1080p quality video, choosing a video card with a fast read/write speed is essential, because a tremendous amout of raw data needs to be transferred from the video camera to the memory card every second as you're recording. When it comes to video, memory card read/write speeds are divided into four classes—class 2, class 4, class 6, and class 10.

Class 2 memory cards can store data as it's being recorded by your camcorder at a rate of just 2 megabytes per second (MBps). A class 4 memory card can store data at a speed up to 4 MBps, while a class 6 memory card can store data at a speed of up to 6 MBps. You'll probably discover much better performance from your camcorder when recording HD 1080p quality video if you use either a class 6 or class 10 card (which is capable of storing data at a rate of up to 10 MBps).

Be consistent with your memory cards. If you start filming a video using a class 10 SDHC memory card, for example, and you run out of storage space, replace it with

MORE ON MEMORY CARDS, CONTINUED

an identical card and keep shooting. Don't try using an inferior card to shoot a portion of your video. You may notice a quality difference when you try to edit all of the footage together on your computer.

When you begin shopping for memory cards, the card's class may be displayed on the front of the packaging, or in the fine print about the card's technical specifications, often printed on the back. Some companies like Sandisk have branded the various categories of their memory cards. Its SDHC cards are marketed as Advanced (the best), Extreme, Ultra, Standard, and Wireless.

In a nutshell, SD memory cards are great for shooting standard quality video, while SDHC memory cards (rated as class 6 or class 10), are much better suited for shooting HD 1080p quality video. However, there's yet a more modern alternative.

Some newer HD camcorders are compatible with newer SDXC memory cards. From the outside, these cards look the same as SD or SDHC memory cards, but they're capable of storing much more data (up to 2 TB or more), and are capable of read/write speeds up to 300 MBps. Expect to pay a premium for them, and understand that they're only compatible with the newest, most advanced camcorders.

Another nice benefit of using flash memory card storage with a camcorder is that you can swap out cards for each video project you're working on. Different camcorders use different formats of memory cards, so be sure that the card you buy is compatible. You'll find compatibility information on the camcorder packaging.

Pocket Camcorders

For some YouTube video productions, a pocket camcorder may offer a viable option. These camcorders typically cost less than $300, and they're designed specifically for shooting HD video on the go that can easily be edited and uploaded to YouTube. These camcorders are small, lightweight, and versatile. Most have either a built-in flash drive or utilize memory cards.

They use an industry-standard video file format (such as MPEG-4), have a built-in microphone, and a built-in USB port to which you can connect a USB cable to transfer your raw footage to your desktop or notebook computer.

Even though many of these pocket camcorders can shoot HD-quality raw footage, their low-quality lenses and built-in microphones typically result in video quality that's inferior to what's possible using a full-size, mid- to high-end consumer camcorder. And they typically only offer digital zoom and don't have an optical zoom lens.

The pocket camcorder category first became popular when a product called the Flip camera was released. The company that manufactured the Flip was later purchased by Cisco, which ultimately pulled out of the business altogether. The Flip cameras, including the Flip Slide HD and MinoHD, will continue to be sold while supplies last. However, the company will discontinue any and all support for them by the end of December 2013.

Other manufacturers of pocket camcorders—sometimes referred to as "shoot and share" camcorders—include: Samsung, GE, Vivitar, Creative Labs, Kodak, Sanyo, Sony, 3M, and JVC. You'll find these devices sold online and through consumer electronics retail stores.

Each of these companies offers several different models. Look for one that offers HD 1080p video recording capability, a long battery life, and the option to connect an external microphone. If the pocket camcorder utilizes an internal hard drive or flash drive, the larger the capacity, the better.

A larger size display is also useful, because this will be used both as a viewfinder and for video playback. If you're on a tight budget, a pocket camcorder may be a better option than a point-and-shoot camera or a webcam.

SEMIPRO OR PROFESSIONAL-QUALITY VIDEO CAMERAS

Beyond the mid- to high-end consumer camcorders you'll find at consumer electronics superstores such as Best Buy, there's another category of professional-quality camcorders that start at around $4,000, and go up considerably from there. These cameras are used to film TV shows, commercials, and some movies.

These professional-level camcorders offer many features not found in even the highest-end consumer camcorder models, including interchangeable lenses and powerful optical zoom capabilities. Professional camcorders are heavier and more cumbersome, but offer unparalleled HD-quality filming capabilities.

In addition to buying or renting a professional camcorder, you'll probably need to hire an experienced camera operator, and need a high-end tripod, lighting equipment, and external microphones. Beyond needing a substantial budget, you'll also need to learn how to utilize this type of equipment.

SPECIAL-PURPOSE CAMCORDERS

You may need a camcorder that can withstand harsh climates, that's waterproof, or that can be clipped onto your own body so you can perform some type of action or sport and shoot it from a first-person perspective. For these tasks, you'll want to get your hands on a specialty camcorder, such as the Hero3 Black Edition from GoPro.

This camera weighs 2.6 ounces and can clip onto your body or directly onto sports equipment. It has a waterproof housing and a built-in microphone; you can also attach an external microphone. Sony, Samsung, Kodak, Bell & Howell, and Panasonic also make consumer-quality camcorders designed for underwater use, for example. Splashcam offers several professional-quality camcorders designed for filming underwater (www.splashcam.com/underwater_video_cameras.htm), such as the Deep Blue Pro, which is designed specifically for TV and film production.

Liquid Image (www.liquidimageco.com) has Scuba Series HD video cameras that are built into scuba masks, allowing for hands-free underwater photography.

If your needs include aerial photography that's shot using a remote-controlled, unmanned aircraft, check out the camcorder and video production solutions offered by PhotoShip One (http://photoshipone.com).

TRANSFERRING VIDEO FOOTAGE TO YOUR COMPUTER

You'll need to transfer footage from whatever camcorder you're using to your primary computer for viewing, editing, archiving, and publishing online. Depending on the camcorder you purchase, this can be done in one or more of the following ways:

- Connecting a USB cable directly between the USB port of the camera and the USB port of your computer. In some cases, a Firewire cable can be used, if both the camera and your computer have a Firewire port. Firewire works the same way as a USB cable, but allows for much faster data transfer speeds.
- Removing the camcorder's memory card from the camera and inserting it into an external memory card reader that's already connected to your primary computer via its USB port. For less than $30, you can purchase a memory card reader that's compatible with the type of memory cards you'll be using.
- If your camcorder has Wi-Fi file transfer capabilities, the video footage can be transferred wirelessly to your computer if the camera and computer are connected to the same wireless network.

When you purchase your camcorder, determine if the appropriate cables and equipment for transferring the video footage you shoot are included with the camera (they often are). If necessary, purchase the additional cables, memory card reader, or other equipment you'll need to handle this important task.

Many video cameras have a built-in A/V port or HDMI port that allows you to directly connect a specialty cable between the camcorder and your HDTV set in order to view the video footage you shoot directly from the camera without first transferring it. This allows you to see exactly how your footage will look on an HDTV.

When you do this, however, the footage remains stored on your camcorder. It will still need to be transferred to a computer for viewing, editing, archiving, and publishing.

One of the very first things you should plan to do after you shoot important video footage is to transfer it to your computer. However, before you start the editing process, immediately make a backup of the raw video footage, which you store on an external hard drive or on an online file storage service. This way, if something goes wrong during the editing process, or your computer crashes, you know you have a full backup of the original video footage.

Never delete the raw video footage from your camcorder or its memory card until you are certain that the file transfer was successful and that you've backed up the footage somewhere other than your primary computer.

MONEY-SAVING TIPS WHEN CAMERA SHOPPING

Consumer-grade camcorders are available from consumer electronics stores and photo/ video specialty stores. While you will pay more at retail photo/video specialty stores, the expertise of the salespeople tends to be top-notch, so you will receive excellent advice and get hands-on product demonstrations prior to making a purchase.

However, if you're looking for the best deals on these cameras, you'll probably want to shop online. Camera/photo specialty stores, such as B&H Photo/Video (www. bhphotovideo.com) and Adorama (www.adorama.com), not only offer competitive pricing, but also tend to maintain a great inventory selection.

These companies also offer telephone sales and support departments, which you can call for advice about what to purchase. Online photo/video retailers also sell a wide selection of video-related accessories and the other equipment, such as a tripod and lighting and sound equipment, so you can often acquire everything you need in one stop.

If you already know the exact make and model of the camcorder you're looking for, or what additional equipment and accessories you need, consider an online price comparison website like Nextag.com (www.nextag.com). Enter the exact make and model of what you're looking for into the site's search field for a list of retailers and prices, plus customer ratings for the retailer and product reviews.

Another savings option is to seek out used equipment from a reputable photo/video specialty store. This equipment typically comes with some type of warranty, and you're guaranteed it'll be fully operational when you first take possession of it. Some camcorder manufacturers' websites, as well as photo/video specialty stores, sell refurbished equipment as well. This is equipment that has been returned by the original purchaser, but has been refurbished by the manufacturer to meet its original specifications.

And consider seeking out the advice of experts. For example, you can hire a freelance camera operator or video producer using a service like eLance.com, and then pick their brain. Or, you can rely on the advice offered by the salesperson at a photo/video specialty store. You can also contact other YouTube video producers and discuss what equipment they use.

Learn More from Video Production Magazines and Websites

Reading special interest video production magazines, such as *HDVideoPro*, will also help you learn about the latest video equipment and provide you with reliable product reviews. *HDVideoPro* is a monthly magazine that's available from newsstands, however, the publication's website (www.hdvideopro.com) offers a vast amount of free information, including past articles and reviews.

Videomaker magazine is another "must read" monthly publication if you're interested in learning more about video production and want access to reviews of the latest camcorders and equipment that's available. This, too, is a print publication available from newsstands, but the publication's website (www.videomaker.com) offers a vast amount of useful and free information.

Videography magazine (www.creativeplanetnetwork.com/videography) is targeted more to professional-level video production, but is also highly informative.

You'll find plenty of free how-to information available from YouTube. For product reviews and demonstrations of newly released camcorders, cameras, and video equipment, visit websites such as Video University (www.videouniversity.com), Studio Daily (www.studiodaily.com), The DV Show (www.thedvshow.com), Reviewed.com (owned by *USA Today*), and Kelby Training (http://kelbytraining.com/online/courses/video).

Once you know which camcorder make and model you'll be using, visit the manufacturer's website. You'll often find free video-based tutorials about how to use that specific camcorder, plus other useful information that can help you dramatically improve your video productions' quality.

Filming YouTube Videos

IN THIS CHAPTER

- Putting the production elements together
- Get ready to start filming
- Shooting your videos

You've probably put a lot of thought into the concepts for your videos, and then invested additional time storyboarding the ideas and/or writing scripts. Now that the pre-production phase is completed, it's time to gather up your production equipment, cast, and crew, and get ready to shoot your videos. This chapter focuses on the production phase or filming aspect of your overall videos.

PREPARING FOR YOUR SHOOT

First and foremost, you'll need to consider what approach you want to take with each of your videos, and then consider how you'll want them to look and sound once you've finished editing then. Keep in mind, consistency between videos, your YouTube Channel page, and your overall online presence on other services (including your website) is important. These initial decisions will also help you determine where you should do your shooting and what production equipment you'll need to use in order to achieve the best possible results.

Envision how you want the final videos to look and sound once you add titles, credits, background music, sound effects, and other production elements, such as animated graphics, digital photos, and/or graphic charts, which are added during post production.

If you'll be shooting indoors, you'll need to set up and use proper lighting and sound equipment, plus a simple background—whether it's your office, factory, or a solid-color backdrop.

Especially if you're first starting to learn about video production, the best strategy for success is to keep your videos simple from a production standpoint, and really focus on the content—your key message, call to action, and whatever other important information you plan to communicate within your videos.

For example, the promotional videos on Apple's website typically feature an executive wearing a solid-colored outfit, looking at the camera from a slight angle, while sitting in front of a solid white background. Visually, you can't get simpler than that. But the videos are informative, engaging, cater nicely to their audience, and are perfectly integrated with the rest of the website.

Saddleback Leather (www.saddlebackleather.com) uses a different approach. Its website and YouTube channel use a much more grass-roots, raw approach in promotional and product demonstration videos. One of the company's owners simply sits or stands in their office, while discussing or demonstrating Saddleback Leather's handmade bags and accessories. The products can often be seen in the background as well. To reinforce that "homemade" approach, sometimes there's a pet roaming around in the videos, and the featured person speaks extemporaneously to the audience while wearing casual attire. While the video is clearly carefully planned, there's no script or teleprompter.

The videos work extremely well because they reflect the company's core message, that Saddleback Leather is a small company that handcrafts all of its high-quality products. The goal is to personalize the company and make existing customers feel like part of the Saddleback Leather family, while also showcasing the company's products.

Videos for major corporations are much more likely to be professionally produced and suitable for broadcast on TV. Even their product-demonstration and promotional videos have a slick look that's almost like watching a high-budget TV show or music video. The Honda Channel (www.youtube.com/user/Honda) and the Coca-Cola Channel (www.youtube.com/user/cocacola) on YouTube both use this approach. Most of the videos on these channels are highly produced, extended-length commercials created by well-known advertising agencies.

Figure out what approach will work best for your company and that will allow you to effectively and efficiently communicate to your intended audience your core message and call to action as quickly as possible. Try to personalize your company and those people featured within your videos to quickly establish a connection with your audience.

In the production phase, your focus should be on shooting the live-action scenes or elements that will be used within your videos. "Live action" is the scenes or sections of your videos that will feature people or content shot in the real world. Titles, logos, graphics, music, sound effects, computer animations, and other multimedia content will be added later, during post production.

Let's take a closer look at some of the things you'll need to consider as you begin shooting the live-action video elements of your productions. While you want to achieve the highest production quality you can, your content is what matters.

Where You'll Be Shooting

Whether it's indoors or outdoors, select a shooting location that can help you tell your story, communicate your message, and set the scene, without distracting your audience. As you choose your setting, consider what lighting and sound challenges you'll encounter, and make sure you have the right production equipment to overcome these challenges.

Ideally, you want to be able to control the environment within and around your shooting location so you can easily light the set and capture only the sound you want to include in your videos, without cars, airplanes, machinery, or other distracting ambient noises.

As you're shooting, ensure what you're filming is in focus and well lit. While you can slightly improve some aspects of a video's quality in post production, ideally you want to capture the highest quality raw video footage possible.

Based on what will be happening in your video, make sure your location will allow you to achieve the shots you need, whether it's showing your subject in motion, sitting at a desk or on a stool, or positioned with your company's products in the foreground or background.

If you're shooting a product demonstration, a solid backdrop will be less distracting, because you want the audience to focus on the product or spokesperson. However, if you're shooting a news-style report or a tour of your factory, your background will be a key part of the message you're trying to convey.

There will be challenges wherever you shoot. Indoors, when using artificial lighting, you'll need to deal with unwanted shadows; outdoors, the challenges might include reflections from the sun, ambient noise, and wind. The right equipment is essential.

Consider the Stars of Your Video

Next, consider who will be appearing in your videos and how you want to present them. Pay attention to every aspect of each person's appearance, as well as how they'll be positioned, what they'll be doing, what persona or personality they'll convey, and what they'll be wearing. Wardrobe, makeup, and hairstyle will all play a critical role in establishing that all-important first impression and ongoing rapport with your audience.

People often come across best wearing solid colors, and simple outfits that don't blend in with the background. Avoid flashy or shiny jewelry, including watches, that reflect light. If your subject wears glasses, get anti-reflective lenses, especially if you'll be using artificial light, to avoid eyeglass glare.

The people in your video should also have their hair nicely styled, so you may want to hire a professional. Messy hair can detract from their professional appearance and be distracting to your audience. As for makeup, more is less, especially if you're shooting in HD or plan closeups. You want the people in your videos to look natural. A professional makeup artist understands how to do makeup for video shoots.

Next, think about what your presenters will be doing, and how they'll be positioned. Figure out what props will be needed to help them appear natural in front of the camera. Will they be holding or interacting with specific products? If so, do their appearance and the background complement those products? Will they look more natural and comfortable sitting or standing? Will they be more appealing to your audience looking directly into the camera, or slightly away from it?

Your stars' appearance should reflect their personalities, fit the image you're trying to convey, and appeal to your audience.

Lighting

Depending on where you're shooting and the lighting challenges, you'll likely need to use a semi-professional or professional lighting kit, as well as light diffusers and/or reflectors. A basic lighting kit will include three or up to five individual lights that will ultimately be positioned around your subject(s) to create even, shadow-free lighting.

If you use too much light, your videos will appear overexposed, and everything will look washed out. If there's too little light, everything will appear dark, and colors and visual details will be obscured.

Even if you're shooting outdoors, artificial light, reflectors, and/or diffusers can help create optimal lighting around your subjects. When the artificial lights aren't enough to control the lighting, a diffuser can help to eliminate unwanted shadows or glare, while a reflector redirects light onto your subjects.

For most video shoots, a basic, three-point continuous lighting system will work fine. One light is positioned in front of your main subject, while the others are to the left and right of the subject. If you access YouTube and use the search phrase "video lighting," you'll find multiple tutorials for how to best utilize a basic three-point lighting system.

Refer to Chapter 8, "The Equipment You'll Need," to learn more about semi-professional and professional lighting kits, reflectors, and diffusers. B&H Photo-Video (www.bhphotovideo.com), Adorama (www.adorama.com), and PhotoBasics (http://fjwestcott.com/photobasics) offer a selection of affordable lighting kits that are easy to use. Don't mix different types of lighting, such as incandescent, fluorescent, or LED lights, when filming your video.

Sound

Close your eyes and listen carefully to whatever ambient noises you hear in the background. Can you hear the fan from your computer, clocks ticking, the sound of distant traffic, airplanes flying overhead, telephones ringing, people walking and talking in neighboring rooms, or the sound of an air conditioner?

If you were to start filming right now, your camera would pick up all of these ambient sounds. When you actually start filming your videos, these are the distracting sounds you want to notice upfront and eliminate. Chances are, the microphone that's built into your camcorder or video camera can't adequately achieve the high-level audio quality you'll want and need, so you'll need to attach an external microphone to your camera.

There are different types of microphones, each with a specialized purpose. Some are designed to pick up only the sound of people's voices, or the sound that's directly in front of them, while others are designed to pick up all ambient noise in the area where you're filming. There are also different styles, such as handheld, lapel, and shotgun microphones, each of which is suitable for recording audio in different situations. There are also both wired and wireless variations, as well as specialized accessories, such as pop filters and wind screens, that can help eliminate unwanted noises. For help making the right decision, B&H Photo-Video's website (www.bhphotovideo.com/indepth/category/tags/microphones) offers a library of how-to tutorials about recording audio. You'll also find similar tutorials on YouTube and the PhotoBasics website (http://fjwestcott.com/university).

Camera Preparation

Before you set out to start shooting your videos, learn how to properly use your camera and all of its functions. This small investment of time could mean the difference

CONSIDER SHOOTING WITH MULTIPLE CAMERAS

More often than not, your video production will benefit if you simultaneously shoot each scene in your video using two or three cameras at once, each set at a different angle. Then, you can pick and choose which shot you want to use, and be able to switch between shots to create a more visually interesting video.

If you don't have the budget to shoot with multiple HD cameras, you can always shoot the same scene several times and position the camera differently for each take. This too will provide you with options when it comes to editing your videos later.

Using multiple cameras also requires added crew members. You'll also need to use video editing software that allows you to more easily edit multi-camera shots and video using multiple video feeds.

For more information about how to shoot multi-cam videos, search for "shooting multi-cam videos" on YouTube for tutorials on how to use this shooting technique. For example, visit www.youtube.com/watch?v=1ItW5yz9L6M to view a four-minute tutorial video.

There are also editing techniques that allow you to use one camera for shooting, but during the editing process, fake a multi-cam shoot approach. A tutorial for how to do this can be found at www.youtube.com/watch?v=PZmV0YNObAQ.

between shooting a clear and professional-quality video, and a total mess that will require re-shoots.

Be sure to begin your shoot with fully charged batteries for your camera. Ideally, you want to have two or three extra fully charged batteries on hand. If your camera uses recordable media like memory cards, be sure to have an ample supply so you can shoot plenty of video, including multiple takes of each scene.

It's also essential that you clean your camera lens before shooting. Even the smallest speck of dust, fingerprint, or water drop on the lens can result in shooting unusable video. Use a lens cleaning cloth—not a paper towel or your shirtsleeve—to carefully clean the lens.

Finally, practice using all the camera accessories you'll need for the shoot, including a tripod or a camera stabilizer or support rig, an on-camera monitor, and/or an external microphone.

LIGHTS, CAMERAS . . . ACTION!

Even if your goal is to create a two- to three-minute video, you'll wind up shooting a lot of extra video that you'll then edit during post production. The more planning you do before you start shooting, the more efficient your shooting time will be. Because you can reorder shots using your video editing software, there's no need to shoot your video in sequential order. In fact, you'll often find it more advantageous to shoot out of sequence.

As a video producer, you'll need to pay continuous attention to every detail during your shoot—lighting, sound, and continuity-related issues. For example, if you start shooting one day and then pick it up on another day, be sure the visual is identical from one day to the next, from your players' appearance to the lighting, the set, the position of props, and anything else that can be seen or heard.

You'll also need to make sure that you properly present your message and call to action, and get your other key points across quickly. To make your video more visually interesting, you'll want to use different shooting angles, and maybe incorporate a small amount of motion into your production. Let's take a look at some of these important considerations.

Define, Present, and Repeat Your Message

During the pre-production phase, you should have clearly defined the message you want to get across to your audience. Now that you're actually shooting a video, be sure to:

- Present your core message very early in the video—within the first 10 to 15 seconds.
- Repeat your message, using different wording or a slightly different approach, several times.
- Make sure that the message is presented in a natural and organic way that fits into the video as a whole.
- As you're filming, put yourself in your audience's shoes to make sure that your approach is appealing and easily understandable.
- Repeat or emphasize your core message multiple times. Try to do this every 30 seconds, if possible, without making it look forced or sound too much like an infomercial.
- Avoid taking a hard sell, commercial-style approach. On YouTube, the soft sell almost always works better.

Incorporate Your Call to Action

Your productions should all have a call to action, or tell your audience exactly what you want them to do and when as a result of watching your video. It might be, "For an extra savings of $100, click here to visit our website and order our new [insert product name]," or "To receive $50 off of your first order, call us right now at 800-555-1234." It might also be to get the viewer to click on the "Like" button, post a comment about the video on your YouTube channel page, or to share it via Facebook or Twitter.

Here are some tips for presenting your call to action:

- Present your call to action near the start and at the end of your video, and repeat it during your video. Most people won't be watching your video from start to finish, so don't wait until the very end to present your call to action for the first time.
- State the clear benefit or reward first, and then explain exactly what the viewer needs to do.
- Make sure your call to action is easy to understand and straightforward. Tell the viewer exactly what to do, how to do it, and when to do it.
- In addition to stating your call to action within the video itself, embed links or annotations in your video during post production and use titles to reinforce what you're saying.

Get Your Key Points Across Quickly

YouTube viewers have short attention spans and are constantly bombarded with links or invitations to watch new videos. It's essential that you capture their attention within the first five seconds, so think about your opening shot very carefully.

Then, within the first five to 10 seconds, be sure to inform the viewer about what your video is about, and exactly what they can expect from watching it. At the same time, communicate your core message and, potentially, your call to action.

Within that first five to 15 seconds, a viewer can determine if your video is of interest and offers a benefit. Then, even if someone stops watching after 15 seconds or so, at least they were exposed to your core message.

While there is no optimal length, perfect formula, or format to follow—it depends on who your audience is, what you're trying to communicate, and what approach you're taking—you should still keep your videos short and to the point.

You're better off creating a series of shorter videos, of one to three minutes, than producing one long video. Shorter videos capture and keep your viewer's attention, plus create a quality interaction. You also improve the chances of someone finding your videos when doing a search on YouTube or Google.

With more videos listed within your channel and on Google, your overall SEO rankings will improve, plus you'll receive separate listings for each of your videos. This increases your chances of someone finding your channel using YouTube's or Google's search function.

For each of your related videos, make sure you use similar titles, descriptions, keywords, and tags, as well as the same category. Then, from your YouTube Channel page, you can link the related videos into a playlist for your audience.

Use the Rule of Thirds When Shooting

Invest time learning some basic principles of cinematography. One core concept is the "Rule of Thirds." Instead of pointing your camera directly at your subject and keeping them centered in the frame, position your main subject off-center.

Envision a tic-tac-toe board is overlaid over your camera's viewfinder, with nine equally sized boxes that together make up your shooting frame. The box in the center represents the center of the shot, where most people position their subject.

Instead, line up your main subject at one of the interaction points within the grid, and pay attention to whatever is in the foreground, background, and/or to the sides of your subject within the shot as well. The goal is to move your main subject out of the center of the frame to create a more visually interesting shot.

You don't need to position your camera directly in front of your subject or head-on. Shooting from a different perspective or angle creates a much more visually compelling shot. Position your camera slightly above, below, or to the side of your subject, and shoot from an angle.

Utilizing your camera's zoom lens allows you to switch between closeup, mid-length, and wide-angle shots. You can switch shots using a manual zoom as you're shooting, or stop the action, reposition and refocus your camera, and then restart shooting. Later, you can also edit in scene or shot transitions as needed.

Part of being a skilled cinematographer is to tap your own creativity and experiment. Select shots and perspectives that will be visually appealing and potentially artistic, but not distract your audience from your message. Study popular YouTube videos that take the approach or format that you intend to use.

If you plan to add a company logo, titles, or other graphics into a shot, be sure to leave room in the frame as you're shooting the core live-action footage so there's room for those post-production elements. Instead of using a closeup shot, for example, you might need to use a medium or wide shot.

Keep Your Camera Steady by Using a Tripod

While MTV and most reality TV shows use handheld cameras to create a "you are there" perspective with a lot of camera motion, you'll probably want to use a tripod or Steadicam. These allow you to hold the camera perfectly still and also use smooth, slow camera movements to show motion without amateurish shakes and jerks.

Refer to Chapter 8, "The Equipment You'll Need," to learn more about tripod and Steadicam accessories. Especially if you're shooting people or "talking head" scenes,

CONSIDER SHOOTING IN FRONT OF A BLUE OR GREEN SCREEN

As you become more proficient using your video equipment and want to tap your creativity to produce more visually interesting videos, you can try a technique called "chroma key." This is technically a post-production special effect that's relatively easy to use with even the most basic video camera and video editing equipment.

With chroma key, you shoot all of your live-action content in front of a special blue or green background. Then, using specialized video editing software, you can remove the background digitally, and replace it with anything you want: animated graphics, other video, or a still image. Whatever was shot in front of the blue or green screen will then be digitally superimposed over the background. The trick to using this effect well is to ensure proper lighting when shooting and then selecting the best video editing software.

123 Video Magic (www.123videomagic.com), NCH Software (www.nchsoftware. com), Pinnacle Studio (www.pinnaclesys.com), and Magix (www.magix.com) are some of the many companies that offer video editing software that includes the chroma key effect. The feature is also included in more advanced video editing software packages, like Final Cut Pro X and Adobe Premier Pro CS 6, which you'll read more about in Chapter 11, "Editing Your YouTube Videos."

Here are a few of the free YouTube tutorials that showcase how to use chroma key:

- Chroma Key Studio Set Up HD—www.youtube.com/watch?v=GjvqsB2EAuc
- Green Screen Tips, Tricks and Materials—www.youtube.com/user/ tubetape?v=q3PZO_ICBkw
- How To Set Up A Green Screen—www.youtube.com/watch?v=20U86p2ceEc
- Green Screen Tips, Tricks and Materials—Chromakey Tutorial—www.youtube. com/watch?v=M_WdLkaOUic

To find more videos that showcase creative ways to use chroma key, simply search for "chroma key."

keeping the camera perfectly steady is essential. Otherwise, you'll wind up with a video that is distracting or annoying.

Don't Forget About Branding

Regardless of your video's purpose—be it promotional, instructional, or to demonstrate a product—make the look, sound, and overall feel of your production consistent with your other videos, your online presence and company website, and your real-world image.

To ensure you include your own branding showcase your company logo and website URL within the video or display products, even if they're in the background or on someone's desk. Think about how to communicate your branding or core message visually. It can be subtle or blatant.

Also consider how to use product placement to better promote or showcase your own products, brand, or image. The person in your video can wear a T-shirt that clearly displays your company's logo, or place a computer in the shot and display the logo or photos of your products as its screen saver.

Develop strategies that will appeal to your target audience without being distracting. Nobody wants to watch infomercials, but people will invest their time to watch videos that offer useful information about products or services they're interested in, as long as the viewer perceives what they're watching to be valuable, accurate, and credible. More often than not, taking a very subtle approach to branding within your videos works the best.

NOW, EDIT YOUR VIDEOS IN POST PRODUCTION

Once you've shot your video and assembled any other multimedia content, you're ready to begin post production. Using your video editing software, you'll edit down your footage and create the video production that you'll upload and share with your audience on YouTube, your company's website, and other services, such as Vimeo.

It's during the post-production phase that you can piece together your production, add special effects and animated transitions, incorporate titles, credits, and animation, and insert music and sound effects.

Then, once you upload your video to your YouTube channel, you can add annotations and embed links.

Editing Your YouTube Videos

Each phase of a video's creation is important, including its post production, after the footage has been shot and you're ready to edit and add other production elements. Post production involves several key steps, including:

- Reviewing, cataloging, and editing footage
- Adding titles, such as an opening title and end credits
- Incorporating voice-overs, music, sound effects, and other audio elements
- Importing multimedia elements, such as animated charts, graphs, tables, and PowerPoint slides
- Adding effects and scene transitions
- Cutting or trimming content to make it an acceptable length

- Exporting the fully produced video into an industry-standard file format
- Uploading and publishing the video on YouTube

You'll do much of the post-production work using video editing software on your Windows-based PC or Mac. Consumer-oriented editing applications are designed for ease of use, but lack a vast collection of editing and post-production tools, and range from free to under $40. There are also consumer-oriented applications that offer scaled-down versions of professional tools that can allow for near professional-quality results and are priced around $100.

You'll also find consumer-level online video editing tools. To use one of these services, you'd first upload your raw video footage and other content to the service, and then take advantage of the online-based video editing tools available. This option eliminates the need to install video editing software on your computer. Another benefit is that you can edit your videos from any compatible computer or device that's connected to the internet, regardless of where you are.

WeVideo.com (www.wevideo.com) is an example of a fee-based video editing option that's based online. You'll read more about this service shortly. As you'll discover, YouTube itself also offers a handful of basic video editing tools you can use to edit and enhance your videos once they're uploaded to your YouTube Channel.

Yet another category is designed for semi-professional videographers and editors. These tend to be feature-packed, extremely powerful, and require a significant learning curve. They typically cost several hundred dollars, and require more advanced computer hardware.

To create truly professional, broadcast-quality results, you'll need professional video editing tools and either high-end computers or specialized editing equipment. Plan to spend thousands on this type of setup, and to hire a professional editor.

You may be able to get by with higher-end consumer-oriented video editing software, but for higher-quality videos, it's best to go for semi-professional video editing software, such as Final Cut Pro (for the Mac) or Adobe Premier Pro CS6 (for the Mac or Windows-based PCs).

Depending on the video—its complexity, the amount of raw footage and multimedia elements, the type of software you're using—plan to spend between several hours and several full days to edit each of your YouTube videos. You may also need to use other software to create production elements, for example, Microsoft PowerPoint to create animated digital slides showcasing charts, graphs, tables, and lists—that can be imported into your video as pre-produced multimedia content.

You'll need digital audio production software and equipment to record your own music and sounds effects, photo editing software to incorporate digital photos, and other

MOBILE VIDEO EDITING

If you shoot video footage on your mobile device, you can use a video editing app to edit your raw video, handle many post-production steps, and then directly upload your fully produced video to YouTube.

While the quality isn't the same as that of a desktop-edited video—nor will you have the same caliber of editing tools available— what is possible using a smartphone or tablet with wireless internet capabilities is adequate for many YouTube video producers.

For an Apple iOS mobile device, purchase, download, and install Apple's own iMovie app to handle many post-production steps. Many third-party apps are also available from the App Store within the "Photo & Video" category. Among them are SpliceVideo Editor, Magisto Magical Video Editor, Camera Awesome, Viddy, Videolicious, 8mm Vintage Camera, and countless others.

software to incorporate animated elements, such as an animated company logo. Each of these elements will be imported into your video editing software to add to your video.

WHAT VIDEO EDITING SOFTWARE CAN AND CAN'T DO

In just the past few years, the capabilities of consumer-oriented video editing software has dramatically expanded. Once you import raw video footage into the software and then import your other multimedia elements, video editing software allows you to transform the raw content into a slick-looking, fully professional production.

While each has its own set of tools, most of the popular editing packages include the ability to:

- Add animated titles to your production, including scrolling credits
- Edit, trim, or crop footage, with control over one frame at a time
- Add professional-style, animated scene transitions
- Make minor fixes to raw footage, such as shaky footage or lighting, or make subtle color adjustments
- Incorporate pre-recorded music, voice-overs, and sound effects
- Add pre-produced multimedia elements
- Incorporate special effect filters

- Use optional plug-ins available from third parties that expand the video editing tool set
- Preview your edited movies
- Export your edited/produced videos
- Upload your videos to your YouTube channel

To speed up the video editing process, many consumer-oriented video editing software packages offer pre-created themes into which you can drag and drop your raw video footage and multimedia elements.

Video editing is both a skill and an art form. The skill needed includes knowing how to use your computer and video editing software. This means discovering what's possible, and then learning how to use the various menus, commands, and features built into the software. You'll ultimately decide what your audience will see and hear during every second of your video, and have many tools available to transform your creative vision for the video into a finished production that caters to your target audience.

Yet another option for editing videos is to upload your raw video footage directly to YouTube and use its video editor to edit your productions before making them public.

COMPUTER HARDWARE CONSIDERATIONS FOR EDITING HD-QUALITY VIDEO

The digital files for HD video footage are massive, and most consumer-oriented editing software that run on basic Windows-based PCs or on Macs running OS X Mountain Lion can't handle long videos because of the file size. If you attempt to load one into a standard PC or Mac, the editing software might crash, or the computer may slow to a crawl.

To avoid this, keep your videos short and only load 15 or so minutes of raw video at a time, especially if you're using an older computer. If you know you'll need to edit longer HD videos, consider upgrading your computer with a faster, more powerful microprocessor, graphics, and sound cards, increasing the amount of RAM, and using a large-capacity external hard drive with a fast read/write speed.

Try to meet or exceed the hardware requirements listed by the software's developer. If you're looking to use more advanced video editing software, such as Adobe Premiere Pro CS6 on a PC or Mac, the system requirements are rather extensive; you can find them at www.adobe.com/products/premiere/tech-specs.html.

The editing functions are limited, but for editing vlogs (a video where one person is looking into a camera and speaking, using a digital diary-like format) and other short videos that don't need to be polished, this is certainly a viable option, especially if you need to upload and edit a video while away from your primary computer.

What Your Software Can't Do

While some video editing software packages offer tools that allow you to manipulate the quality of raw video, there are limits to what's possible. Especially with lower-end software, there's only so much you can do post production to fix video that is shot out of focus, is extremely shaky, or is over- or underexposed. Before editing and adding production elements, you'll want to discover what your software is capable of and what features it offers.

CHOOSING THE RIGHT SOFTWARE

Choosing the best video editing software will come down to a handful of decisions early on, including:

- Your budget
- Your computer knowledge and comfort using technology
- How much time and effort you want to invest in editing your videos
- How much control you want to have when editing your videos, including the selection of post-production tools you want or need in order to achieve your video's objectives
- The level of production quality you're striving for
- The capabilities of your Windows PC or Mac computer
- The file format(s) of the raw video and multimedia content to be incorporated into your videos, and the file format(s) and data compression you'll use when you export your final productions

If you're already proficient editing or enhancing digital photos on your computer, you already have some of the core skills needed to edit video. When editing video, however, you're dealing with 20 or more individual frames per second, plus audio content, so there's a lot more to consider and the software-based tools you'll be using are more robust.

Even if you opt to use the most user-friendly and basic video editing software on your computer, such as Microsoft Movie Maker for Windows or iMovie for the Mac, there's still a learning curve with discovering how to use the software, its features and tools.

Should you opt to use semi-professional level video editing software, such as Apple's Final Cut Pro or Adobe Premier Pro CS6, the learning curve is much more significant, because the editing tools are far more extensive and advanced.

Start off with basic software that has tools to achieve the production quality you'll need to achieve your objectives and creative vision. You can always upgrade down the road.

Overview of Popular Software Packages

There are literally hundreds of video editing software packages, as well as optional add-ons and plug-ins available that allow you to transform raw video footage and other multimedia elements into a cohesive and professional-looking video presentation that can be published on YouTube or elsewhere.

Both Microsoft and Apple offer basic video editing software either bundled with their operating systems or available as free downloads. Microsoft Movie Maker (http://windows.microsoft.com/en-US/windows7/products/features/movie-maker) and Apple's iMovie (www.apple.com/ilife/imovie) are both very easy-to-use, yet powerful consumer-oriented editing tools that offer a nice selection of features and tools for creating decent-looking HD-quality productions that can be published on YouTube with a few mouse clicks.

Using the Online-Based YouTube Video Editor

Another option is to upload your unedited, raw video footage directly to YouTube, and then use the service's own online-based Video Editor (http://www.youtube.com/editor), as well as YouTube's info and settings, enhancements, audio, annotations, and captions options (available through the Video Manager) to handle many post-production tasks.

You can find the Video Editor by accessing YouTube and logging into your YouTube channel. From the menu that's displayed, click on the "Video Manager" option, and then click on the "Video Editor" tab. You'll first need to upload your raw video footage to YouTube and ensure that you don't publish it. To do this, access the Video Manager, select the video, click on the "Info and Settings" option, and then, using the "Privacy" pull-down menu, select the "Private" option.

The editing tools offered by YouTube's Video Editor (Figure 11–1 on page 153) aren't as robust as those available in most video editing software. While these tools will help you edit a personal or company vlog entry, they probably aren't adequate for editing a video aimed at representing your company, product, or service. But they can be used on a fully produced video that's already been uploaded to YouTube.

The Video Editor offers tools for:

- Editing and manipulating video footage that's been uploaded to your YouTube channel, including raw video that you've labeled as private. For example, you can trim your video footage to custom lengths, and then merge scenes that have been shot and edited separately into one production.
- Enhancing the video footage using effects and other controls, such as "Brightness and Contrast," "Stabilize Video," and "Black and White."
- Accessing and remixing YouTube Creative Commons video content. These videos are produced and uploaded by third parties that have granted permission for anyone to use, edit, and incorporate. When you use Creative Commons video, YouTube automatically attributes the content to its creator. To learn more about using Creative Commons content within your videos via YouTube's Video Editor, visit: www.youtube.com/t/creative_commons.

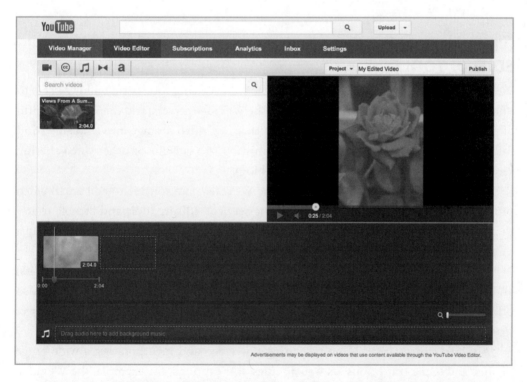

FIGURE 11–1. YouTube's Online Video Editor Offers a Handful of Useful Tools for Editing and then Publishing Your Videos Online. Start by Uploading Your Raw Video Footage and Other Pre-Produced Content to Your YouTube Channel and Marking Them as Private.

- Adding music and sound effects to your videos using the "Media Picker." This grants you access to content from YouTube's vast library of free audio content. You can't edit audio tracks using the Video Editor; you can only determine when it starts and stops playing.
- Incorporating animated transitions between scenes or shots.
- Inserting titles into your videos.

Like many video editing software packages, YouTube's Video Editor uses an intuitive, drag-and-drop interface. While these tools are accessible via any internet-capable device, it's best to use them on your computer. You'll have a difficult time editing a video on a small screen.

When you're done using the Video Editor, click on the "Publish" button displayed near the upper-right corner of the screen. Then, access the Video Manager options to adjust the various settings associated with that video. See Chapter 12, "Uploading Your Videos to YouTube," for more information about using YouTube's Video Manager options.

WEVIDEO.COM OFFERS ADDITIONAL ONLINE VIDEO EDITING TOOLS

WeVideo.com (www.wevideo.com) is an online video editing toolset that allows users to upload their raw SD or HD video footage to the WeVideo servers, and then use a handful of powerful video editing tools to transform that raw video footage into a polished and fully produced video that's suitable for submitting to YouTube or other video sharing services (such as your company's website or blog).

Individuals and small businesses can use WeVideo.com for free to edit small video projects. However, to gain access to all of the service's editing tools and be able to use them on all of your videos (regardless of their length or file size), you'll need to pay a monthly fee, starting at $20.

WeVideo offers two different video editors—the Super Simple Editor (for amateurs) and the Full Featured Editor (which offers much more functionality). The service also offers tools so two or more people can collaborate on editing or reviewing a video project from separate locations.

As you'd expect, in addition to editing raw video and incorporating a wide range of shot and scene transitions, as well as titles and captions, for example, the WeVideo service allows users to easily add music and sound effects to video productions. WeVideo includes a library of more than 400 royalty-free music tracks that can be included within a video for free, or you can add your own music or sound effects (assuming you have obtained the rights or license to use that content).

POWERFUL, FREE EDITING SOFTWARE

There are plenty of free open-source and shareware software packages that can be downloaded and installed on your PC or Mac. There's Wondershare Video Editor that supports dozens of popular video formats and offers hundreds of Hollywood-style effects and scene transitions you can incorporate into your productions. You can also edit and enhance your media files by trimming, cutting, splitting, merging, rotating, and fading videos, while also having the ability to adjust things like contrast, saturation, brightness, and the hue of your raw footage.

Wondershare Video Editor includes tools for inserting and editing audio tracks, plus creating and incorporating text, subtitles, and credits into your productions. What's great about this particular video editing software is that it's available for free, as shareware. Simply visit www.wondershare.net/ad/video-editor-win to download and install the award-winning software.

OpenShot Video Editor (www.openshot.org) is another example of a free, simple-to-use, yet powerful Windows-based video editor that supports HD video and a wide range of visual and audio effect tools.

Another shareware video editing software package for Windows-based PCs is Ezvid VideoMaker for Windows (www.ezvid.com). This software, which works with more current versions of Microsoft Windows (XP SP3, Vista, 7, and 8), is easy to use and offers a handful of tools designed specifically for people creating YouTube videos. Ezvid can create videos up to 45 minutes in length, assuming you have computer hardware capable of supporting large video files sizes.

For a list of free video editing software, as well as links for downloading and installing the software, go to:

- Free Video Editing Software—http://tv.isg.si/site/?q=node/873

- Multimedia and Audio Software—www.osalt.com/multimedia-and-audio

- Video Editing Software—http://en.kioskea.net/download/video-editing-76

For PCs and Macs, you'll find a listing of editing software—some free, some not—at CNET's Download website (http://download.cnet.com) or Wikipedia (http://en.wikipedia.org/wiki/List_of_video_editing_software).

The service supports all popular video, audio, and graphic formats, so uploading and adding any type of multimedia content to your video projects is very easy. Then, once you've edited your videos using the service's online tools, transferring the finished video projects to YouTube or another video-sharing service requires just a few clicks of the mouse.

In addition to the collaboration features built into WeVideo, another great feature is that once your raw video and other multimedia content is uploaded to the service, you can edit your video using any computer or mobile device, such as a tablet or smartphone, and work from anywhere there's an internet connection.

Once your raw video content is uploaded to your WeVideo account, it's securely stored and achieved there. You can only access it if you or your collaborators know your account login information. Storing your raw video footage, as well as your final edited videos on WeVideo (or a service like it), also allows you to conserve storage space on your computer's internal hard drive (or flash drive). As you know, HD video files can take up a lot of storage space due to their large file sizes.

Also, if you own one of Sony's newer model camcorders (released after 2012), you're automatically entitled to use the WeVideo service for 90 days for free. So, whether you use a Sony camcorder or your own camcorder or video camera to shoot SD or HD video footage, using online editing tools from a service like WeVideo, as opposed to video editing software that's installed on your computer, offers several potential advantages.

COMMERCIALLY AVAILABLE VIDEO EDITING SOFTWARE

These packages can be purchased and downloaded directly from their developer's websites and in some cases are also available through retailers that sell software. Many of the more expensive video editing applications, including Adobe Premier Pro CS6 and Apple's Final Cut Pro, offer a free, 30-day trial version that can be downloaded from the developer's website. Before investing hundreds of dollars, download and use the trial versions of several packages to help you decide which work best for you.

Adobe Premiere Pro CS6

Available for both PCs and Macs, Adobe Premiere Pro CS6 (www.adobe.com/products/premiere.html) is one of the most advanced semipro to professional video editing packages available. It is available as a stand-alone package but also integrates perfectly with the other applications in Adobe's Creative Suite.

Adobe Premiere Pro CS6 supports all popular audio and video file formats, and allows for HD-quality video productions to be created on a standard PC or Mac. The latest edition of Adobe Premiere Pro features a newly redesigned user interface that's more intuitive, because there's less on-screen clutter as you're working with your video content.

FIGURE 11–2. Adobe Premiere Pro CS6 Running on a Mac Gives You Tremendous Creative Control Over Your Video Editing and Post Production.

Adobe Premiere Pro CS6 (shown in Figure 11–2) is a higher-end application and is priced that way. Adobe's CreativeCloud option grants unlimited access to the software and to other tools for a monthly fee; for more about the different pricing options, visit www.adobe.com/products/premiere/buying-guide.html. Optional plug-ins and add-ons from third-party companies are also available to enhance specific features of this software.

Apple iMovie

Apple's iMovie software (www.apple.com/ilife/imovie) is part of its iLife '11 suite of applications that comes bundled with all new iMac and MacBook desktop and notebook computers. It's a consumer-level video editing application that's extremely intuitive, thanks to its drag-and-drop interface. iMovie (shown in Figure 11–3 on page 158) allows you to edit HD-quality videos, as long as they're relatively short.

This software works much better on newer Macs that are running the latest operating system (at this writing, OS X, Mountain Lion). If you have an older version of iMovie, there may be an upgrade fee to acquire the latest edition. What's nice about iMovie is that it works seamlessly with other Apple iLife and iWork applications, including GarageBand, iPhoto, Pages, Numbers, and Keynote. It's also compatible in

ADOBE PREMIERE ELEMENTS OFFERS
SCALED-DOWN VIDEO EDITING FEATURES

For digital photographers, Adobe's Photoshop CS6 is one of the most advanced, popular, and feature-packed photo editing tools available. The company also offers a lower-priced, consumer version of Photoshop, called Photoshop Elements, that offers a more user-friendly and easy-to-use interface.

For video editors, many of the most powerful and popular features built into Adobe Premiere Pro CS6 have also been incorporated into a consumer-friendly version of the software, called Photoshop Premiere Elements (www.adobe.com/products/premiere-elements.html). This scaled-down version of the software for PCs and Macs offers a much more intuitive drag-and-drop interface and a shorter learning curve than Adobe Premiere Pro CS6. It also offers a bit more creative control than Microsoft Movie Maker or iMovie.

FIGURE 11–3. The iMovie Software Is Part of Apple's iLife Suite that Comes Bundled for Free with all New Macs. You Can Purchase a More Recent Version of iMovie from the Mac App Store.

many ways with iMovie for iOS, which is an optional video editing application for the iPhone and iPad.

For companies looking to define and promote their corporate image through their YouTube videos, iMovie probably doesn't offer the post-production capabilities and creative control that you'll need. However, if your business would benefit from producing and showcasing animated slide shows, iMovie is a great tool for putting these types of presentations together quickly.

If you're a Mac user, this is an excellent introductory application that's also suitable for online personalities who need to create more basic, but impressive-looking videos for YouTube.

To make the video editing process less time consuming and more intuitive, iMovie also relies heavily on templates. When you begin working on a new video project, you're encouraged to select a fully customizable template to which you can add your video footage, photos, and other multimedia content.

The drawback is that unless you spend a lot of time customizing every aspect of the template, your videos will start to look similar to every other video edited using iMovie.

Apple's Final Cut Pro

While iMovie is very much an introductory, consumer-oriented application for video editing, Apple also offers its Final Cut Pro package (www.apple.com/finalcutpro), which features many more advanced tools designed for achieving semipro to professional-quality results when working with HD video content.

To fully utilize Final Cut Pro, you'll need to run it on a higher-end Mac that's equipped with an Intel Core 2 Due microprocessor (or better), 4 GB of RAM (or more), one of Apple's higher-end graphics cards, and plenty of internal or external hard drive space. You'll also want to run the latest version of the OS X Mountain Lion software. Final Cut Pro will benefit by running on a Mac that's equipped with the more advanced Retina Display being incorporated into the latest iMac and MacBook computers.

Many companies that produce YouTube videos can easily take advantage of the editing and post-production capabilities that Final Cut Pro offers. These functions are pretty much in line with what's offered by Adobe Premier Pro CS6, although individual features and effects vary.

Because Final Cut Pro offers more advanced and professional-level tools, the software requires a much more significant learning curve than iMovie, as well as a better understanding of video editing and production principles. What's nice about this software is that it gives you excellent creative control over the visual and audio aspects of your production, and is compatible with a wide range of popular audio, video, and image file formats.

One of the tasks that Final Cut Pro handles very well is organizing and managing raw video content and pre-produced multimedia elements that will ultimately be incorporated into your video productions. The software uses a dynamic editing approach, which offers greater creative control compared to applications that use timeline-based tracks. This software is also designed to help you view multiple video feeds simultaneously during the editing and post-production process. This allows you to more easily assemble and edit multi-cam projects. You can also simultaneously work with multiple audio channels and have total and independent control over each channel.

Apple also offers a vast library of royalty-free music and sound effects, as well as photo libraries and graphic backgrounds and textures that can be used to polish your project. A large selection of optional plug-ins and add-ons from third-party companies are also available.

Avid Video Editing and Production

Of all the post-production and video editing tools available to professionals, Avid's are the most widely used when it comes to producing broadcast-quality content for TV, motion pictures, and the internet.

This suite of professional-level tools requires a tremendous learning curve, as well as a working knowledge of video production. You'll also need to operate the software tools on high-end computer equipment, especially if you'll be working with HD video.

While the editing, finishing, and post-production tools available from Avid are top-notch, they're also extremely costly. For example, the Avid Media Composer 6.5 software is priced at $2,499, plus has a variety of add-on and plug-ins that are sold separately. To learn more about Avid video editing and production tools, visit www.avid.com/US/categories/Professional-Video-Editing-Finishing.

The video editing tools available from Avid are designed for professionals looking to create broadcast-quality content. It is not meant for use by amateur or even semi-professional video producers.

Microsoft Movie Maker

For Windows-based PC users, Microsoft offers free video editing software called Movie Maker, which provides for a quick and easy solution for taking photos and video footage, and creating animated slide shows or professional-looking video productions.

Like iMovie, Movie Maker is theme-based. A theme is just like a template that was designed by a professional graphic designer or videographer. You pick a theme, drag-and-drop your content into the selected theme (template), add special effects, titles, and a soundtrack, and then export the produced video into a file format that's suitable for whatever destination you plan for the movie, such as uploading it to YouTube.

Some of the basic video editing tools Movie Maker offers includes the ability to easily trim the beginning and end of your videos. One nice feature is that you can easily split longer-length videos into shorter ones for easier editing, and then regroup the video elements before exporting the final production.

Movie Maker is an excellent tool for quickly editing videos, although the software lacks the more advanced features of higher-end consumer-oriented packages like Adobe Premiere Pro or Final Cut Pro, for example. Movie Maker for Windows 8 can be downloaded from Microsoft's website (http://windows.microsoft.com/en-US/windows-live/movie-maker-get-started), and works seamlessly with other Microsoft Windows applications, such as Photo Gallery and Windows Media Player. It also works with Microsoft SkyDrive, which is used for storing and sharing your productions in the cloud (online).

Video Editing Applications Offering (or that Offer) Specialized Functionality

Specialized video editing applications such as Camtasia from TechSmith offer advanced screen recording and editing tools. Camtasia is ideal for recording software or presentations as they're being used on your computer, adding narration, and then editing that content into video tutorials or software demonstration videos. Companies often use software like Camtasia to record PowerPoint slide presentations, software demos, and web pages; edit in live-action video footage or other multimedia content; and record custom voice-overs or an audio track, in order to produce their final video productions.

Screen recording software that allows for editing and exporting into a commonly used video format has many uses to help promote online sales or promotions, showcase product demonstrations, and to adapt in-person training or workshop sessions into videos that can be watched online.

Camtasia Studio is available for Windows-based PCs, while Camtasia for Mac offers similar functionality for Mac-based computers. Both are available for purchase and download from the TechSmith website (www.techsmith.com/camtasia.html).

Camtasia is one of many screen recording and editing applications available. Other popular applications are Adobe's Captivate 6 (www.adobe.com/products/Captivate), CamStudio (free, http://camstudio.org), and Movavi Screen Capture Studio for Business (www.movavi.com/screen-capture). They can export content into a file format that's compatible with YouTube. To find others that may offer a different assortment of tools or features, search for "screen capture software" on your search engine.

IMPORTING FOOTAGE AND OTHER PRODUCTION ELEMENTS INTO YOUR VIDEO EDITING SOFTWARE

Whichever video editing software you opt to use, it's this software that provides you with the tools to edit the raw video, audio, photos, and/or multimedia content that you create and record using other equipment. For example, you'd use your camcorder to record raw video footage and then transfer that video footage from your camera into your computer. It would then be imported into the video editing software to be edited and exported into a file format that's suitable for what you'd be using the video for, such as presenting on your company's YouTube channel.

Some software will automatically facilitate the transfer of your raw footage, audio, and other multimedia content from the recording device to your computer and ultimately into the software. Other video editing software, however, will require you to first transfer the raw footage and other content to your computer manually, store it on your computer's hard drive or external drive, and then import it manually into the software for editing.

START EDITING

Virtually every video you produce will require at least some level of editing and post production, even if you're going for a grass-roots or raw, low-budget look. Plan on spending considerable time editing and re-editing your videos until every second, scene, and every shot all work together to achieve your goals, adhere to your company's image, and cater to your audience.

Editing a video is a technical as well as creative process. But before you start, back up all raw footage and pre-produced elements on an external drive. Then, as you finish editing each scene, save and back up your work. Because you'll be working with extremely large files, it's not uncommon for the computer or software to periodically crash. If that happens, you don't want to lose more than a few minutes' work.

Begin by launching your editing software, and importing your raw video and other multimedia assets. As you do, write detailed notes about what you've recorded and where each component is stored. Catalog how many times a scene was shot or if you used multiple cameras, so that when you're editing the scene, you can review all the footage for the best takes. Refer to your storyboard and shooting script as you assemble each scene and string them together.

Use the worksheet in Figure 11–4 on page 163 to help you more efficiently catalog your project's footage, pre-produced content, and audio components.

Refer to your storyboard and shooting script as you assemble each scene and string them together. Begin to edit the raw video using the software's tools and features. You can trim sections of the video, separate footage into scenes and reorder them, and begin to shape the production. After the raw video has been edited, insert video effects and filters and insert animated transitions. Import other multimedia, such as PowerPoint elements.

Video Title: _____

Scene Name: _____

Scene Number: _____

Content Details	Description/ File Name	Time Code	Storage Location	Production/ Creation Date	Edited Date	Edited Length	Notes
Raw Video (Angle/Shot #1)							
Raw Video (Angle #2)							
Raw Video (Angle #3)							
Music Track							
Music Track							
Sound Effect(s)							
Sound Effect(s)							
Digital Photo(s)							
Pre-Produced Content							
Pre-Produced Content							
Pre-Produced Content							
Other							
Other							

FIGURE 11–4. Worksheet for Cataloging Your Raw Video and Pre-Produced Multimedia Components

Once the main components are assembled, create an opening title sequence and any closing credits, and insert any captions and other text-based elements throughout the video.

Make sure your message and call to action are clearly and cleverly incorporated and that the nearly finished product speaks to your target audience.

12 EDITING STRATEGIES FOR A MORE PROFESSIONAL PRODUCTION

1. Make sure each scene in your video flows nicely into the next, from a visual, audio, and context aspect.

2. Ensure that the overall audio levels are consistent throughout the video.

3. Avoid static images or "talking-head" shots. If you use them, keep them short and switch camera angles or shooting perspectives often.

4. If you forgot the Rule of Thirds when shooting your footage, use the software's cropping and editing tools to reposition your main subject off center in the frame. This is particularly important if you'll be presenting your video in widescreen format on YouTube.

5. As you're editing each scene, incorporate different shots and camera angles, but make sure you use appropriate transitions that allow the video to flow. Most editing programs have dozens or even hundreds of scene transitions that you can drag and drop into a scene to blend two video clips. A jump cut— when one scene abruptly cuts into another—is the one used most often. But alternate with animated transitions so your video isn't too choppy. Two of the most common editing mistakes are overutilizing elaborate transitions, and using the same transition repeatedly in a relatively short video. The goal of a transition is to help one scene flow smoothly into the next, not to distract the viewer.

6. Make text-based titles, credits, and captions short and succinct, so that your viewers can easily read them even on their smartphone's tiny screen. Likewise, keep horizontally and vertically scrolling text moving slowly and steadily.

7. Don't overuse visual effects and filters. While they do make your videos more visually appealing, too many can distract your audience from your core message and call to action.

8. Choose your background music wisely. It can set a mood, keep momentum going, or just be entertaining, but mostly can help convey your message— or detract from it. Think about what genre, volume, tempo, lyrics, and, of course, specific piece of music are most appropriate, and, once you're sure there are no copyright issues, then choose where best to incorporate it.

12 EDITING STRATEGIES FOR A MORE PROFESSIONAL PRODUCTION, CONTINUED

9. Keep production elements simple and straightforward. Your message and call to action are your video's key components, not the visual or audible bells and whistles you can throw in as eye or ear candy.

10. Remove ancillary content. You're much better off with a short, coherent video that succinctly achieves your goals than a long-form masterpiece full of the snazzy production elements that your editing software makes so easy to add.

11. Consider animated slide shows of photos or PowerPoint presentations in addition to live-action footage. You can control how long a slide is displayed, and add animated transitions between slides as well as an audio track. One common technique included in almost all editing software packages is the Ken Burns effect, which makes digital photos appear almost as moving video.

12. Don't be afraid to promote your company's website, Facebook page, Twitter feed, blog, and other online activities. Their URLs can be cited by the video's host, announced in a voice-over, and displayed in the credits and captions. You can also include these links on your YouTube channel page and outside the main video window on YouTube. Within the videos themselves, they can be included within annotations. To learn more about using YouTube Annotations, visit http://support.google.com/youtube/bin/answer.py?hl=en&answer=92710. Keep in mind, however, that a viewer who clicks on the annotation will quit watching your video to follow the link. This may or may not be a goal for your video. For example, you may want someone to click on a link and immediately visit your website to place an order. However, the goal of your video might be for the viewer to watch the entire thing before following a specific call to action.

Once the visual elements have been edited and you've got a rough cut, start mixing in the audio components, like background music, sound effects, and voice-overs. Each audio component should be placed on a separate audio track so you can independently control and adjust each one.

Once you've uploaded your videos to YouTube, you can also incorporate visual effects using the service's online tools. Access your YouTube channel's Video Manager,

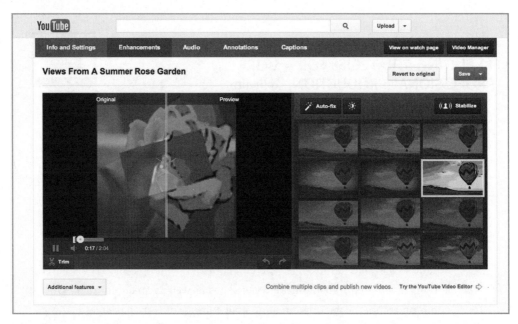

FIGURE 11–5. A Selection of Optional Video Effects Can Be Added to Your Video Once It's Been Uploaded to YouTube Using Online-Based Tools.

select one of your uploaded videos, and then click on the "Enhancements" button displayed near the top of the window (shown in Figure 11–5). One useful effect, on the "Additional Features" menu, is "Blur All Faces," which obscures the identities of people featured in your video whose written consent you haven't obtained—for example, people in a crowd shot.

Uploading Your Videos to YouTube

In Chapters 10 and 11, you learned all about what it takes to shoot and edit a professional-quality video. Once the video is ready to be shared, you'll need to upload it to your YouTube channel, customize the settings, and then present it to the public via your channel.

YouTube offers a handful of methods for uploading one or more videos at a time to your channel. In addition, however, you can also record "live" video using your computer's webcam, and then use YouTube's online editing tools to edit and publish the video. Another option is to use Google+'s "Hangout" feature to present a live online broadcast that can also be recorded and offered on YouTube.

In this chapter, you'll learn how to upload videos using any internet browser. Keep in mind, you can upload HD video files up to 20 GB in size. To watch the sample video used throughout this chapter to demonstrate how to upload videos, visit www.youtube.com/user/JasonRichChannel, and select the "Views From a Summer Rose Garden" video.

PREPARING YOUR VIDEO FILES

YouTube is compatible with a wide range of video file formats, such as: WebM, .MPEG3, 3GPP, .MOV, .AVI, .MPEGPS, .WMV, or .FLV.

After editing your video, either use your editing software's built-in "Share" feature or its "Save As" or "Export" command to convert the file to one of YouTube's compatible file formats. If you attempt to upload a video file to YouTube, but receive an error message that says "Failed (Invalid File Format)," this means you'll need to first convert the video file into a compatible file format before uploading it. This is easily done using your video editing software.

Always upload your videos at the highest resolution possible, and in the video's original quality. If given the option, choose to save the video file using a 16:9 aspect ratio with the highest bitrate possible. Also, do not change the frame rate of the video. If the video was captured at 24 or 30 frames per second, which is standard, keep it at that frame rate when exporting the files from your video editing software and then uploading it to YouTube.

Many video editing software packages, including iMovie for the Mac, have a built-in "Share" option that allows you to upload your edited videos and adjust the settings from your computer directly to your YouTube channel. If your video editing software doesn't have the feature, save the video files on the computer's internal or external hard drive and then follow the steps outlined in the next section of this chapter to upload your video file to your YouTube channel.

Video files captured on your mobile phone or tablet can also be uploaded directly to YouTube via an app that comes bundled with your mobile device or a specialized third-party app. For the iPhone and iPad, the iMovie app, available from the App Store, offers powerful tools for editing, viewing, and sharing video footage, including an option to upload files directly to your YouTube channel.

If you become a YouTube Partner, there is no limit to a video's length, as long as its file size is 20 GB or less. If you're not a YouTube Partner, a video can't be longer than 15 minutes, although you can obtain permission to upload longer videos. To do this, go to the "Upload" page, click on the "Increase Your Limit" option, verify your account, and then follow the on-screen prompts. If you know you'll be uploading videos longer than 15 minutes in length, verify your account right from the start. This enables you to upload longer videos. Visit this link: www.youtube.com/my_videos_upload_verify, and follow the on-screen prompts.

As your video is being processed, YouTube determines if its content violates any copyrights. If it does, the video will be blocked from being posted. And if you suspect that someone has violated your copyrights in their videos, file a complaint

ULTIMATE GUIDE TO YOUTUBE FOR BUSINESS

online with YouTube by visiting http://support.google.com/youtube/bin/answer.py?hl=en&answer=140536.

HOW TO UPLOAD VIDEOS FROM YOUR COMPUTER

When you're ready to upload your first video, follow these steps:

1. Log into YouTube (www.youtube.com) with the Google account information that was used to create your YouTube Channel account.
2. From the main YouTube home page, click on your username or profile photo that's displayed near the upper-right corner of the screen.
3. Click on the "Video Manager" option (shown in Figure 12–1).
4. Click on the "Upload" button that's displayed on the left side of the screen, and choose the "Upload a Video" option (shown in Figure 12–2 on page 170).
5. When the "Upload Video Files" screen appears (shown in Figure 12–3, page 170), click on the "Select Files From Your Computer" option to find and select the video file(s) from your computer. Or, simply open another window on your computer's desktop, locate the video file(s), and then drag and drop the video file(s) anywhere onto the "Upload Video Files" page.
6. The uploading process will then begin, and you'll need to enter the title, description, and tags for your video, plus adjust various settings.

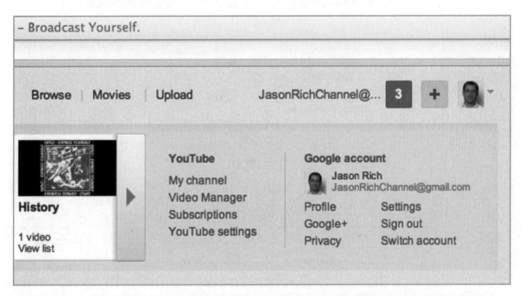

FIGURE 12–1. Click on the "Video Manager" Option to Access the Uploading Options on YouTube.

CHAPTER 12 / UPLOADING YOUR VIDEOS TO YOUTUBE ■ 169

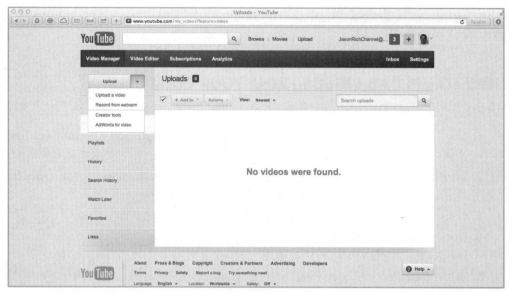

FIGURE 12–2. Click on the "Upload" Button to Access the "Upload Video Files" Screen.

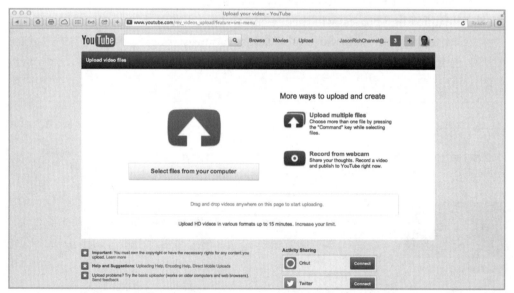

FIGURE 12–3. The "Upload Video Files" Screen Is Used to Upload Your Videos and then Add the Relevant Title, Description, Tags, etc.

7. Near the top left of the "Uploading Video" window (shown in Figure 12–4 on page 171), you'll see the "Basic Info" and "Advanced Settings" tabs. By default,

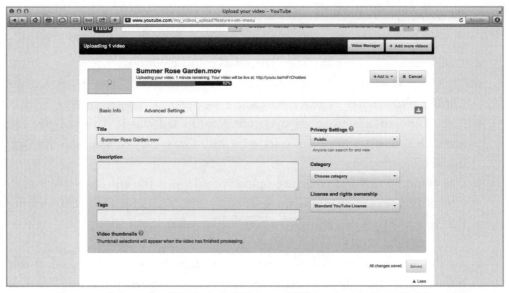

FIGURE 12–4. Select the "Basic Info" Tab and Fill In the Various Fields to Give Your Video a Title, Description, Tags, a Thumbnail Image, and Associate Other Information with the Video File.

the "Basic Info" tab is selected. Begin filling in each field with the appropriate information. See the next section, "Providing Details About Your Video" (page 172), for more information about what to enter into each field.

8. After the video has uploaded, it must then be "processed." Depending on its quality and length, as well as YouTube's upload traffic at the time, this will take anywhere from a few minutes to several hours. Once the processing is done, a message under the video's title will be displayed that says, "Upload complete! Your video will be live at:" and a custom URL for the video will be displayed.

9. Once you have customized the options displayed within the "Basic Info" and "Advanced Settings" windows, click on the "Video Manager" button that's displayed near the upper-right corner of the screen. Your video is now online and viewable.

10. From the "Uploads" screen that appears, you can view basic stats about your video on the right side of the screen, or click on the "Edit" button to further customize your settings. You'll have the opportunity to add annotations and/or captions to your video, change the audio (background music), and/or add visual enhancements to it.

Overcoming Uploading Problems

Here's what to do if you experience a recurring problem using the YouTube uploader:

- Make sure you're using the latest version of your web browser.
- Try using another web browser: Internet Explorer (PC), Safari (Mac), Google Chrome (PC/Mac), or Firefox (PC/Mac).
- Point your web browser to www.youtube.com/upload_classic. This will give you access to YouTube's Basic Uploader, which is more widely compatible with various web browsers.
- One common cause of recurring upload problems is the anti-spyware or anti-virus software that's running on your computer. Try temporarily deactivating that software, but don't forget to reactivate it after the video uploads to You-Tube.
- Another common cause of video upload problems is a poor wifi signal. If this is the case, try moving your computer closer to the wireless router so the signal improves, or connect your computer directly to the router using an Ethernet cable. If you're using a 3G or 4G cellular network to access the internet, move to where the signal is stronger and retry the upload.

Once a video file is uploaded, it will take time to process. As a general rule, videos shot in high definition (720p or 1080p) resolution will take longer to process than a standard-quality 480p resolution video. When uploading a large HD video file to YouTube, if processing takes longer than eight hours or so, a problem could have arisen. Access the My Videos section of your YouTube account and see if the video is listed. If so, remove the video and try the upload process again.

PROVIDING DETAILS ABOUT YOUR VIDEO

As your video is uploading, you'll have the opportunity to create and enter your video's title, description, tags, privacy settings, category, and license and rights ownership information when you click on the "Basic Info" tab that's displayed on the "Upload Video" screen (see Figure 12–5 on page 173).

Within the "Title" field, enter the title of your video. As you create the title, remember your goal is to entice a potential viewer to watch it, so choose something that's catchy, descriptive, and to the point. The video's title will be displayed on YouTube, along with your description and other information, and is separate from whatever titles you incorporated in the video itself when shooting or editing it. The title you create (in conjunction with the description and tags) is also used for search engine optimization purposes, by YouTube's search feature and Google, to determine how and where your video will be listed. Thus, be sure your title is short, highly descriptive, accurate, and highly targeted by incorporating tags or keywords into it as applicable.

In the "Description" field, enter a few sentences that describe your video and why someone would want to watch it. This is your video's marketing tool, so use as many Tags in the text as possible to increase the probability that someone will find your video when performing a keyword search.

The "Tags" field is used to compile a list of keywords or phrases that best describe your video; separate each with a comma and include as many relevant keywords or phrases as you can think of to improve its discoverability in a keyword search. There are a variety of online tools available to help you compile an appropriate and highly targeted list of applicable keywords or tags. For example, you can use the free YouTube Keyword Tool (https://ads.youtube.com/keyword_tool).

After your video has processed, YouTube will automatically select and pull three thumbnail images from your video. Below the "Tags" field, click on the video thumbnail you want to accompany your video's title and description. Choose the thumbnail that you believe will capture the most attention and that visually communicates the most about the content of your video.

Over on the right side of the video upload window, under the "Privacy Settings" option, choose from "Public," "Unlisted," and "Private." By selecting the "Public" option (shown in Figure 12–5), anyone who visits your YouTube Channel page will see a listing

FIGURE 12–5. Select a Privacy Setting for Your Video, Based on Who You Want to Be Able to See It.

for your video and be able to watch it. It can also be viewed via its unique URL and if it's embedded in another website or blog. Your video will also be listed within keyword search results.

By selecting the "Unlisted" option, the video will be viewable only to those who have its unique URL; it won't be listed on your public YouTube channel page, nor will it show up in search results. (As the channel operator, however, you will be able to access your own Unlisted videos.)

If you select the "Private" option under the privacy settings, only people you specifically invite to watch your video will be granted access to it. It will neither be displayed on your public YouTube channel page nor show up within search result listings.

Also displayed on the right side of the "Upload a video" screen is the "Category" pull-down menu. When you click on it, 15 YouTube video categories will be displayed (shown in Figure 12-6).

YouTube video categories include:

- Autos & Vehicles
- Comedy
- Education
- Entertainment
- Film & Animation

FIGURE 12–6. Every Video You Upload Needs To Be Placed Into a YouTube Category.

- Gaming
- How To & Style
- Music
- News & Politics
- Nonprofits & Activism
- People & Blogs
- Pets & Animals
- Science & Technology
- Sports
- Travel & Events

Choose a category that your video best fits into and click on it. You might not always be able to choose a category that matches perfectly, so choose the most relevant option. Your selection will now be displayed in the "Categories" field. If your YouTube channel has multiple videos, each video can be placed into a separate category.

Finally, click on the "License and Rights Ownership" pull-down menu if you want to change the default setting, which is "Standard YouTube License." The alternative is to choose the "Creative Commons—Attribution" option. Here's what each means:

- *Standard YouTube License.* Within YouTube's "Terms of Use" document, which can be found online (www.youtube.com/t/terms), you'll find information pertaining to publishing videos on the service. It explains what content can and can not be used in a video.
- *Creative Commons—Attribution.* If you activate this feature, you give other people the right to take clips from your video and incorporate them in their own videos without violating any copyrights. You can only choose this option if you own the rights to 100 percent of your video's content, including the rights to the visuals, sound effects, content, and music.

As you update the information on the "Upload a video" page, YouTube will auto-save your information. Near the lower-right corner of the screen, the "Saved" button should be inactive, and next to it will be a message that says "All Changes Saved." If you don't see that message before leaving this page, manually click on the Save Changes button.

ADJUSTING THE ADVANCED SETTINGS FOR YOUR VIDEO

From the video upload page, you can further customize the settings for each of your videos via the Advanced Settings option. The more detailed the information in the basic and advanced settings, the more likely people will find and view your video.

Once you've filled in all of the fields on the "Basic Info" screen, click on the "Advanced Settings" tab (refer to Figure 12–7). Some of these options are listed under the "Comments and Responses" heading. Each has a checkbox to activate or deactivate it. These options include:

- *Allow Comments.* Check this box to allow viewers to post comments about the video and, from the pull-down menu that's displayed to the right of this option, choose "All" or "Approved." By selecting "All," all comments that are submitted will be displayed with the video. If you select the "Approved" option, you can read and approve each comment before it's published.

- *Allow Users to Vote On Comments.* When you activate this option, your viewers will be allowed to read each other's comments and then "vote" on them by clicking on the "Thumbs Up" or "Thumbs Down" icon. They'll also be able to post a reply to someone else's comment.

- *Allow Users to View a Video's Ratings.* While anyone who watches a video can rate it, you can choose whether others will be able to view those ratings. If you want people to do so, check the box associated with this option.

- *Allow Video Responses.* When you activate this option, any of your viewers will be able to create and publish a video-based "response" to your video. Their response will be linked to your original video, so when someone views your video, they'll also be able to view the "responses" from other people. Using the pull-down menu

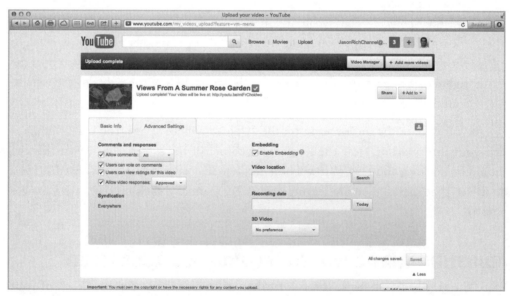

FIGURE 12–7. The "Advanced Settings" Tab Allows You to Further Customize the YouTube Settings Associated with a Specific Video.

that's associated with this option, you can allow "All" responses to be viewable, or you can choose the "Approved" option and first preview and select which responses will be viewable by the public.

■ *Enable Embedding.* By adding a checkmark to this option, you allow others to embed your video within their website, blog, Facebook page, etc., so your video can be viewed without accessing your YouTube channel page. You'll also be able to embed your own video into your own website or blog. If you remove the check-mark from this option, users will need to access the video directly from YouTube in order to view it.

■ *Video Location.* Use this field to manually enter where your video was shot. You can be as specific here as you'd like: You can enter an exact address or simply cite a country, city, or state. A Google Map of the location will be created and displayed with the video, and people will be able to find your video using a geographic search.

■ *Recording Date.* The date your video was recorded. This is useful if the date is relevant to the content, or if you want people to be able to search for your video based on the date.

■ *3D Video.* From the pull-down menu, you have a variety of options related to whether or not 3D effects have been incorporated into the video as you were shooting, or if you want YouTube to add 3D effects and compatibility after the fact.

MAKING FURTHER ADJUSTMENTS TO YOUR VIDEO FROM THE VIDEO MANAGER PAGE

As the operator of your YouTube channel, at any time you can click on the Video Manager, select "Uploads" from the left side of the screen, and adjust each video's customizations and settings (shown in Figure 12–8 on page 178).

Any time after a video is uploaded and made public, you can alter any of the YouTube-related options (such as its title, description, tags, or category), add or modify links or annotations, or re-edit the video and then publish a new version of it. In fact, if you track the YouTube Analytics information relating to a video and discover that at a specific point, say 24 seconds into the video, many people are clicking out of it, you can re-edit the video to help keep a viewer's attention beyond the 24-second mark. Or, you may discover that by tweaking the title or tags list, you'll attract more viewers.

This screen displays a listing of each video on your channel, including how many views, likes (thumbs-up icon), dislikes (thumbs-down), and comments it has received.

To adjust the settings, click on the "Edit" button for the following options:

FIGURE 12–8. At Any Time, Access YouTube's Video Manager to Edit or Change the Settings Related to a Specific Video.

- *Info and Settings.* Edit the video's basic info or advanced settings, including title, descriptions, tags, privacy settings, and category.
- *Enhancements.* You can insert a wide range of video special effects into already uploaded videos using YouTube's online tools (shown in Figure 12-9 on page 179). After adding enhancements, click on the "Save" button to publish your changes. From the "Enhancements" screen, you can also access more video editing tools, including the "Blur All Faces" feature, by clicking on the "Additional Features" button.
- *Audio.* Use this option to alter the background music used in your video. There are more than 150,000 music tracks available on YouTube that can be used without violating copyrights. By searching the web for "background music," you can also find music and sound effects that are either free or available for a flat licensing fee.
- *Annotations.* These YouTube tools allow you to add text into specific sections of your video after it's uploaded. You can also incorporate "hotspots" and active links within the video itself, so if someone clicks on a specific area of the screen while watching your video, they'll be able to access another video, website, blog, online store, or a Facebook page. For more information about how you can utilize annotations into your videos, visit http://support.google.com/youtube/bin/answer.py?hl=en&answer=92710.

FIGURE 12–9. Using YouTube's Online Video Enhancement Tools, You Can Add Special Effects to Your Videos After They've Been Uploaded and Before They're Made Public.

- *Captions.* You have the option to incorporate subtitles into your video. For directions on how to do this, visit http://support.google.com/youtube/bin/answer. py?hl=en&answer=100079.
- *Download MP4.* Download the video file (in MP4 format) to whatever computer you're using to access YouTube.
- *Promote.* Set up a Google AdWords campaign (or an AdWords for Video campaign) to help promote your video on YouTube, Google, and its online partners. Though there is a fee, it's a very fast and cost-effective way to drive traffic to your YouTube channel or to a specific video.

ADD INTERACTIVE ELEMENTS USING ANNOTATIONS

The Annotations Editor available from YouTube becomes available once you have uploaded a video; you don't need to edit or re-load the video to add these features. These tools allow you to overlay text within the video window as your videos are playing. Plus, you can add hotspots and active links within your video: for example, "Click here for more information..." with a link to a website or another video.

Using annotations allows you to make videos more engaging and interactive. But use annotations correctly and sparingly, or you could wind up confusing or distracting your viewers.

Consider using annotations if they will enrich the video's content without distracting the viewer. The hotspots and links should always be directly relevant, and displayed only as long as it takes someone to use them. Don't allow the text to block important content within the video itself. YouTube recommends placing annotations around the border of the video, not near the center of the video window, and never using more than two annotations at a time.

Many producers use annotations at the end of their videos to point viewers to other relevant videos on their channel, or point them to their website or Facebook page. Annotations can also be used to break up a long video into shorter videos that can then be presented as a series that can be watched in any particular order.

In addition to hotspots and active links, an annotation can be a text bubble in the video, or a text-based title. You control when and where the annotation appears in your video, as well as its color, font, size, background color, and dimensions.

When you access the Annotations Editor, your video will be displayed in a window with a timeline displayed beneath it. Use the timeline to select the exact moment(s) when you want text, hotspots, or active links to appear and disappear as overlays on your video. You can create and customize annotations via the "Annotations Properties" panel on the right side of the window.

To add a new annotation, click on the "Add Annotation" button and choose between one of the five types: speech bubbles, spotlights, notes, pauses, titles, and labels.

A speech bubble is a pop-up text window. You determine what it looks like, when it appears and disappears. A spotlight allows you to make text appear only when someone waves their mouse cursor over that area of the video's window. A note is a pop-up text window that you can make appear and then disappear at will. The "Pause" option allows you to pause the video automatically at a specific point as someone is watching it. The "Title" option allows you to overlay a text-based title.

The "Label" option allows you to create a text callout that you can use to focus the viewer's attention on something. It can be an arrow, another symbol, or alphanumeric text.

YOUR VIDEO'S WORLDWIDE PREMIERE

As soon as you've uploaded your video and have made it public, it will be displayed on your YouTube channel page and available for anyone to view. Figure 12–10 on page 181 shows what the video looks like playing on YouTube. Notice that below the video, you can access the "Thumbs Up," "Thumbs Down," "Add To," "Share," and "Flag" buttons as a viewer. If you scroll down, you may also have the ability to post a comment about the video, based on how you've adjusted the video's settings.

FIGURE 12–10. Here's What a Newly Uploaded Video Looks Like to an Average User on YouTube.

To tell the public about your new video, click on the "Share" button that's displayed below the video, and then click on the Facebook, Twitter, or Google+ logo, one at a time. A pop-up window will appear, allowing you to compose a message to your online friends and followers to announce the video. The message will have a link directly to your video embedded within it.

Figure 12–11 on page 182 shows the message composition window that's created when you click on the Facebook icon; Figure 12–12, page 182, shows the tweet-composition window that appears when you click on the Twitter icon. Notice that a link to your video is already embedded into the message.

Sharing details about your video via Facebook and Twitter, or through the use of Google AdWords, are just three options for promoting your videos and building an audience. The focus of Chapter 6, "Promoting Your YouTube Videos," explores these and others in much greater detail.

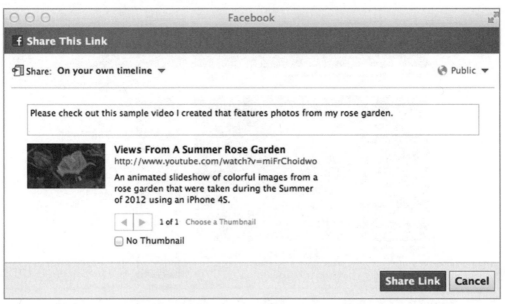

FIGURE 12–11. Click on the "Share via Facebook" Icon within a Video's Listing to Share Information About It on Your Facebook Account.

FIGURE 12–12. Click on the "Share via Twitter" Icon within a Video's Listing to Compose and Send a Tweet About It to Your Followers.

PART III

Expert Advice

These final three chapters feature advice and insights from a diverse group of successful YouTube veterans and experts—from a stand-up comedian to an attorney specializing in copyright issues, and from a software developer to the director of a film about the underground culture of YouTubers.

Learn from Business Owners and Entrepreneurs

Small-business owners and entrepreneurs are often on a tight budget and have limited time and resources, yet want to reach a broader audience to boost awareness of their company, products, or services, or to connect more deeply with existing customers. In this final section of the book, you'll read exclusive interviews with a handful of YouTubers who discuss planning, filming, editing, publishing, and promoting videos. All of them know firsthand how challenging it is to create YouTube videos that attract a significant audience, and most have become experts at overcoming the obstacles involved.

MEET STAND-UP COMEDIAN/ACTOR DAN NAINAN

Even if you're not a stand-up comedian, and never plan to become one, you can still learn a lot about utilizing YouTube for your own business from someone who has already achieved success—in this case, Dan Nainan.

Nainan stumbled on stand-up comedy and acting later in life, after working in a senior engineer position at Intel for several years. While at Intel, some of his job responsibilities involved participating in press conferences and product demonstrations all over the world with the company's top-level executives. Early on, Nainan suffered from stage fright, so he took stand-up comedy classes to help overcome his fear of being in front of crowds. He ultimately discovered a hidden talent.

Eventually, Nainan decided to leave Intel and pursue stand-up comedy and acting full time. Today, he travels around the world performing for the public and at corporate events. A listing of his recent appearances can be found at www.danielnainan.com/index. php/shows.

Nainan has performed for U.S. presidents, numerous government leaders and dignitaries, and for hundreds of sold-out crowds. He credits much of his success to YouTube. By posting clips of his performances online, Nainan uses YouTube, as well as Facebook and Twitter, to stay in contact with his global fan base. Some of his YouTube videos have received millions of views each, and he has more than 250,000 followers on Twitter.

Those YouTube videos have resulted in bookings worldwide. While at Intel, Nainan discovered the power of online social media as it was first evolving. It's how he's used these tools more recently that has allowed him to achieve success in his second career.

Rich: *What made you walk away from a successful career at Intel to pursue a much riskier career as a stand-up comedian and actor?*

Nainan: "To become more comfortable in my job at Intel, I took a comedy class to get over my fear of being on stage. I was always told that I was funny. I took the comedy class and, in a nutshell, I wound up performing comedy for 2,500 people at an Intel sales conference, and it was amazing. I ultimately got promoted to a boring job at Intel, so I decided to quit and become a full-time comedian. Since then, I have performed all over the world, in something like 25 different countries. I currently fly more than 200,000 miles per year. These days, I make my living performing clean stand-up comedy, as well as doing occasional acting and voice-over jobs. Looking back, I can easily credit YouTube for much of my success in terms of building my fan base and landing show bookings."

At what point did you discover that YouTube could become a valuable tool to help launch and expand your comedy career?

"I originally started uploading and sharing videos using the now defunct Google Video service. The problem was that back then, you needed to be an engineer to figure out how to upload videos to it. When YouTube came along, it was so much easier to use. I was a very early adopter of YouTube. One of my first videos, which has since received well over 1 million views, was first uploaded in 2005. I saw the potential for this service and have been using it as a promotional tool ever since.

"When I uploaded my first video to YouTube, it was 25 minutes long. Today, it's highly recommended that you keep videos under five minutes in length. People who use YouTube rarely want to watch something that is longer than one or two minutes, because they have very short attention spans. They're much more apt to click on a shorter video to view it."

How do you use YouTube on an ongoing basis?

"In addition to uploading clips from my performances around the world, I also constantly post short videos showing where I am and what I am doing, especially if I am in an interesting place. For example, I have posted travel video logs of myself skiing in Dubai. I also have posted clips of famous people, including President Obama, Mayor Bloomberg, and Steve Wozniak, endorsing my comedy.

"If you post a video that's good and that people like, it is much more apt to go viral, which is what happened to one of my very first videos that I posted on YouTube. It included clips of a performance. Since then, whenever I publish a new video on YouTube, I focus on creating a really good title for it, and then associate appropriate keywords with it. For example, I work very extensively with an extremely famous comedian, so when I post new videos of my work which somehow relates to this comedian, I always put his name as one of my video's keywords or tags. That way, when someone using YouTube enters his name into the search field, they stumble upon my videos as well and ultimately discover who I am as a comedian."

What has been the biggest perk or benefit to using YouTube?

"By far, it's been the bookings I've received for shows all over the world as a direct result of people seeing my videos. When someone contacts me about a booking for a show, one of the first questions I ask is, 'How did you hear about me?' and the response I get the most is, 'From a YouTube video.' This has been true for almost every international gig I have done. I've been lucky enough to do shows all over the world because people have seen me perform on YouTube."

Have you discovered any useful tips for making your videos more popular on YouTube?

"Yes. One thing I noticed with many popular videos, including the original Psy *Gangnam Style* video—which has become the most viewed video ever on YouTube—is that the publishers of those videos allow for video responses, and do not stop other people on YouTube from posting parodies or other videos related to theirs. People find the parody videos, for example, and then want to view the original, which helps that original video go viral.

"I have heard other stand-up comedians complain that audience members record clips of their performances and post them on YouTube without permission, and then that comedian constantly needs to write new material. I believe that if that happens to me, it means I am achieving success as a comedian and it helps my overall popularity. I try to discourage people from filming my entire performances, because I don't want all of my material online, but I do allow people to post short clips of my performances, because in essence, these people are helping to promote and market me for free. As a stand-up comedian, it's part of my job to continuously write new material. It keeps me from becoming complacent."

Do you encourage your fans to post comments on YouTube?

"Definitely. However, I do review all comments first before they're posted on my YouTube Channel page for everyone to see. I think the comments can be a powerful tool for a YouTube video producer. If many people comment on one thing, even if it's critical, those people may have a point. It's good to take that information to heart. Sometimes, it is very hard for people to take criticism, especially if it's mean-spirited. If someone posts a comment that is very harsh, I have learned not to respond directly to those. Responding often just leads to more and more anger."

Do you use YouTube Analytics to track information about who is watching your videos?

"I look at that information once in a while, but I don't really have time. I use YouTube to communicate with and expand my global fan base. As long as I see more and more people watching my videos, and I keep getting booked for new gigs as a result of people watching my videos, I know I am doing something right. For me, the information YouTube Analytics offers isn't critical to how I am using the service. I invest my time creating and uploading new YouTube videos regularly, and I am also active on Facebook and Twitter. I try to use my time as efficiently as possible when it comes to managing what I do online."

How do you use Facebook and Twitter to cross-promote your YouTube videos?

"Using Facebook and Twitter, for example is absolutely essential. When I post a tweet about a new video, it generates a ton of new views within a short time. There is so much more I could be doing when it comes to managing my online social media activities, I just don't have time to do it all. I do use my Facebook and Twitter accounts to promote my YouTube channel and latest videos, and then have links within my YouTube videos and on my YouTube channel page to get people to like my Facebook page and/or follow me on Twitter. Everything I do online has become synergistic and is treated accordingly."

What type of equipment do you typically use to shoot and edit your videos?

"I have spoken with the vice president of talent at Comedy Central, and she receives hundreds of videos from stand-up comics that are shot in HD-quality video, but the audio quality is so bad, it's almost impossible to make out what the comedian is saying. All too often, people rely on the microphone that's built into their camera. When you try to film a stand-up comedy routine and have the camera set up in the back of the room, the microphone that's built into the camera picks up everything, not just what's being said on stage.

"What I learned from that conversation is that I needed to edit and produce videos for people who have never seen me and who don't know my act. Part of that means having crystal-clear audio within the videos, in addition to a high-resolution picture. Now, when I record performances, I will set up a camera in the back of the venue, for example, but I will connect an external microphone directly to the sound board in the venue to pick up my on stage microphone's audio directly. This allows me to record crystal-clear audio of myself. I sometimes set up a second camera and have it record video from another angle, plus record the ambient sounds from the audience. I can then edit all of this together. When I do this, it provides viewers of my videos with an honest representation of what happened during my show at that venue. Viewers can see and hear me clearly, but also hear the roar of the crowd and their other reactions.

"These days, I think people expect videos to be shot with multiple cameras and switch between several different camera angles, for example. Expectations are very high. However, with that being said, I still use an inexpensive Flip camera and my iPhone to shoot many videos that go on my YouTube channel. These cameras offer HD-quality video. If you're using a lower-end camera, you just have to be conscious about the sound quality.

"If you want your videos to become popular on YouTube, having really good production values is essential. One additional lesson I have learned is that certain types of clothing do not translate well on video. Now, I try to wear solid colored clothes when I am shooting myself in videos for YouTube.

"I have a technical background, so I edit all of my videos on my laptop computer using Adobe Premiere Pro CS6. I highly recommend this video editing software, although for some people, they can easily get away with using the less expensive Adobe

Premiere Elements software, which costs less than $100. With the high-end video editing software, I wind up using only about 20 percent of what the software is capable of when it comes to editing my own YouTube videos. Adobe Premiere Pro CS6 is great for editing multi-cam productions."

What other advice do you have for small-business operators or entrepreneurs who want to begin creating and publishing videos to share on YouTube?

"I think you should not worry too much about how much you spend initially on a camera, as long as the inexpensive camera can shoot in HD-quality. I do think, however, that you need to have good lighting and crystal-clear sound in conjunction with all of your video productions. Although, if something is truly funny, valuable, or entertaining, it does not require a tremendous amount of production. It just needs to be content people want to see and in a quality that's good enough for them to understand and appreciate. When it comes to publishing your videos online, choose the correct category for your video and then use keywords to your advantage. Also, try to associate each of your videos with other videos or online personalities that are already well known on YouTube so you can piggyback off of their audience or fan base.

"Another useful tip is to make sure that all of your videos, and your YouTube channel page, as well as your Facebook page and Twitter feed, make it very easy for people to contact you. Within all of my videos, on my webpage, and in conjunction with everything I do on the online social networking sites, I always blatantly post a message that says something like, 'For booking info please call 212-414-2129 or email comediandan@gmail.com.'

"I have seen people who use YouTube in hopes of finding new customers or clients, for example, but their videos and YouTube channel page don't offer an easy way to make contact. People who watch your videos are lazy. Make it as easy as possible for people who watch your videos to reach you by phone and/or email. Do not create barriers for people to find you and make direct contact with you."

MEET TEA SILVESTRE, EXECUTIVE PRODUCER AND HOST OF *PROSPERITY'S KITCHEN*

After seeing the incredible popularity of YouTube and what was possible with Google+'s Hangouts, Tea Silvestre developed a unique concept for a live, online training program based on a reality show-style competition. The program is called *Prosperity's Kitchen* (http://prosperityskitchen.com), and it's an innovative way for small-business owners and entrepreneurs to learn about marketing through hands-on activities and challenges that are taught and judged by a panel of experts.

To make her online training concept unique, she combined a live web-based broadcast with an online competition that it ultimately recorded, edited, and then offered on YouTube on demand and for free. In its first season in early 2013, 15 contestants competed for a $10,000 price package and the opportunity to be mentored by a team of marketing experts.

Everything that happens before and during the competition is streamed live over the internet via Google+ Hangout (www.google.com/+/learnmore/hangouts); soon thereafter, the video is offered on YouTube. Companies that want to utilize Google+ Hangouts with YouTube for online training, or to host conferences, meetings, or panel discussions via the web, can learn from Silvestre's experience.

Rich: *What is your background, and how did you come up with the idea for Prosperity's Kitchen?*

Silvestre: "I have more than 20 years' worth of marketing experience. As a marketing coach and consultant, I have discovered that companies have more money to spend on training than they do to hire someone to do a task for them. Most of my work is done by teaching classes and doing group coaching. When I compared teaching classes in person to teaching classes online, I quickly discovered that there was a big difference in terms of people's attention spans and retention.

"If someone is supposed to be attending a class or seminar online, they can often be found simultaneously checking their Facebook page or emails, or surfing the web. What happens online is that people tend to drop out and lose interest a lot faster than they would attending a similar class in person, where the teacher is looking them in the eye.

"In my search for a way to fix this problem, I began doing a series of classes called *The Test Kitchen* back in 2010. During this period, I closely monitored what worked and didn't work. I also learned about gamification. When a traditional class is transformed into an interactive game, there's more accountability and follow-through on the part of the participants. There's also the element of people putting themselves out there, in a public way, to win something. This makes the participants much more dedicated and attentive.

"I combined what I learned about teaching online with what works in transforming educational content into a game, and came up with the idea for *Prosperity's Kitchen*. It's a reality-web series that's 13 weeks long, but it's also a class. We have 15 people participating as contestants, while an unlimited number of people can watch how things unfold online, learning at the same time. Everyone winds up learning about marketing."

How are you combining Google+ Hangouts with YouTube?

"Google+ Hangouts is a way for people to meet up in one online forum and broadcast their interactions live over the internet. It's a form of video conferencing for groups, sort of like GoToMeeting, but it offers seamless integration with YouTube as well. We looked into using other video conferencing and live-streaming services, but all offered limitations. We opted to go with Google+ Hangouts because it allows us to stream content live over the internet. Each episode of *Prosperity's Kitchen* is presented live over the internet via Google+ Hangouts, but then made available on-demand via YouTube. This makes the programming much more accessible to the world, because when all is said and done, we're producing a YouTube video.

"I have been playing around with YouTube for years, by producing tutorial and promotional videos, but *Prosperity's Kitchen* is the first time I am producing and hosting an entire web series. On the show, we've taken our 15 contestants and divided them into five teams. Throughout the 13-week season, the teams need to hold team meetings on Google+ Hangouts to develop their strategies. If someone wants to, they can watch the main episodes of the series at any time on YouTube, but can also watch the behind-the-scenes strategy meetings, which offers additional educational content that's packaged in a fun way. We're offering a lot of different learning opportunities."

Are you doing your own production and editing for the live web broadcasts and videos?

"All of the contestants are using their own computers with their own webcams and microphones to link from their respective homes or offices to the Google+ Hangout for each episode and training session. After we present each live show, I take the content and edit it into more easily watchable YouTube videos.

"As part of the editing process, I add opening and closing credits, take out dead air, or edit out mistakes that detract from the show's process. However, I take great efforts to keep the videos looking as real and raw as possible. At any one time, up to 10 contestants, hosts, and special guest mentors can participate in a Google+ Hangout. However, that saved web broadcast can then been seen on YouTube by an unlimited number of people.

"To do the video editing, I use a PC that's running the Camtasia software." [See Chapter 11, "Editing Your YouTube Videos."]

What challenges have you encountered producing live web programming via Google+ Hangouts and then presenting it on YouTube for the masses?

"So far, the challenges have been few. However, I am trying to do something that is rather unique. One of the limitations is that YouTube does not have a tech support phone number to call to get questions answered as technical challenges arise. Thankfully, I have been working with a Google+ Hangouts expert who has been very helpful navigating through the ins and outs of how to make my programming idea work technologically. My biggest challenge has been making sure all of the participants and contestants are on the same page technologically, since not everyone is savvy yet when it comes to video conferencing on the web."

Does creating your content live on the internet make the overall process easier or harder?

"There's a lot more pre-production that goes into creating a live web program, because there are people watching the show live, and we can't go back and re-shoot something or add in special effects on the fly. However, once it's done, transforming it into a YouTube video is a straightforward process."

What have you been doing to build an online audience for Prosperity's Kitchen?

"I started generating online hype about the program about five months before we actually started the 13-week season. I created a Facebook page and dedicated email list to build and cater to the show's audience. Once the first episodes began airing, the popularity of the show and our YouTube channel grew very quickly.

"It's important to understand that when it comes to putting together a comprehensive marketing plan, there are a lot of separate pieces involved. To help cover the costs of this project, I sought out a presenting sponsor. We also generated income from people who signed up for the 'play at home' membership, which offers a more interactive experience than just watching the live web broadcasts or YouTube videos.

"To help with the marketing, I put together a 10-person advisory panel, comprised of high-profile people. I also brought in 10 high-profile guest mentors, as well as the 15 contestants. Each of these people is using their own Facebook page, website, and Twitter account, for example, to promote each new episode of the series and each new video that goes onto YouTube. We also have recruited a team of volunteers who are using online social media to help spread the word about *Prosperity's Kitchen*. So, when you combine the fan bases of these people, and their online followers and friends, we're reaching over 1 million people with our promotional mentions for the project."

Once the videos are published on YouTube, what are you doing to make the viewing experience more interactive?

"People are encouraged to post comments on the YouTube channel page, and we monitor those comments. What we're doing here is ultimately an online teaching tool, so we're reviewing all of the questions that are posed by viewers very carefully, and using those questions as we develop new online content. For promotional reasons, we're also encouraging viewers to like and share the YouTube videos."

What happens next?

"We're already planning for future seasons. For season two, for example, instead of inviting small-business owners to participate as contestants, we are going to focus on having marketing experts as our contestants.

"I think more and more businesses are going to start using Google+ Hangouts to host live internet broadcasts and then publish those recorded shows on YouTube to give viewers on-demand access to the content. There are plenty of other services that allow companies to produce live broadcasts and then save them to be shown later, but Google+ Hangouts in conjunction with YouTube is free, has the fewest limitations, and ultimately makes the content accessible to the widest audience.

"Once videos are published on YouTube, if they're uploaded and published correctly, they become very easy to find online, in part, because the videos get listed automatically within the Google search engine. What I am doing is certainly something any business can do as a way to open up their closed online training events and make them more readily available to the public. This concept can also work for companies who have been hosting online-based panel discussions, conferences, and webinars, for example."

If a businessperson wants to explore what's possible with Google+ Hangouts in conjunction with YouTube, what should they do first?

"The first step would be to attend some live Google+ Hangouts events or meetings, and then try hosting some on a smaller scale yourself. Beyond that, building an audience for your online programming or videos all comes down to basic marketing—how you're going to get the word out and knowing who is out there who can help you. You need to define your message, and then use the resources available to you to communicate that message to as many people as possible."

MEET ADAM SCHLEICHKORN, ONE OF THE ORIGINAL YOUTUBERS

When YouTube first started becoming popular, a small group of people started creating videos, hosting their own YouTube channels, positioning themselves to be online personalities, and building what became massive audiences. These people became known as YouTubers, and over time, their numbers grew dramatically. Adam Schleichkorn was one of YouTube's very first popular YouTubers. He was inspired by the MTV series *Jackass*.

Back in 2007, Adam Schleichkorn was the first YouTuber to gain national media attention for a video he created called *Fence Plowing*. As a result of this video, which can still be found on YouTube, he has appeared on *20/20, FOXNews, ABC News, The New York Times*, and other major media outlets, which ultimately resulted in an incredible number of video views and subscribers to his YouTube channel.

Schleichkorn's YouTube channels have attracted more than 20,000 subscribers and 47 million video views. At the height of his online popularity, he was receiving more than

50,000 video views per day. For a while, being a YouTuber was his full-time, well-paying job. A recent YouTube channel focuses on Mylo the Cat. The videos feature a real cat whose comic voice and edgy personality are provided by Schleichkorn.

Now in his early 30s, the Long Island, New York, native still produces the occasional video for one of his YouTube channels, and Mylo the Cat continues to entertain audiences worldwide. Schleichkorn also consults small businesses on how to gain popularity on YouTube. He has a unique perspective about how YouTube really works, because he's been part of it since the very beginning and has seen it evolve firsthand.

Rich: *Why did you first get started making videos for YouTube?*

Schleichkorn: "I was making and sharing videos for years before YouTube ever existed. Basically, I discovered YouTube when I was a grad school student and wound up posting a bunch of stuff up there. I always knew that YouTube would change the way people viewed programming and media.

"One of my videos became a major news story that was picked up across the country, and I very quickly gained tremendous popularity on the up-and-coming YouTube service. It was then that I discovered just how powerful YouTube could be as a way to reach a massive audience. Originally, I was simply making videos for myself that I wanted to share with my real-life friends. For a career, I always knew I wanted to do something relating to video production, because video editing was an interest of mine. All of my early videos, which ultimately were posted on YouTube, were made to be seen by my friends. I never planned for millions of people to see them."

Where did the ideas for your early videos come from?

"Ideas for my videos came from everywhere and everyone around me. I did so many different videos over the years, and each was inspired by something different in my life."

What skills does a businessperson need to utilize YouTube for their own purposes?

"First and foremost, the content of the video is the most important. A lot of people say that the production quality of the video is the most important, but I don't believe that's the case. I always focused on great content, as opposed to amping up the production quality of my videos."

Have you discovered a formula for success to create a video that will generate an audience?

"For a while, being a YouTuber was my full-time career. The only reason I was able to achieve this level of success on YouTube was because I remained an individual. I never hired actors or tried to be someone that I wasn't. I was honest and open with my audience, and I developed an online entity that my audience really related to. A business operator who is looking to build an online following should also focus on setting themselves apart and showcasing what they represent as a company in an open and honest way."

What are some of the biggest challenges you had to overcome on YouTube in order to build your audience?

"Especially in the early days of YouTube, one of the biggest challenges was dealing with all of the 'hater comments.' As a video producer, you're putting your heart and soul into your videos, yet there are a lot of people who watch YouTube videos that enjoy berating them, often without cause.

"For me, reading those mean comments was difficult, but I learned to focus on the positive comments and the fact that my videos were being watched and enjoyed by people all over the world. Don't focus on any negative comments you receive for your videos. There are always going to be people who are harsh critics who post comments on YouTube. Some of them have very valid points, while many others do not. They just hate for the sake of hating. I recommend that you simply ignore those comments and those people.

"As a YouTuber, I was able to get away with calling out those haters, and my fans loved me for it. However, for business operators, you do not want to alienate anyone on YouTube. You're much better off simply ignoring negative comments and feedback.

"At the same time, if the videos you've produced for your company are consistently getting the same types of negative comments, that's worth looking into. However, if it's just a few negative comments here and there, ignore them. You may ultimately find that the commenters are your competition trying to sway your audience and hurt your reputation."

YouTube has evolved a lot in recent years and that evolution continues. How do you think this impacts what videos become successful?

"Currently, YouTube favors high-quality content that's well produced, that viewers watch in full, and then interact with, by posting comments or liking them, for example. This is referred to as 'user engagement.' YouTube is also favoring long-form content these days in an effort to compete against Netflix and Hulu+. Part of this change has resulted in YouTube favoring the major corporations that produce videos, and not the individual users.

"In terms of video content, YouTube viewers have become much more savvy and particular. In my opinion, videos on YouTube that use an infomercial-style format never come across well, and they don't go viral. You're better off making more informative and interesting videos. I think companies should go with more realistic, unscripted, traditional YouTube-style videos if they want to capture the attention of the YouTube audience.

"People on YouTube don't access the service to watch infomercials or commercials. These people will connect more to a real person talking about their company, product, or service in a down-to-earth, real way."

Can hiring a popular YouTuber help a small business's videos gain popularity, or can it help a company promote a product through paid product placement opportunities?

"That kind of stuff is like buying Twitter followers. It's cheating, and it doesn't always work the way you hope it will. If the YouTuber you hire appears in one of your videos on your channel, for example, only a small percentage of that YouTuber's followers will most likely watch your video. It might help you generate some quick attention, but it's not how to build your own online audience in a natural way. Ideally, you want people to subscribe to your YouTube channel and watch your videos because of its unique or valuable content—not because someone told them to watch it."

You mentioned that it's better to build an online audience the "natural way." What does this mean?

"It means providing consistently good content that people want to watch and become invested in. It all comes down to creating fresh and frequent content that's of interest to your audience. As soon as you fail to do this, you'll lose your audience very quickly."

What type of production equipment do you recommend?

"I am a firm believer in the content being key. However, you need to have at least good production quality. Having higher-quality production if you're representing a business or product, for example, is more important. I have seen a lot of companies invest their production budget into producing one single video that's longer in length. Instead, I recommend using that same budget to produce a bunch of shorter videos. Publishing multiple videos on YouTube increases your chances of being found by your target audience, plus the shorter lengths make it easier to retain your audience.

"To edit my videos, I always use Final Cut Pro X on a Mac. However, the mid-priced, intermediate video editing applications are adequate, and most are getting better with each new version that's released. I see a lot of small businesses try to edit videos themselves, even with little or no knowledge about video production. That usually doesn't work out too well. It's a good investment to have your YouTube videos edited by a professional or highly experienced video editor."

How active are you currently on YouTube?

"My own YouTube channels are still online and I try to provide new content at least once per month, just to keep them going. In terms of my own online presence, I am focused a lot more on Facebook these days. I still love YouTube. I was immersed in it for so many years, and it's still an important part of my life. However, I have shifted gears a bit and now work as a consultant to small businesses looking to fully utilize YouTube.

"What I do now is help small businesses step up their YouTube game, or I step in and help companies plan their YouTube strategies from scratch. I often go into companies and assist them in planning, filming, editing, publishing, and/or promoting their YouTube videos and building their YouTube channel.

"Even if a company manages to do everything right in terms of planning and producing their own videos, I still find that, more often than not, they wind up using nondescriptive titles, a poorly written description, and/or badly chosen keywords and tags when uploading their content to YouTube. It's this information, however, that is so important if you want your videos to be found on the service and properly listed on the Google search engine. Creating a properly designed YouTube channel is also important for a small business that wants to build an audience. These are tasks that small businesses tend to need a lot of help with, and that I know how to do extremely well."

What are some of the misconceptions small businesses have about YouTube and online marketing/ promotions as a whole?

"For small businesses, their biggest concern is often their search-engine results. They have been fooled by all of these so-called SEO experts. Many people are shocked to discover that Google owns YouTube, and that by implementing YouTube videos into your website, for example, you can easily improve your Google search engine rankings.

"In other words, if you have a YouTube channel or integrate YouTube videos into your website, your Google ranking is always going to improve and be higher than any competition that does not utilize YouTube effectively. Thus, one of the easiest ways to improve your SEO results is to implement YouTube videos into your company's online strategy.

"Another problem I see with small businesses is that they all know they need a Facebook page, but few know how to create content for it. Once again, it's a good strategy to integrate your YouTube videos with your Facebook page. On your company's YouTube channel page, you need to provide new and fresh content on a regular basis in order to keep people coming back. It's important to understand that YouTube videos can be used for so many things by a small business, but everything that's done online should be consistent and somehow integrated.

"One other major misconception people have about YouTube is that you can include whatever content you want within your videos. In reality, you are not allowed to use content that you don't own the copyright for. In other words, you can't steal music, photos, video clips, sound effects, or other content and simply call it your own.

"I have seen companies and individuals get themselves into a lot of trouble for stealing content. YouTube is getting better and better at catching copyright violations. You are much better off creating and owning all of your own content."

How often should new content be added to a YouTube channel to build and maintain an audience?

"This all depends on the company and its goals. It also depends on what your company has to offer. You don't want to be redundant with your content. If a company has a continuous lineup of new products or plenty of information to offer, and can present it in an entertaining way, it should be producing videos more frequently.

"I have worked with companies that publish new YouTube videos once a month. I personally recommend adding new content at least once per week. However, you need to create a schedule for your audience and then stick to that schedule. Ultimately, the more videos a company has online, the more different search engine results their content will show up in, which means a better opportunity to generate new business or expand your audience.

"Small-business operators truly have many different opportunities when it comes to creating YouTube videos and building a successful YouTube channel. If a company doesn't truly understand what's possible or know how to do it themselves, they should hire someone who does to get them started.

"These days, a company's online social networking activities should spread across YouTube, Facebook, Twitter, and Google+. These are sites that people spend a lot of time on every day. Most people discover new YouTube links as a result of Facebook or Twitter posts, not from searching YouTube directly. As a result, you want to have a presence where your potential customers or clients are, and be able to reach them in the least intrusive and most constructive way possible. That's why integrating all of your online activities is so important.

"In most work situations, people are not allowed to spend lots of time surfing around YouTube. That's frowned upon. However, for whatever reason, it's acceptable in many business environments for employees to spend time on their Facebook page or managing their Twitter accounts from work. If you can link a YouTube video to your Facebook presence, for example, you're more apt to get views from people while they're on the job.

"Right now, Facebook is the number-one place to have an online presence for a small business. If you have a well-done Facebook presence and simultaneously integrate it with your YouTube videos, you'll be in good shape in terms of building your online presence without spending a fortune. Remember, it's all about providing valuable, unique, and engaging content."

MEET IMAN JALALI, PRESIDENT OF TRAINSIGNAL

As the president of TrainSignal, Iman Jalali has more than a decade's worth of internet marketing experience. The company was started in 2002, with the goal of providing a better learning experience and an alternative to classroom IT training. Since then, TrainSignal has generated a total of more than $30 million in revenue as a result of training-course sales throughout the world.

TrainSignal offers online IT training in Microsoft, Cisco, VMware, and Citrix. The training programs are also used by IT professionals as a go-to resource.

Rich: *How do you utilize YouTube in your business?*

Jalali: "We use YouTube to increase awareness of our company, drive traffic back to our website, and ultimately to help sell our training programs. We have been actively using YouTube as a marketing and sales tool since 2007."

What have been some of the biggest benefits or results to using YouTube?

"With over 2.3 million video views so far, YouTube has helped us to advertise TrainSignal for free. Since we're already creating so much video content for our training programs, we're able to utilize some of it directly on YouTube as a lead-generation strategy. YouTube not only helps drive thousands of visitors a month to our website, but it's also helped drive thousands of dollars of revenue that we directly attribute to YouTube video traffic."

What obstacles have you encountered using YouTube?

"It's always a challenge and almost a game to constantly change up your video content strategy and the optimization of different factors on YouTube to maximize the views. You need to understand what people are searching for, what's actually getting the views on YouTube, and what's not in your niche or industry.

"After a small-business operator has a clear understanding of the type of content that performs well on YouTube, they also need to know how to optimize and utilize certain factors, like the video title, a video's description, and tags to ensure the videos rank high for the search terms that are getting the most traffic."

Who handles your video production, and what advice can you offer to companies looking to improve the production quality of their videos?

"We handle all video production internally. It's not something we'd outsource to anybody. Since video is a core of our business, we like doing it ourselves. However, if someone is looking for a company to handle production, always ask for a video reel of past work, and then talk to their previous clients to see how happy they were with the services performed. Also video production is definitely something where you get what you paid for."

On your YouTube channel, how do you handle YouTube comments, likes, shares, ratings, etc.?

"We pay close attention to engagement on YouTube as we've noticed that engagement with videos is definitely becoming a factor in how well YouTube videos rank in YouTube searches. We also look at comments daily and promptly comment back when necessary. Our goals are to create and maintain an engaging channel, to facilitate discussions, and to promote engagement within the videos."

What are some of your best tips for marketing a YouTube channel or promoting videos?

"Marketing your YouTube videos and YouTube channel shouldn't only be done on YouTube. Promote your YouTube videos and channel on your website, as well as within your email newsletter and via your other social media activities. Many of your customers or potential customers might not even know you have a YouTube channel."

What are some of the biggest mistakes you've seen people make when trying to promote their videos?

"One of the biggest mistakes I've seen are companies who use YouTube to upload videos, but they never build out their channel. Spend some time and money with your web designer in order to build yourself or your business a custom channel that fits your brand. A well-designed YouTube channel page will help to get people to subscribe and come back for more videos in the future.

"Another huge mistake for businesses utilizing YouTube is not knowing their audience and failing to cater the right content to those users. Determine what your goals are for your YouTube videos, and make sure to deliver on those goals with every video.

"Have a call to action within each video and make sure to provide a link to your website. Whatever your call to action is, make sure to mention it in your videos via annotations and early on within the video itself.

"Also, don't upload and never come back to the videos and stats. Sometimes it's best to try out different video titles until you see which title performs the best in terms of traffic and video views. Look at YouTube Analytics to see which videos are performing and which aren't. Learn from the data to make better videos in the future. Discover what worked and what didn't."

How have you seen YouTube evolve, and what trends do you see now and over the next year or two?

"After Google, YouTube has turned into the second busiest search engine in the world, and it'll be that way for a long, long time. Too many companies ignore YouTube and by doing so are missing out on a huge marketing opportunity for their company.

"I see channels and playlists really evolving in the next few years. More people will be finding niche channels that they follow a lot more closely than they do now. I expect to see a lot of original, high-quality content being produced for YouTube channels as well. I am referring to the type of content that will continue to disrupt traditional TV programming whose viewership is quickly falling."

What does it take to achieve 1 million or more views for a video?

"Ninety-nine point nine percent of the time it takes a great plan before the video is created to achieve 1 million or more views for a video. You have to find the perfect mix of audience size, quality, and searchability to get millions of views on YouTube. You want to make videos that people actually want to share. The more your viewers share, the more your videos get watched. It's a continuous cycle that builds. However, unless you're a major musician or celebrity, for example, you also need to get really lucky."

Do you have any tips for using pay-per-click ads to promote a video?

"Google AdWords can be a great way to really target the users you want finding your videos, but don't expect your videos to go viral or gain more traction because you're buying views. It's great for businesses who want to target specific search terms and audiences."

Is there any other advice you'd like to share?

"The best advice I can give to a business using YouTube is to research extensively before creating your video content. Then, after you upload your videos to YouTube, test different titles, descriptions, and tags. Refer to YouTube Analytics often to check the data before making more videos. Constantly optimize your content strategy, target different audiences, and test until you find the perfect sweet spot that works for your particular business model.

"Also, to start on YouTube, you don't need to get all crazy and spend a ton of money. Start small and scale up your production. For example, start with an inexpensive Flip cam in order to get the hang of the type of content you want to create, and over time, upgrade your equipment and get more professional and sophisticated from there."

MATT PETERSON, OWNER OF BIG SHOT BIKES, TAKES YOUTUBE FOR A SPIN

Matt Peterson created a company around an activity he's truly passionate about, with a creative twist that sets his products apart. Big Shot Bikes (http://bigshotbikes.com) manufactures and sells customizable fixed gear bicycles via an interactive website and a retail-based dealership network.

From the company's website, customers can select the color scheme for their bike and then order it online. They can also use one of Big Shot Bikes' interactive kiosks at a growing number of bicycle dealerships throughout the country. Big Shot Bikes targets several different audiences, including high school and college kids. To reach this younger, hipper, and more tech-savvy audience, Peterson uses YouTube videos and other multimedia content both on the company's YouTube channel page and its website.

Big Shot Bikes has developed a loyal group of customers, who film their own videos of their custom-made bikes and publish them on their personal YouTube channels, Facebook pages, and blogs. These customer videos have helped build and promote the Big Shot Bikes company, brand, and its products, and expand its customer base.

The next phase of Big Shot Bikes' YouTube marketing strategy will include a fan video contest. Even though Peterson still considers his online activities to be in their early stages, he's already seen tremendous success using YouTube videos as a sales and marketing tool.

Rich: *How is Big Shot Bikes different from other bicycle manufacturers?*

Peterson: "Big Shot Bikes is a manufacturer of customizable fixed gear bicycles. What we do is offer a unique shopping experience. We allow our customers to customize each component of their bicycle online, and then we build it based on their selections. A customer can choose from a variety of colors for each component in order to create a bike that perfectly matches their own personality.

"We've been in business since 2009. Our style of fixed gear bike is considered the hottest new style of bikes, so there's been a strong demand for them among college students and young people in particular. Fixed gear bikes have recently become something of an urban phenomenon as well.

"It's our customer's ability to customize their bike online that sets our products apart. Using YouTube and other online resources, we have put a lot of effort into branding our product. I have always had an entrepreneurial spirit, and Big Shot Bikes allows me to combine my passion for bicycles with my skills at marketing and branding.

"Founding and running this company has been a wild ride so far, but it's been a fun one. We've developed a very strong and loyal following of fans, and using online video has been a powerful tool for communicating our brand image to our target audience, while also showcasing our products."

What have you done with video so far to promote your bikes and brand?

"Our experience has been somewhat unique when it comes to using video, because we've had some very talented video producers approach us who have been willing to create our promotional videos on a barter basis. In other words, to keep costs down, we've traded bikes for video production, and this has worked out very well. We've been able to produce videos that we otherwise could not have been able to afford.

"Beyond using the barter system to have our own videos produced, our customers continue to produce their own fan videos, which continue to be published on YouTube, as well as on Facebook and other online social networking sites. This serves as free and extremely powerful advertising for us, because the fan videos are unsolicited testimonials from very happy customers.

"One of our more recent videos was a highly produced, professional-looking promotional video, which looks very much like a 30-second commercial spot. It will initially be presented on YouTube, Vimeo, and other online services. However, my long-term goal is to be able to afford to have the commercial air on TV.

"Another one of our videos was produced to drive customers to visit our point-of-sale interactive kiosks which are available at our authorized dealers. This, too, has proven to be a good sales and marketing tool, with a very different type of call to action.

"I have to admit we're still in the infancy of what we could be doing on YouTube to promote the company, its brand, and our bikes. But, with our limited resources, I am very proud of the successes we've had thus far.

"A third category of videos we've produced for YouTube have been how-to related and targeted to people who have already purchased one of our bikes. Using video, in addition to a printed manual, we're able to demonstrate how to assemble the bike and use it properly. These videos have dramatically reduced the number of technical support calls we receive from our customers, and has reduced the amount of troubleshooting we need to do on the phone with our customers. Ultimately, this has reduced our customer support costs rather significantly."

Based on the sales videos you've posted on YouTube, what have been the results?

"I would like to be able to tell you about the solid correlation between video views, visits to our website, and sales, but we haven't tried too hard as of yet to track this data. With the limited time and resources that I have, my goal has been to get videos online and promote them on our YouTube channel and on our website. In the near future, I plan to use YouTube Analytics to better track YouTube video views more closely.

"Without looking closely at traffic details related to our videos, I know that the ones in which we get our brand and marketing message across near the very start of the video tend to perform much better. One of my employees has been in charge of our pay-per-click advertising campaign, which is one of the major tools we use to drive potential new customers to our website, and he is starting to focus more on using YouTube as a sales and marketing tool for us.

"There are so many tools out there that allow us to track our ROI for online advertising, as well as traffic to our website, I just haven't gotten around to really using YouTube Analytics yet, but I understand the importance of doing this as we move forward building up our YouTube presence.

"Because we've done the majority of our videos on a barter basis with video producers, getting each video done in the time frame we'd like has been a challenge. This is an obstacle we could avoid if we were paying the video production company. Not being able to schedule video productions has made it more challenging to keep to a schedule for publishing new content on a regular basis. However, our barter production approach has kept our costs way down."

Where else have you distributed your promotional videos?

"We embed the videos on our company's main website, plus publish them on Vimeo, as well as on our Facebook page. I do know, however, that there are a lot of other things we could be doing to build a larger audience for the videos faster. I have discovered firsthand that you can spend a lot of time and effort producing an awesome video, but those efforts are worthless unless you also heavily promote the video once it's published online.

"I must admit, in addition to everything we've done to produce and promote our own videos, we've seen tremendous results from our customers publishing their fan videos and showcasing our products. For other small-business operators, I can't emphasize enough how much of a positive impact this has had. All of these videos show our bikes in a very positive light. In the future, I do plan to develop a video-based contest for our customers. In the past, we have done photo contests through our Facebook page and website, and those have gone very well. We've encouraged customers to submit photos of themselves riding or interacting with their customized bike. The next logical extension of those contests is to host a video contest as well.

"Part of our overall marketing plans includes us setting aside a certain number of bicycles to use as prizes for upcoming contests and online promotions. We have maintained an email list of our existing customers, as well as people who have expressed interest in our bikes and our company, so we'll also use email to promote the video contest when we kick it off.

"Another part of our marketing strategy involves donating bikes to certain charities, participating in events, and taking part in trade shows. These are all things that could be filmed in the future and leveraged as promotional content within YouTube videos.

"Based on my own experience running Big Shot Bikes, I have discovered that YouTube is just one of several online resources that, as a small-business operator, I need to be utilizing. I have also seen the need to integrate our usage of these services, including Facebook and Twitter. I think it would be a mistake to focus solely on just one of these services or sites."

Hiring Help: The YouTube Services Industry

IN THIS CHAPTER

- Micah Kohne, marketing director at High Impact, shares his experience helping clients use YouTube.
- Stephanie Belsky, founder and president of Lucid, discusses how her company helps nonprofit organizations utilize YouTube and other online social networking services.
- Get online reputation advice from Brent Franson, vice president at Reputation.com.
- Learn how large companies use YouTube and how to apply those strategies from Andrew Hirshman, the founder and president of 360i.

When developing and implementing a strategy for managing your online presence—from your YouTube videos, to your blog, to every tweet you type—you can save a lot of time and potentially avoid costly mistakes by hiring experts. And an entire industry has evolved comprised of companies and consultants proffering specific services for producing, editing, publishing, and promoting YouTube videos. This chapter offers just a small sampling of the types of companies and services for hire for some or all aspects of your online activities.

MEET MICAH KOHNE, MARKETING DIRECTOR AT HIGH IMPACT

High Impact (www.highimpact.com) is a video production and animation company that works with medium to large businesses in a wide range of industries to produce videos for sales presentations, trade shows, and as training material on YouTube.

Micah Kohne, the company's marketing director and visual media consultant, offers tips and strategies about how to produce quality, high-impact videos for YouTube.

Rich: *What is High Impact and what services does it offer?*

Kohne: "We are a multimedia company that specializes in illustrations, animations, and interactive presentations. One of our specialties is producing marketing videos for pharmaceutical and medical device companies. We're good at taking any type of product or service that might be difficult to explain, and simplifying those concepts by explaining them in an illustration—animated or video format.

"The nice thing about videos and animations is that the content can be used in so many different ways. Once we produce a marketing video, for example, there are many ways it can be deployed, including on YouTube or through a company's website. YouTube provides companies with a free marketing tool that can easily be linked with other social media sites. These tools combined make it easy and inexpensive to market to your clients or customers."

What are some of your key steps in producing videos for clients?

"It all depends on the project. We typically begin with a written storyboard and script, which gets provided to the client. Once the concept gets approved, we move on to create a visual storyboard, which includes rough sketches that outline what the final piece will look like. We work with award-winning video producers, who each have a unique approach for creating marketing videos for our clients.

"For example, when a video will include an interview with a spokesperson or executive from a company, we never provide that person with a copy of the questions they'll be asked in their interview. We want to capture off-the-cuff responses from them. We never want it to look like someone is reading a script or reciting a memorized monologue. Internally, however, we have a team of people that think carefully about the questions that will be asked in order to solicit the responses we need to showcase within the video."

Once you're hired, how long does the process take?

"That varies, depending on the project and whether or not travel is involved. I would say the average is three to four weeks from start to finish. Whether you hire a professional video production company to shoot your videos, or you do it yourself, production quality is key. You want to showcase your company, product, or service in a professional way. Keep in mind, any YouTube user can always tell the difference between a professionally produced video and one that was created by someone in-house who has little or no video production experience.

"When a company hires a video production company like ours, we use high-end production equipment that's best suited for the specific project. This allows us to achieve a unique look and feel within a video that you can't achieve with a low-end camera. If someone is interested in producing high-quality videos that will represent their company, product, or service, I recommend hiring a video production company to create your videos for you.

"We have experience and the equipment to achieve that all-important professional look within your videos. The price for hiring a professional video production company to create a three- to five-minute video varies, based on how many different scenes are required to be shot and how much travel in involved. Typically, if we're hired to do a shoot, we will shoot multiple videos at once to maximum our time and the money our client is spending.

"We typically do a one- to two-day shoot. Depending on the goal of the video, we'll try to incorporate interviews with multiple executives from the company, plus include customer or client testimonials within the production. Cost-wise, our fees start at around $10,000 per shoot, which includes the editing of the video, but costs can go up a lot from there."

Do you help a company promote its videos to establish an audience?

"We're mainly a video production company. We recently started offering web design services as well, but our focus and expertise is in video production, not on the deployment or promotion of the videos. There are other companies that specialize only in video marketing. When we do website design for our clients, we often create specialized websites or webpages to be used specifically as a forum for showcasing the videos we're creating for them. It's a website that's very sticky and that offers interactive content to support the video. We believe that to properly communicate with people online, incorporating video elements into a website is extremely important."

With so much video content out there, is it difficult to attract attention for a new video?

"We are very aware of the short attention span that a YouTube user has. As a result, we try to keep our videos short and sweet. They're often shorter than two minutes in length. If we have a bunch of content to convey, we'll divide it up into a series of videos that can be spread out onto YouTube or throughout a website.

"One benefit to creating multiple, short videos, as opposed to a single long one, is that for each video, we can attach a separate set of tags or keywords, a different title for each, and a variation for each video's description. This makes the video series, as a whole, more searchable and easy to find. Of course, each video in the series then promotes the others."

Do you have any tips to help someone quickly capture a viewer's attention?

"It all depends on your objectives and audience. It's important to engage your target audience right away. One thing that tends to work well is to quickly incorporate a call to action. Also, at the very start of the video, make sure you set up and quickly explain what you'll be talking about.

"When someone decides to watch a video on YouTube, they make that decision for a reason. We try to address that want or need as quickly as possible and as efficiently as we can. One of the biggest challenges anyone faces when creating a YouTube video is keeping the viewer engaged. Keeping the video as short as possible, while still getting the message across, is a good way to achieve this."

When you're working with a new client, how do you help them establish realistic goals for attracting an audience?

"This is always a challenge. We try to demonstrate to the client actual examples from our past clients. We show them what we did and how we did it, and then provide detailed information and hard data about the outcome, in terms of viewership and actions taken by the video's viewers.

"We always recommend that a client fully utilize all aspects of online social media, including Facebook, Twitter, LinkedIn, and Google+, in order to promote their videos efficiently. These are all free vehicles for promoting videos, but they also offer paid advertising options. Our clients have also had success using email campaigns to promote their videos. This works particularly well if the client has a large database of email addresses for their customers or clients who have opted into a mailing list.

"When a company incorporates videos into the website, we strongly recommend that they implement SEO coding within the website that will help attract viewers to the videos on that site. We have also seen tremendous results from pay-per-click advertising to promote videos, using Google AdWords, or AdWords for Video, for example."

As a video producer, what tips can you offer on improving the production quality of self-made videos?

"Simple is always better. In terms of shots, you don't want any complicated or busy backgrounds. The people appearing in your videos should always wear solid colors that do not blend into the background. If someone is wearing a shirt with thin stripes, for example, it can distract the viewer, especially if the person is moving around, even a little bit.

"We always spend a lot of time researching and choosing the ideal background for each shot within a video. The background can help set the overall scene and convey information to the viewer. Lighting and sound quality is definitely important as well.

"Regardless of what type of video we're shooting, we typically shoot with three cameras simultaneously. Most video production companies will only use one or two cameras. This gives us a much greater selection of shots and angles when it comes to editing the video later. How often you should change shots is a creative decision. It often works when there's a topic change related to what the person in the video is saying. If you stay on the same shot for too long, it gets boring for the viewer. Sometimes, if the person in the video is saying something that's intimate or important, switching to a closeup works well.

"Switching between shots is another way of keeping a viewer engaged in a video. It can also set your videos apart from others' competing videos that were shot by amateurs."

What advice do you have about using background music in a video?

"Background music is almost always good, as long as it's subtle and appropriate music. This all depends on the type of video you're shooting and the content you're trying to present. Sound can affect the feeling the viewer gets when they're watching a video, even if that sound is just barely perceptible. In almost every video we produce, we incorporate at least some type of background music.

"As for video transitions and effects, it's very easy for amateur video editors to overuse these elements. Just because you can drag and drop really cool-looking effects into your production using iMovie, for example, this does not mean you need them in your video. If you explore YouTube and watch a bunch of videos, it's easy to find many examples that overuse transitions or use them improperly. If they're not used correctly, animated transitions can be very distracting to the viewer. It all goes back to keeping your video simple. Don't go crazy with the music, sound effects, or visual effects you use in your videos."

What advice can you offer to someone looking to hire a video production company?

"Do your research. Make sure you see actual examples of videos that the company has produced for other clients. It all comes down to professionalism and creating a video that will be produced at a quality suitable for your company and its intended audience. If you look at two similar videos from two competing video production companies, you can usually quickly determine which is the better video in terms of production quality and professionalism.

"YouTube is free. Use it. In conjunction with YouTube, there are a ton of free resources out there that can help you produce great videos. However, if you have the budget, there are also plenty of paid options, too. Take advantage of what's available to you for free, especially the promotional opportunities available through online social media networks.

"YouTube videos are readily searchable via Google, for example. So, if they have a good title, description, and the right keywords associated with them, you can increase traffic to your website and other online activities as a result of people finding and watching your YouTube videos."

MEET STEPHANIE BELSKY, FOUNDER AND PRESIDENT OF LUCID

Stephanie Belsky began her career in public relations at Weber Shandwick Worldwide. She's had numerous professional accomplishments related directly to YouTube. In 2007, she launched the marketing and social engagement department at CollegeHumor, where she managed all syndication platforms and grew the CollegeHumor YouTube channel to more than 3.5 million subscribers and more than 1 billion video views.

In 2011, Belsky moved to head audience development and channel marketing for Big Frame, which represents YouTube channels and YouTubers. She also helped launch one of YouTube's first 100 programming channels.

In 2012, she founded Lucid, a content strategy consultancy that connects creatives with nonprofits and is focused on YouTube optimization and engagement across all social platforms.

Rich: *Big Frame works directly with popular YouTube channels and helps them become even more popular. What were some of your responsibilities and accomplishments when you worked there?*

Belsky: "Big Frame is one of the newest YouTube networks, and I was their first employee. The company was founded in 2011 by Sarah Penna and Steve Raymond. The co-founders poached me from CollegeHumor to head up their audience development and channel marketing.

"As part of the 'YouTube 100,' YouTube's new original programming initiative, Big Frame launched their channel Bammo in March of 2011. The company represents some of the top YouTube talent, including MysteryGuitarMan, Dave Days, DeStorm Power, TheWingGirls, Tyler Oakley, the award-winning web series Squaresville, and many more. They are a full-service media agency and a YouTube partner."

What do you currently do that relates to YouTube?

"I handled promotions for a documentary about YouTubers called *Please Subscribe*, which was directed by Dan Dobi. [See Chapter 15 for an interview with Dan Dobi.] I also work with nonprofit clients on channel creation and development, plus help to broker relationships with web properties to get YouTube talent featured in more original content."

How can small-business operators take advantage of hiring YouTubers to be spokespeople or for product placement? What have you seen work well?

"As an entrepreneur myself and a friend of the YouTube community, I can tell you YouTubers typically won't work with small businesses, and they shouldn't. Their responsibility is to make the best content they can for their audience and promote it. If that involves a product from a small business, so be it. But unless the product is really amazing and the small business can somehow convince the creators that this brand-new product will enhance their production value or is something that their audience will truly love and will use, it's not really worth their time or the time of the small business, because it won't be organic.

"The business often ends up with a video with lower views than anticipated, and the YouTube talent has created a piece of content that he/she is not 100 percent on board with. This often also results in hundreds of thousands of disappointed fans. This is why many brands get in trouble."

What are some of your best tips for marketing a YouTube channel or promoting videos?

"Keep it short—two to three minutes maximum. Use a lot of quick cuts. Get creative. Make it personal when you can, and engage with your audience. Leverage YouTube as another platform in your social media arsenal. If the video is really good and relevant, then send it out to various blogs and website editors, and ask if they'll watch it and promote it.

"I value my relationships with bloggers and editors; they're the gatekeepers and the ones that will determine whether or not they want to embed your video."

What are some of the biggest mistakes you've made in promoting videos?

"Forcing a piece of content on an audience that didn't ask for it and didn't want to see it in the first place. Just because the eyeballs are there doesn't mean they'll be automatically receptive to what you put out there. What it all comes down to is engagement. Ask your audience what they would like to see, create your videos accordingly, and then they can't complain about it because you've given them exactly what they asked for."

How have nonprofits effectively used YouTube?

"The best case study I have is one of my first clients, 'Because I Said I Would,' a 501-C3 founded by Alex Sheen. I discovered Alex through his post that made the front page of Reddit.

"Alex Sheen created the organization in honor of his father, a man of his word. In 2012, Alex created 'promise cards,' that he shipped for free to anyone that requested them, no matter where they were in the country or in the world. On his promise cards, he wrote 52 resolutions that he would complete throughout the year. Each week, he would choose another card and would give himself a one-week deadline to complete each task.

"I gave him two additional resolutions: starting a YouTube channel from scratch, and then to upload one new video per week after he'd completed each task. The key to YouTube success is consistency and commitment. If you can commit to uploading at least one new video a week and let your viewers know which day they should expect to see your video, and you stick to it, you'll do well. I have discovered that Wednesday is an optimal day to upload a new video if you're on a weekly schedule."

How have you seen YouTube evolve in recent years? What trends do you see now and over the next year or two?

"YouTube is changing literally every day. New layouts, new channels, new ways to annotate videos, plus new tools and features are constantly being added. It's hard to keep up.

"Everyone is making a fuss over YouTube taking over TV, but really, it's the medium that is the most engaging and enhances the traditional media experience. It's not taking it over—it's making it better."

What does it take to achieve 1 million or more views for a video?

"Ah, yes, I believe the kids call it 'viral' these days. The ultimate success stories are those that have the following elements: relevancy, for SEO purposes and just general discoverability; a good thumbnail that will draw your viewers in; a title with keywords that they'll be searching for; and an audience that is excited to watch and share your video."

What tips can you offer companies that produce their own videos?

"If you have the budget, absolutely get a production team on board. The quality will be so much better. But if you're going to bootstrap it, just be a straight-up vlogger and put your face of the company in front of the camera.

"The YouTube community is creative and fun, so if your product isn't the most exciting thing in the world—let's say a hedge fund, for example—make fun of the fact that you're a hedge fund making a YouTube video.

"Transparency goes a long way in the YouTube community; even if you hire a YouTuber as a spokesperson, they'll call out the fact that this particular video was sponsored by your company or product by saying something like, 'Thanks, McDonald's, for making this video possible!' If they don't, they come off as a sell-out to their users."

BRENT FRANSON ON PROTECTING YOUR ONLINE REPUTATION

When it comes to doing business on the internet, there are a lot of things that can quickly tarnish your company's reputation or sway customers from purchasing your product or service in favor of your competition's. Negative reviews, comments, feedback, or ratings can all be detrimental, as can negative tweets and unfavorable Facebook posts.

And negative reviews or ratings you receive on independent services, like Yelp!, especially if you're a local business, can also be extremely damaging. As you begin to develop your company's online presence, it's extremely important to actively build and maintain a positive online reputation.

Reputation.com offers fee-based services to manage the information that appears online about its clients. Brent Franson, a vice president, shares some advice about protecting your company's online reputation—on YouTube and beyond.

Rich: *What is Reputation.com?*

Franson: "Reputation.com was founded in 2006, and has developed proprietary tools and strategies that can help any business or individual build, protect, control, and manage the information that appears about them on the internet.

"Reputation.com offers a few different product areas. For example, we offer a privacy technology that helps individuals understand exactly where their personal information is appearing on the internet, and then we will help them remove that information so it can't be sold to marketers or used by identity thieves.

"We also have a service called Reputation Defender. It is used by small businesses and individuals, such as doctors or lawyers. Its typical use helps them fix situations in which there is information appearing on the web that they don't like or that's inaccurate. For example, if you Google the name of your company and search results that are not favorable pop up, we can proactively help create positive information to help bury the negative information, and strategically have what we create appear in search results. This will make the negative information much less prominent.

"To be very clear, we will not work with companies that are disreputable and make them appear legitimate. We have a whole set of guidelines that dictate who we will work with and who we won't. If a company or individual deserves the negative reputation that they have, we will not work with them.

"Our job is to help you create honest and accurate information about [you], your product, and your business, and then strategically place that information throughout the internet in a way that's optimized. We do not create fake reviews or ratings, however."

What are some of the things a company needs to be mindful of when it comes to managing their online reputation?

"YouTube is just one of the many online services on which a small business needs to maintain a positive reputation. You never want to utilize methods for generating fake views, comments, or ratings, for example, when trying to promote or expand your YouTube audience.

"What I recommend to clients is that they need to take a proactive approach to monitoring everything that's said about them on the internet, and pay particular attention to online reviews that appear in places like Yelp! These services can have a large impact on a local business.

"Second, a company needs to pay attention to what appears when someone googles their company or product name. The search results that come up need to provide an accurate representation of their business. These days, just having your own listing with a high ranking on the search engines is not enough. You need to be mindful of what else pops up when someone does a search for your company or product name. Ideally, you want to own the top 10 or 20 results that pop up on Google, Yahoo!, and the other popular search engines.

"Third, a company needs to properly manage their social media. This includes correctly using services like YouTube, as well as Facebook, Twitter, Google+, and LinkedIn, for example. If you choose to utilize online social media, what you do with these services needs to be consistent with the rest of your messaging and branding. You also want to make sure that if you're going to use these services, you need to go all of the way with them.

"Simply creating a YouTube channel or Facebook page for your business is not enough, if you opt to utilize online social media. It's essential that you regularly update your content and use these services as a forum to create positive interactions with your audience.

"Finally, a company needs to properly manage the content of a blog, website, and anything else they're doing on the web. What most people don't fully understand is that once something gets published on the internet, it is there forever. Even if you try to delete a video that you've previously posted on YouTube, for example, chances are it's already been copied or distributed elsewhere on the internet.

"Anything you say or do on the web essentially becomes part of your permanent record. It is permanently attached to you or your business. Just as you would carefully think about a tattoo that you might want to put on your body, that same level of thought and critical thinking needs to go into absolutely everything you choose to publish on the web.

"If you want to use YouTube to somehow enhance your business, you need to pay attention to all aspects of how that video will be perceived by the public. Thus, you need to consider your message, production quality, content, how the public will perceive the video, and how it will impact your company's overall reputation and image.

"YouTube can be an excellent tool for helping to personify your business. You can show, through your videos, that your company is made up of real people, plus provide an accurate visual representation of your products or services."

What are mistakes that you've seen companies make on YouTube?

"We have seen companies try to artificially inflate video views, likes, and comments, for example. These are short-term actions that do not yield a lot of benefit. In fact, if you get caught by YouTube, there can be serious consequences to your YouTube channel and online presence.

"You also need to understand that people who use YouTube can often be somewhat anonymous, which allows them to be much more vocal with their comments. People are more apt to post negative material online, as opposed to having them say something in person if you met them face to face, or if they had to attach their real name and contact information to a comment. So you do not want to take negative comments posted on YouTube too seriously.

"You also want to be very sensitive when reacting to that negative material. If you post a reaction to a negative comment, for example, the ramifications can make a situation much worse. Plus, this all happens in a public forum. If you react too strongly to negative material on the web, you can exacerbate the issue. This is particularly true when dealing with video-related comments on YouTube. If you react strongly to a comment, that will often incite additional comments, and you wind up making the situation much worse.

"In most cases, it's better to simply ignore very negative or angry comments in a public forum, while you focus your energies on interacting with people who leave positive comments and who support your online endeavors."

What does a company need to know about forming a positive online reputation?

"When you begin using any form of online social media, including YouTube, as an organization, you need to make a decision early on about the personality of your organization. If you are a small technology company in the Bay Area and your company is comprised of people in their mid-20s, and you're targeting customers in their mid-20s, you have the ability to be a bit edgy or sarcastic. However, if you are a tailor in New York City, the public personality your company showcases online needs to be vastly different.

"Make a decision about the personality of your company and decide how you want and need to represent yourself at all times on the internet. Be very careful about posting anything whatsoever that could be construed as offensive, political, or sexual in nature. Take the long view with anything that you're posting, keeping in mind that public attitudes change quickly about many issues."

How does Reputation.com work?

"We begin by identifying the issues that need to be addressed with each potential client. We determine if we need to create or expand upon your online reputation, or if we need to do damage control. We provide the tools and technology needed to help control what's being said about your company on the web. The first step is knowing what information is already out there. The next step is proactively publishing more positive and accurate information, using a systematic process that results in information appearing in all of the right places on the web.

"For example, we never publish fake reviews, nor do we encourage or incentivize anyone to write favorable reviews. We do, however, encourage your customers or clients to write reviews about your company, without giving them any guidance whatsoever about what to say.

"We have discovered that 80 percent of reputation damage risk comes from a mismatch of offline vs. online. This means that the reality of your positive offline reputation is not being accurately represented online. That's where the majority of a company's reputation risk comes from. Ideally, you want your positive offline reputation to be consistent with your online reputation.

"To accomplish this, we use a combination of proprietary automated tools, as well as personalized services. We offer options for our clients to use our tools by themselves, or we can use our tools for our clients on their behalf. We are a technology company, and at the core of everything we do is our unique technology and tools, although we also provide managed services to our clients."

What is one aspect of a company's online reputation that often gets overlooked by a small business?

"More and more people are accessing the internet, as well as services like YouTube, using their wireless mobile devices. As a small business, it's becoming increasingly more important to make sure that you're paying attention to the ways your business is being represented via a mobile device. The biggest trend we're seeing is the transition to mobile as a way consumers are gathering or accessing information.

"This is particularly important for local businesses. More and more smartphones, for example, have GPS and map-related apps that not only display addresses for businesses, but also automatically display reviews, ratings, and comments. It's important that the information that automatically pops up on people's phones or tablets as they're navigating their way around is accurate and favorable.

"If someone is using their iPhone for example, and seeks out a local hair salon, using the Maps or Yelp! app, in addition to seeing all of the salons in the area displayed on the map, the user can instantly access detailed information about that business. This information can potentially include a link to a website, YouTube channel page, or individual video, which can then be viewed from the mobile device.

"As a small business, it's becoming increasingly more important to monitor and proactively manage all aspects of your online reputation, and to understand that everything you do online is interrelated."

360I FOUNDER ANDREW HIRSHMAN ON USING A BIG-COMPANY STRATEGY FOR YOUR SMALL BUSINESS

Andrew Hirshman is the founder of 360i, an advertising and marketing firm that caters to a handful of big, high-profile companies. Hirshman has been using YouTube since 2007, in his first advertising job at Ogilvy, and has discovered many innovative ways for his clients to use this service for things like product launches, events, and direct-response campaigns. Here, Hirshman discusses how small businesses can leverage the same strategies that he's employed for his big clients.

Rich: *What fascinates you about using the internet, and particularly, YouTube, as a marketing, sales, and advertising tool?*

Hirshman: "Back in college, I hosted a public affairs radio show on which I interviewed numerous authors, actors, poets, musicians, and politicians. All of my friends said they'd be interested in listening to my show, but they didn't have access to a radio when my live show was on. They wanted me to put the radio show online in the form on an online, on-demand podcast. I then worked with a friend to create a website for the show that allowed people to download and listen to the show at their leisure.

"Google Analytics had just been released, and I was able to track how the popularity of my podcasts grew over time via the internet. In the summer of 2007, I landed an internship at the *Charlie Rose* show. At the time, their web producer was trying to figure out how to reach more young people online. We wound up working together to develop video-based segments related to the *Charlie Rose* show that were available only via the web. It was through this experience that I discovered the power of YouTube and how it could be used to effectively reach an audience.

"When I landed my first advertising job at Ogilvy, the account I was initially assigned to was one of the world's largest computer companies. My responsibilities included handling the company's search-engine marketing. As a result, my client was one of the first major companies to begin using what is now AdWords for Video on YouTube. We also developed specialized tools for measuring engagement around messaging, long before this was offered as part of YouTube Analytics.

"Unlike selling something like soda to customers using a traditional 30-second commercial TV spot, my client needed to explain very technical things, like cloud-based computing and database query tools, to its higher-end business customers. For that, we decided to use three- to five-minute YouTube videos in order to explain what my client's products were and how they worked. We knew that many of the people we were trying to reach were visual learners, so using video was the right tool.

"Some people like to learn about things visually, and video is a great way to teach those people. Instead of repackaging an online, text-based blog, for example, we needed to quickly illustrate our highly technical message using video. We ultimately developed a highly targeted YouTube channel that achieved the results that the computer client needed. The same concept was later adapted to one of the world's largest shipping companies, and to a major chemical company.

"What's possible using YouTube and video in general is powerful and highly trackable, which makes it a very attractive marketing, sales, promotional, and advertising tool for businesses of all sizes."

What experience do you have buying advertising on YouTube for your clients?

"We have extensive experience using paid online advertising and YouTube advertising as tools for helping our clients reach their customers. When using YouTube, whether you're a large or small company, the strategy is basically the same. First, you need to figure out who is your audience and then determine where they are. If you own a local diner, your audience is probably within a 20-mile radius of your location. Using YouTube-related advertising, you can geo-target specific cities or regions in an effort to get your message seen by the right audience. Using this type of advertising is much more controlled and targeted, as well as less expensive, than even making a local TV ad buy."

What advice do you have for a company that's about to create a YouTube channel?

"Think of your YouTube channel page as a landing page. As you name your channel, and then give titles to each of your videos, it's important to know that the Google search engine, as well as others, focus on the first 40 to 60 characters within the title for video search engine optimization and ranking.

"Many companies don't put enough thought into the titles for their videos and this causes them to lose out on viewers. For example, if you're publishing a video that features your company's vice president of development demonstrating how to use a new product, don't bother including that executive's name in your video's title. People who are searching for details about your product will not enter the person's name into the search engine. They're more apt to enter the product name and/or your company's name. This is the information you want to focus on when giving a title to your videos.

"Within the titles, also use as much descriptive language as possible. The titles should focus on outside-in marketing that will appeal to people who don't necessarily know about your product or your company, as opposed to inside-out marketing, which would cater more to people who are already very knowledgeable about your company and its offerings.

"Video titles, descriptions, and tags should all be used to help a total stranger not just find your video, but also encourage them to want to watch it. As you're publishing your videos on YouTube, you also need to select the right category for it in order to help YouTube and Google properly organize it.

"Another strategy I suggest to help a video achieve better search rankings is to attach a full transcript of your video within the YouTube file as you upload it. YouTube has really good automated tools for figuring out what a video is about, but they're not as sophisticated as what it can do with a text crawler when it comes to analyzing text. Thus, associating a transcript of the video with the upload will help your video more easily get discovered by viewers who are using the YouTube search feature or the Google search engine, for example.

"To help you create more descriptive titles, descriptions, and tags, I recommend using some of the online-based keyword tools that are available. There's the Google Keyword Tool [https://googlekeywordtool.com] and SEO Moz [www.seomoz.org], for example, that can help you choose the most popular keywords and phrases used by web surfers to find specific things on the web."

What have you discovered about how YouTube measures engagement?

"In the past, YouTube videos were ranked using a variety of criteria, but the number of views it received played an important role. Much more recently, this has changed dramatically. YouTube is now tracking a video's quality of engagement. More weight is put on videos that have a longer engagement time.

"For example, a video which people consistently watch from beginning to end, regardless of its actual length, will rank higher than a video which viewers click away from watching it partway through. The percentage of people who subscribe to a YouTube channel versus who just watch a channel's videos, as well as the number of likes, a video's rankings, and number of comments it receives all now play a much bigger role than ever in determining a video's popularity and ranking on YouTube itself and on Google.

"At the end of the day, Google makes money on YouTube by selling ads. They only get paid by advertisers when people see the ads. So, YouTube has begun favoring the videos that people are watching the most and that have the best engagement.

"Research shows that people who are subscribers to a channel are much more apt to watch that channel's videos from beginning to end, plus they're willing to view longer format ad content."

What are some of the best ways a small business can use YouTube?

"It all depends on the nature of your business and what your goals are. YouTube is really good at helping companies reach a niche audience. Instead of focusing on achieving an insane number of views for your videos, I recommend trying to create the best user experience possible by more carefully targeting your audience. If you force or somehow trick people who have no interest in watching your videos into viewing them, that's just a waste of time and resources.

"If many people wind up starting to view your video, but clicking away from it due to lack of interest, your quality of engagement scores will go down and you will wind up getting penalized by YouTube when it comes to ranking. You're better off reaching fewer, more targeted viewers who will watch your videos with interest and have a quality engagement experience.

"If you're selling ice cream, and you know everyone loves ice cream, getting lots of video views for your ice cream-related video makes a lot of sense. However, if you're selling something like paintball gun supplies, you'll benefit better by targeting paintball enthusiasts, not the general public. This is where using tags and contextual keywords, as well as well-written descriptions, comes in very handy.

"As a small-business operator, don't focus on getting the most number of video views or trying to make a video go viral. Instead, focus on reaching your potential customers and having some type of value-added, engaging interaction."

How can a YouTube video capture someone's attention?

"You already know that the people who use YouTube have a very short attention span. Research shows that if you don't capture their attention in three to five seconds, you probably won't capture their attention at all. I think too often people produce two-, three-, or four-minute videos, but they don't get to the main point of their video until two-thirds of the way through it, and then they hold off their call to action until the very end.

"If you wait 30 seconds to make your point and convey your call to action, chances are, you've already lost your viewer. I would say that within the first five to 10 seconds, a viewer should know what the video is about and what the key message of the video is. If you wait too long, you'll lose the viewer before they can even make the decision about whether or not the video's content is relevant to them.

"There should be a point very early in each of your videos—within 10 to 30 seconds into it—that the viewer should know and fully understand what the video is about, who created it, and what they can expect from watching the rest of it. If they opt to click out of the video and stop watching it, at least they have a good understanding of it and know what they're clicking away from. This is very different from someone clicking away because they're annoyed or don't know what's going on in the video."

How important is a call to action?

"This should typically be a very important element of a video. When selecting a call to action, clarity is the key. As you convey your call to action, make sure you tell the viewer the clear benefit of taking that action, as well as the action you want them to actually take. For example, if you're selling cars, a call to action might be, "Visit the Bob's Used Car Emporium website right now to discover huge savings on used cars. Just click here to save $500 instantly." You want to include a benefit statement and then describe the desired action, such as 'click here.'

"You want to emphasize your call to action at least once during every 30 seconds of your video. Do not wait until the very end, which is what most people tend to do. Yes, you want to repeat the call to action at the end of the video, but it should be conveyed within the main video several times as well.

"There are many ways to convey a call to action. You can tell the viewer what to do using words or video, or you can use YouTube Annotations and/or embedded links within a video, as well as utilize on-screen titles.

"For many small businesses, you'll benefit from having your company's website URL displayed somewhere on the screen throughout your video, or at least in the text that's displayed immediately below the video window on your YouTube channel page. Give someone the ability to find you easily.

"Unless your video is really well done and extremely relevant, most people will not watch more than one minute of it. Knowing this, make sure you pack all of your key messages and call to action into the first minute."

How important is it to manage video-related comments on YouTube?

"If you're going to have a YouTube channel and populate it with videos, I would recommend assigning someone with the responsibility of being your company's social media manager. Allowing for comments allows your channel to become much more interactive. However, have your social media manager constantly review the comments and moderate the discussions that transpire around your content. If your customers are willing to engage . . . use your social listening skills to discover what they have to say and learn from it.

"It makes sense to get customers to engage with your videos through comments, but for you or someone from your company to be there for them as they're engaging. This also applies to comments posted on a Facebook page or within a YouTube feed."

Does it make sense for a small business to use paid advertising on YouTube?

"Yes. This can be done very inexpensively and your ad message can be highly targeted. No other advertising vehicle offers this level of accessibility. Now is the time to start using paid online advertising, because you can do a lot of experimentation and get a lot of bang for your buck. Over time, I believe the cost of online advertising on YouTube will increase significantly, as more and more businesses discover what YouTube is capable of and the marketplace matures and grows.

"Especially if you're a local-based business, chances are your competition is not fully utilizing YouTube and YouTube-based online advertising, and if they are, they're probably not doing it consistently. This gives you a tremendous opportunity.

"One way to increase local exposure via YouTube is to create a lot of short, but related videos and add them to your channel. For example, if you're a local vinyl siding company, instead of creating one five-minute video that covers the top 10 reasons to buy and install vinyl siding, create a series of five or 10 separate, but very short, videos, each of which will then be searchable separately on YouTube and Google, for example.

"By having shorter videos, people are more apt to watch them, plus producing a group of related videos makes them easier to find. This strategy can help you take over more of the top search rankings in your area. When you do this, make sure each video is optimized for your top keywords to enhance the results you experience."

Specialized Advice

IN THIS CHAPTER

- Learn more about what it takes to be successful on YouTube from Dan Dobi, director/producer of *Please Subscribe: A Documentary About YouTubers.*
- Get more tips for editing your videos from Jonathan Thomas, creator and programmer of OpenShot Video Editor.
- Learn more about avoiding copyright and trademark infringement from attorney Rachel Stilwell.
- Google's YouTube product manager, Eli Danzinger, offers his advice to small-business owners on utilizing YouTube.

This final chapter of the *Ultimate Guide to YouTube for Business* features interviews with YouTube experts on specific issues, including copyright and trademark infringement, the secret society of successful YouTubers, and what works for small business from a YouTube product manager's perspective.

Once you're done reading, it'll be time for you to tap your creativity, start thinking about your goals and strategies for YouTube, and then begin planning your own videos. YouTube is a very robust medium with few barriers to entry, so it's also crucial that you keep up with the latest YouTube tools and features, as well as digital trends and technologies.

DAN DOBI REVEALS THE SECRETS OF SUCCESSFUL YOUTUBERS

Producing video content for YouTube is vastly different than producing movies, TV shows, and commercials. TV networks, movie studios, Hollywood directors, as well as the world's most influential advertising agencies, public relations firms, and Fortune 500 companies, have all tried to produce YouTube videos, often without success.

In fact, it's often teenagers and young adults who create and star in the videos that ultimately go viral on YouTube and attract millions, or in a few cases, billions of views—without big budgets, state-of-the-art studio equipment, and often with very little experience.

The *Gangnam Style* music video is one example of a single video that's achieved more than 1 billion views. There are also a few companies, organizations (such as the NBA), recording artists (such as Lady Gaga and Justin Bieber), celebrities, and public figures who have YouTube channels that have earned in excess of 1 billion viewers thanks to all of a channel's individual video views combined.

There's an entire underground culture of YouTubers who have discovered how to capture the interest of the masses, often by producing videos from their bedrooms or basements. Producer and director Dan Dobi has managed to infiltrate this often secretive community.

In his documentary *Please Subscribe: A Documentary About YouTubers*, Dobi goes behind the scenes with some of the world's most well-known YouTubers and provides a unique look at what goes into becoming successful on YouTube.

Dobi, who has also produced music videos, is a successful YouTuber himself and has become good friends with many of the online personalities featured in his documentary. Here, he shares some of his experience and how small-business operators and entrepreneurs can apply it.

Rich: *How did the idea for* Please Subscribe: A Documentary About YouTubers *come about?*

Dobi: "I have been actively producing videos for YouTube for a number of years now, and found that it is driven by what I consider to be a secret society of YouTubers who are popular online, and who are making money producing and showcasing videos on the YouTube service. To establish yourself as a YouTuber who gets accepted within this secret society, you need to prove yourself online by creating videos that attract a tremendous amount of attention.

"Very few YouTubers are willing to share their secrets to success or teach others how to follow in their footsteps. While some of the popular YouTubers are able to generate a rather good income producing and sharing videos that cater to their audience, the majority of these people do it out of a passion for whatever it is they're making videos about, not for the money or even for the online fame.

"Over the years, I have become close friends with many YouTubers. At the same time, I have been fascinated by how the general public watches videos on YouTube but doesn't understand how ordinary people, like themselves, are able to become famous and financially successful by producing YouTube videos. And I discovered that more often than not, the successful YouTubers refrain from participating in interviews with the mainstream media.

"Through *Please Subscribe: A Documentary About YouTubers,* I wanted to share with the general public how I got interested in YouTube and tell the story of popular YouTubers. I think the YouTube community is a very special place, but it's something that few people truly understand. My goal with this documentary is to answer the questions, 'What is a YouTuber?' and 'What are their lives like?'"

What prompted you to become active on YouTube?

"I have produced and/or directed a lot of music videos and TV commercials for mainstream media outlets. What got me interested in YouTube is the fact that anyone can produce video content in HD quality and then share it with the world within minutes. This is truly an open forum that's available to anyone. Once a video is published, the general public can engage by directly sharing their thoughts and opinions about it.

"We are living in a generation where information can be shared immediately. For example, someone can record and edit a video clip on their iPhone and share it with the world in minutes from virtually anywhere there's a wireless internet connection. YouTube has become a DVR or on-demand video service that's always there and accessible to anyone with access to the internet from a wide range of devices."

In your documentary, you feature a handful of very successful YouTubers. What makes these people so successful?

"What I discovered is that those who are successful on YouTube are all entrepreneurs, but just random people with a video camera. They're all hustlers who work hard for their success, and who are extremely passionate about whatever it is they're producing videos about. All of the popular YouTubers have discovered the importance of creating and establishing their unique brand and running with it. Most YouTubers know that their success won't last forever, so they're working hard to take advantage of the opportunity they have right now to produce and share videos that they're passionate about.

"Another thing that I found that the most successful YouTubers have in common is that they all publish videos on a regular schedule, whether it's once a day or once per week. They're consistent, and their audience knows exactly what the new video release schedule is for their favorite YouTubers.

"In addition to sharing their schedule with their fans and subscribers, the most popular and successful YouTubers know their audience well and have inside jokes that they share with their viewers, and all are very active on social media networks. They'll also quickly respond to comments, questions, and emails sent to them through YouTube or via Facebook, Twitter, or their own websites. As a result, the popular YouTubers develop their own form of interaction with their followers, subscribers, and fans, and they do this very well.

"When someone watches a video produced by a popular YouTuber, and the viewer then writes a comment or emails a question, it should generate a prompt response. When this occurs, the viewer becomes a fan for life. All of the successful YouTubers have also discovered something that there is an audience for and that they're passionate about, and they're running with it."

While producing your documentary, what were some of the lessons you learned about YouTube?

"I would say that if you're going to become a YouTuber or you're a businessperson or entrepreneur looking to utilize YouTube, you cannot simply adopt the approach of uploading videos and hoping for the best. It's essential that within the videos themselves, when promoting them, and when interacting with your audience, you have to give it your all. You have to constantly discover new ways of reaching and retaining your audience. This is a highly competitive marketplace, and you can't afford to be complacent.

"Once you begin to establish popularity and momentum with your videos, you can't afford to sit back and relax, or people will quickly lose interest. Everything on YouTube has a shelf life. If you don't clean off the shelf periodically and keep your content relevant and fresh, your videos will simply get lost in cyberspace. Success on YouTube is all about keeping eyeballs on your YouTube Channel and not allowing your viewers to go anywhere else."

Is there a formula for producing a YouTube video that can help ensure its online success?

"The number-one thing about having a successful YouTube channel is being passionate about it. Don't just jump into something that you think people will like. Make sure you're producing videos around something that you absolutely love. Find something that you'd want to continue producing videos about even if you weren't being paid to do it. What do you love doing? What are you knowledgeable about that you love talking about with other people?

"Even if it's something like cooking or gardening, there's a massive hole out there on YouTube that you can fill by producing fun, entertaining, or informative videos that you're passionate about.

"I believe YouTube is a close-knit society. Yes, it's competitive, but it's also a community where many YouTubers can help each other out and work on collaborations together. This allows everyone to expand their audience. I recommend that people who produce videos on YouTube . . . become friendly with as many other YouTubers and YouTube video producers as possible, even if you're not a fan of each other's content. Consider sharing advice, resources, or collaborating on videos in a way that will help everyone expand their audience."

What advice would you give to a small-business owner or entrepreneur looking to produce YouTube videos for the first time?

"Figure out what you want to say within your videos, and then develop your unique voice. Again, the whole passion thing goes a long way. If you're passionate about what you're doing, you'll never have a shortage of things to say in your videos. Also, don't try to blend in with what others are doing.

"Be consistent with your audience and always encourage interaction. Just because you're producing videos for YouTube, as opposed to network TV, for example, take what you do very seriously, and then be prepared to wait. Some people will put up one video and it will go viral quickly. Others will need to produce many videos over time and slowly build an audience.

"Listen to your audience, but don't let them control your channel or content. Take constructive criticism into account, but understand there are a lot of idiots using YouTube who post nasty or harsh comments simply because they can. Those are the people you don't want to listen to.

"Also, invite comments for your videos, but don't allow mean comments get to you. You will get them. You need to realize that a lot of people who are on YouTube are teenagers. Posting comments on YouTube is their only way to experience a sense of power. Your best bet is to ignore nasty comments, and those people will eventually go away.

"If you start a YouTube Channel and it doesn't take off right away, that's OK. Be patient. There are going to be some bumps in the road. Figure out what you need to change, and take time to figure it all out. Then, once you figure out what works, be consistent."

Realistically, how long a period should someone expect for their YouTube channel to build an audience?

"There's no consistent answer to this question. It's different for everyone. Right from the start, I always recommend to people that they be prepared to invest two years of effort into a YouTube channel before they can declare it a huge success or epic failure.

"Every day, thousands of people come to Hollywood in hopes of making it big in the entertainment industry. For a lucky few, it happens quickly. For most, however, they have to pay their dues, stay dedicated, and work hard for a while before they get their big break. There are also many people who never make it. The same is true when it comes to producing videos for YouTube or becoming a YouTuber.

"I have met many YouTubers who became popular quickly because one particular event happened to introduce them to a broad audience. For example, one of Hanna Hart's first videos was featured on Reddit (a popular news article sharing service), and it instantly became popular. One year later, her YouTube channel had more than 31 million views and she had in excess of 328,000 subscribers. If she didn't get picked up initially by Reddit, it might have taken her months or years to gain the same level of popularity. Sometimes, things happen by chance that will impact a YouTube channel's success. It's not just about how much you spend to promote your videos, your production quality, or your content. You never truly know what people are going to like. It is true, however, that on YouTube, there is an audience for everything. You just need to find that audience."

Some companies have found that one way to reach a broad audience quickly is to hire a popular YouTuber to star in their videos or act as a spokesperson, or to pay for product placement in a famous YouTuber's videos. What advice can you share about this?

"Depending on how popular the YouTuber is, most now have representatives who handle their business affairs and serve as brokers between companies and the online personalities. Many also have managers, just like other performers. When it comes to hiring one of these people or arranging for product placement in their videos, the process happens just as it would when trying to hire a celebrity to be a spokesperson or when arranging for product placement within a TV show or movie.

"The popular YouTubers have extremely dedicated and loyal followers and subscribers. As a result, a company can benefit by using one of these online personalities to quickly and affordably tap into that online personality's audience."

What type of video production equipment do you recommend to entrepreneurs who are getting started on YouTube?

"A lot of people and companies are finding success using a midpriced digital SLR camera with a video mode. Nikon and Canon, for example, offer high-quality cameras that offer the features and flexibility needed to achieve professional-quality results from a video production. As far as lighting, I recommend Kino Flo Lighting Systems [www.kinoflo. com]. For a microphone and audio recording in conjunction with a video, I recommend the Zoom H4N [www.zoom.co.jp/english/products/h4n]. It is an excellent external recording device that allows you to produce fantastic audio results.

"As for video editing software, I personally use Final Cut Pro version 7. I have been using this software for more than a decade, and I am very loyal to it. I have produced and edited multimillion-dollar productions using Final Cut version 7 on a Mac. I believe it's as good as if not better than, the most recent versions of Adobe Premiere Pro CS6 or the Avid video editing tools. I think Final Cut Pro version 7 is the easiest, most efficient video editing software out there, and I will probably be using it for the next several years, until it becomes absolutely obsolete."

How is YouTube evolving?

"A lot of people and companies alike are using YouTube as a trampoline to get from point A to point B. It's my prediction that this trend will continue. There will be a lot of early adopters who will move on to other media formats and establish themselves there. For example, there are YouTube personalities who are being discovered by Hollywood or the recording industry, and who are launching more mainstream careers and leaving YouTube behind.

"There are also companies that are using YouTube for low-cost promotion and advertising until they grow large enough to pursue more costly and mainstream forms of advertising and marketing. At the same time, there is a fear that once someone becomes popular on YouTube, if they leave it for any reason, they'll quickly become irrelevant. There's some validity to this.

"As far as YouTube as a thing, it's only going to grow and get better. Companies and individuals are going to put better production value into their videos as expectations and demand from viewers increase. I also think more and more videos on YouTube are going to become more successful than popular network and cable TV shows, as far as audience size. As a result, more and more original programming will be put directly on YouTube as opposed to being broadcast on TV networks. Plus, I predict the movie rental business through YouTube is going to grow dramatically in the near future.

"I also foresee a new format of on-demand, commercially supported programming being produced exclusively for YouTube. The potential for what YouTube is capable of is only in its infancy, and what's yet to come will be truly exciting."

JONATHAN THOMAS, LEAD DEVELOPER OF OPENSHOT VIDEO EDITOR

As you discovered from Chapter 11, "Editing Your YouTube Videos," there are many software options available, and some are ideal for small-business owners or entrepreneurs with little or no video production experience, but who want to create professional-looking videos. Yet another option is OpenShot Video Editor, an open-source software developed by OpenShot Studios, LLC. It's available for free by visiting www.openshot.org.

OpenShot's owner and lead developer is Jonathan Thomas. Here, he discusses some of the options for using the OpenShot Video Editor or other editing software.

Rich: *What is the OpenShot Video Editor and how did the concept for it come about?*

Thomas: "I have more than 16 years of professional software development experience, and a passion for Linux and open-source software. I have successfully led an international team of developers and contributors while developing OpenShot, and deployed the software to hundreds of thousands of users around the world.

"Soon after I switched my operating system to Linux, I realized that there was no easy-to-use and stable video editor. After considering it for a while, I decided I would attempt to develop my own. I also decided to blog about the entire process, and be as transparent as possible. In retrospect, this was one of the best decisions I've ever made. I have met some truly great people that live all over the world, and it's opened many doors for me that would have otherwise remained shut.

"OpenShot started as a very simple editor, with only the most basic features. However, in recent years, some truly unique features, such as 3D animations, have been added."

Who is the target audience for OpenShot?

"The target audience for OpenShot is general computer users, small-business owners, entrepreneurs, moms and dads, and just normal people. I have tried my best to keep the interface simple and free of clutter. Many of the advanced features are only accessible by menus and right-click context menus, in order to keep the interface intuitive.

"Some of the features that OpenShot offers that our commercially available competition does not includes: 3D animated titles, particle effects (a type of visual special effect), custom transitions, and of course, open-source code, which can be modified and extended by anyone, including the users."

Why is OpenShot Video Editor offered for free, when other software costs hundreds of dollars?

"OpenShot is licensed GPLv3, which grants users permission to download, distribute, and even make changes to the source code, all free of charge. I like to think of it as my small donation to the world, and to the many people who cannot afford to buy expensive video editing software.

"Also, developing OpenShot as an open-source application allowed me to recruit developers and contributors, and many other people who volunteer their time and were critical in helping OpenShot achieve success."

How can OpenShot help a small business operator?

"OpenShot is very easy to learn and use, provides a great set of professional title templates, and supports most video and audio formats. Businesspeople who want to save time and save money should take a look at OpenShot."

What is the learning curve for using OpenShot?

"Many video editors follow a basic user interface pattern, and OpenShot is no different in that respect. However, most professional video editors have dozens of buttons, sliders, settings, and other interface elements on the screen at all times, providing a steep learning curve for new users. OpenShot has a very simple and clean interface, and is much easier to learn, yet it ultimately offers much of the same functionality as expensive video editing software."

What editing tips can you offer to make a video look more professional?

"I would suggest keeping it simple. White backgrounds are popular. When creating titles, use a white background with dark text, and leave lots of empty white space around the words in order to make your titles easy to read. Remember, many people who watch YouTube videos will be doing so from the small-size screen of their smartphone or tablet, and you want your titles and text to be readable.

"Most importantly, use a good video camera with good lighting, which can make the difference between an amateur video and a professional video."

What features of OpenShot should someone use to achieve the best possible results for their videos?

"I would suggest using the WebM video format, with a high video bit rate, which is supported on most web browsers and mobile devices. And, of course, use high-quality source video files."

What are some of the pitfalls a business owner might run into when using OpenShot?

"One of the most common pitfalls of producing web videos is finding good, legal music that does not violate the copyright of a musician or music publisher. There are some very good websites that provide Creative Commons licensed music, which can be free to use in many cases."

Which operating systems does OpenShot support?

"As of early 2013, OpenShot is currently available on Linux. It is currently in development for Mac and Windows. If you would like to learn more about the Mac and Windows versions, please follow our blog: www.openshotvideo.com."

What can we expect from OpenShot in the next 12 months?

"We are developing a new cross-platform video editing engine that will power the future Linux, Mac, and Windows versions of OpenShot. It has many more professional features, especially in the animation and compositing aspects.

"The new video editing engine we're developing can also be used by web developers and integrated into websites to provide web-based video editing capabilities, thumbnailing, video transcoding, and other automated video editing tasks."

ASK FOR PERMISSION, NOT FOR FORGIVENESS

For many people, one of the most confusing aspects of producing YouTube videos is figuring out what they can and can't legally incorporate in productions: video clips, photos, graphics, animations, music, sound effects, and other audio content.

YouTube has gone to great lengths to help video producers understand what's permissible by publishing the YouTube *Community Guidelines* (www.youtube.com/t/community_guidelines). And it's always implementing new ways to automatically scan all new video content for copyright and trademark violations.

YouTube's own online community of users actively patrols the service and can report violations by clicking on the flag-shaped Report icon that's displayed below every video. Violators will be flagged and the video—or the subscriber's entire YouTube channel—risk being taken offline.

In this interview, Rachel Stilwell, an attorney with the firm Gladstone, Michel, Weisberg, Willner & Sloane, shares some useful legal advice on the rules of the road.

Rich: *How do you help companies and entrepreneurs protect themselves?*

Stilwell: "In a nutshell, I advise companies on how to avoid infringing on copyrights and trademarks that belong to others. For example, I have advised my clients to obtain licenses for the use of all copyrightable works perceptible in the proposed video, unless the client owns those works.

"For example, one client wanted to utilize a recording of a popular song as background music in his company's video. I advised him that he needed to obtain two licenses—one for the sound recording, and another for the underlying musical composition that has been recorded.

"I dissuaded another client from utilizing an unlicensed photograph showing how their product was utilized. I had to explain that while they owned the product shown in the photo, they didn't own the photo itself and needed permission to include it in the video they wanted to produce. They didn't know who owned the copyright in the photo at issue, and decided it was cheaper to hire a photographer to take a new photograph of the product. I then drafted a 'work made for hire' agreement, whereby my client and the new photographer agreed that my client would own the copyright in the new photograph."

What should video producers know about displaying company logos or other trademarks?

"I advise clients that their videos should not mention or display trademarks that don't belong to them, unless they have received permission from that mark's owner. If my clients need help obtaining the applicable licenses, I help them obtain those licenses."

What if one of your clients discovers that their video content has been used by another party?

"I have sent many takedown notices to YouTube at my clients' request, complaining to YouTube that posted videos infringe on my clients' copyrights and trademarks. Those notices demand that YouTube promptly remove the videos containing my clients' infringing content.

"Occasionally, I correspond with individual YouTube users, explaining how posting videos with my client's unlicensed content is unlawful and subject to criminal and civil liability. Sometimes that requires educating another small-business owner who means well, but who doesn't understand that he/she needs a license in order to use my client's intellectual property."

What legal issues should a small-business operator consider before publishing YouTube videos?

"If you want to use somebody else's intellectual property in your video, then you're going to need to get the owner's permission for that use. If you don't want to go to the trouble, and perhaps the expense, of getting a license, then don't use intellectual property in your video that belongs to someone else. Otherwise you open yourself to risk of substantial liability for money damages.

"The civil penalties for infringement can be fierce, and litigation itself is never a cheap endeavor. Many entrepreneurs want to argue that they are using someone else's intellectual property in such a fleeting manner that it constitutes 'fair use,' or is otherwise harmless. I advise my clients that you can't tell whether a court would decide whether your video is 'fair use' until such time that you are already stuck in very expensive litigation.

"The entrepreneurial spirit often gravitates to the old adage, 'It's better to ask forgiveness rather than permission.' With respect to the use of intellectual property, following such advice is a very risky prospect."

What are the biggest legal mistakes that you've seen companies make?

"The most common mistake that small businesses make is to not think about whether they need a license to use someone else's intellectual property. For example, a concert venue recorded live performances of bands playing at their venue, and then posted those videos on YouTube in order to promote the venue to future audiences. I represented the band. The venue recorded and posted the performance videos without permission from either the band or the writers of the songs being played.

"The venue had previously contracted with ASCAP, a performing-rights organization that provides licenses to businesses who want to publicly perform songs. Consequently, the venue believed that it had a license 'to play music.'

"However, since the posted videos didn't include sound recordings owned by a record label, the venue assumed that they didn't need any further licenses. In fact, since YouTube videos are watched on demand online, a 'sync license' is needed for each song performed in a video, and the ASCAP license doesn't cover on-demand videos, like YouTube, at all.

"Moreover, the band's performance was recorded and posted without the band's permission. That's 'bootlegging,' which is unlawful. Bootlegging is distinct from copyright infringement, but is still subject to substantial civil liability. Just because the venue hired the band to play a live performance, this doesn't mean that the venue automatically acquired a license to record and distribute that performance."

What were the consequences for the venue?

"That venue got lucky. I just sent a cease-and-desist letter on behalf of my client, and once the venue learned that their ASCAP license didn't grant them the right to upload unlicensed performance videos, they stopped the practice.

"Because of the large number of songs and performances involved, the venue could have been liable for hundreds of thousands of dollars in damages, plus substantial attorney fees. They asked forgiveness, and my client granted it in this case, because it was a one-time instance of infringement, and the venue discontinued the practice as soon as it learned that it was violating my client's rights.

"However, my client could have chosen to sue the venue and would have had a very good claim for copyright infringement and bootlegging. Defending such a lawsuit would have been an expensive proposition for the venue."

What does a small-business operator need to know to avoid copyright infringement when using logos and/or music in a video?

"Using a logo that doesn't belong to you is more likely to be trademark infringement than copyright infringement. However, if a logo is visible in the background of a video, it may not actually constitute trademark infringement; that is, if the appearance of the logo is not likely to confuse members of the public about identifying the source of goods or services.

"I always counsel clients to avoid having logos in the background of their videos if permission for such use hasn't been granted by the logo's owner. Defending frivolous lawsuits can be just as expensive as defending lawsuits in which the plaintiff has a valid claim.

"The same goes for avoiding copyright infringement with respect to music;, artwork, including still photographs; and sometimes text, as well. If that intellectual property doesn't belong to you but you want to use it in your video, I recommend consulting an attorney with copyright expertise to discuss how to obtain a license."

What are the consequences for using music or other content without permission?

"Damages can range from very little to as much as $150,000 *per infringed work*, plus attorney fees and court costs. The attorney fees for which you might be liable are not just your own. Potentially the infringer could be liable for the plaintiff's attorney fees as well. So copyright infringement can be very expensive. The owner of an infringed work may also be entitled to injunctive relief, i.e., preventing you from using the infringing video that you may have produced at great expense."

How can a YouTube producer protect himself if someone steals his content or copyrighted materials?

"Assuming the producer is the owner of the copyright in work(s) infringed by virtue of having been distributed on YouTube, the producer can send YouTube a written demand that YouTube promptly remove the infringing content. An easy way to do this is to fill out a form provided by YouTube at the following link: www.youtube.com/yt/copyright/copyright-complaint.html.

"If this form is properly filled out and submitted by the copyright owner of a work that has been infringed on YouTube, then under certain provisions of the Digital Millennium Copyright Act [DMCA], YouTube is legally required to promptly remove that content, or else risk liability for contributory infringement.

"Since YouTube very much wants to avoid liability for the behavior of its users, YouTube has a very good track record of promptly removing content that it has been notified is infringing. In my experience, YouTube usually removes such materials within a day.

"Getting YouTube to remove one's infringing content may not prevent other YouTube users from reposting the video at a later date, however. Keeping your content off YouTube may require repeated monitoring, as well as the searching of YouTube's site, and then sending multiple take-down notices.

"You can always send a note directly to the YouTube user that uploaded the infringing video by using YouTube's 'Send Message' function after logging onto to YouTube, and then by double-clicking on that person's username. In the email you send, you can claim ownership of the copyright or other intellectual property in the video that has been infringed. You can also indicate that if that user continues to infringe your works, you will consider taking legal action. But since that message is sent through YouTube's system, you'll have no way of confirming that the infringer received your communication.

"In order to get an infringing YouTube user's real email address and other contact information, as supplied to YouTube by the user, you might have to actually file suit and subpoena that information from YouTube. That's expensive. Plus, even having a subpoena might not be successful if the infringing content has already been removed by YouTube.

"Unfortunately for copyright owners, the current system under the DMCA 'safe harbor provisions' creates a game of whack-a-mole, whereby copyright owners may have to send many take-down notices about a single video that has been posted on YouTube many times. If you notice that there is a particular user who repeatedly reposts the same video of yours in an infringing manner, be sure to allege to YouTube that such an account belongs to a 'repeat infringer,' and demand that YouTube enforce its terms of service and disable that user's account. If you find that your works are being infringed on YouTube or elsewhere often, it's time to consult a lawyer with expertise in copyright law."

What other legal issues should a small-business owner consider when publishing videos on YouTube or using Facebook, Twitter, etc.?

"Be sure not to use anyone's name, likeness, voice, or signature to promote your products or services without the consent of that person. Doing so can violate that person's 'right of publicity,' and under certain circumstances may also invoke federal Lanham Act claims.

"Don't upload videos of musical performances without the consent of the performers. Besides potential copyright issues with respect to the video and underlying songs, the performances of the band are protected by federal and sometimes state anti-bootlegging statutes.

"Also, keep your message positive in nature. If anything in your video could be construed as defamatory, seek the advice of a lawyer before including it in your video."

If someone publishes videos on YouTube, do they need to do anything special to protect their rights?

"Whether your copyrighted material is published on YouTube or elsewhere, it's always a good idea to register your works with the United States Copyright Office. Doing so is relatively inexpensive, and usually doesn't require a lawyer's advice. For more information on copyright basics and the benefits of registering your copyright, go to: www.copyright.gov.

If a company has a problem with an online stalker or someone harassing them with inappropriate comments, what recourse to they have?

"YouTube's hub for defamation claims can be found here: http://support.google.com/youtube/bin/request.py?contact_type=defamation. If you send a defamation complaint to YouTube and they don't respond in a day or two, consider hiring an attorney to help.

"There's also a growing and disturbing trend involving 'online impersonation' in social media. This is a particularly insidious form of defamation, and it can affect businesses as well as individual people."

Do you have any other advice for a small-business operator for protecting themselves when using YouTube?

"It's a good practice to consult with an attorney familiar with intellectual property and discuss an outline or treatment for your video before you go to the trouble and expense of producing it. Doing this will allow you and your attorney to troubleshoot any needed clearances ahead of time. Under those circumstances, you can always make informed decisions about whether to change your background music, artwork, and other content. Also, if you have questions about registering your copyrights prior to publishing your video, your lawyer can talk you through that process."

How are laws covering online activities changing?

"Relevant case law in the last few years has revolved around the extent to which YouTube and other 'ISPs,' as defined by the DMCA, can avoid liability for infringing works that are posted and accessed by users. The key issues involve the extent to which the ISP, such as YouTube, knows about specific allegedly infringing activity and fails to remove that allegedly infringing material.

"But when a user copies and distributes someone else's copyrighted video or underlying copyrightable material without the consent of the owner of the copyright, you can expect going forward that such activity will be deemed infringement for which the infringer risks substantial liability."

YOUTUBE PRODUCT MANAGER ELI DANZINGER SHARES HIS ADVICE

To wrap up the *Ultimate Guide to YouTube for Business,* we went to Eli Danzinger, a YouTube product manager at Google—which owns YouTube—for advice and strategies from the company responsible for creating and growing the global YouTube phenomenon.

Rich: *What advice do you have for a small-business owner who knows what YouTube is, but doesn't yet understand how to utilize it?*

Danzinger: "My biggest piece of advice is that no matter what your business is, you can find your audience on YouTube. The scale of YouTube is absolutely massive. On the YouTube website, we offer a lot of resources and online help for small-business operators so they can learn how to leverage YouTube as part of their online strategy.

"Knowing that your audience can be found on YouTube, it's important to get started using it sooner than later. What we have tried to do with YouTube is make it super accessible and very easy for businesses to get started using video. Compared to producing video for TV, for example, YouTube is much more accessible, and its power is absolutely incredible when it comes to helping you find and communicate with your audience. The first step is to just get started, because your audience is online waiting for you."

What are some of the really innovative ways that you've seen small businesses utilize YouTube?

"When you first start learning about using video, a lot of what you'll hear says that you need a video to go viral in order to be successful. I think that's a huge misconception. There are countless examples of businesses that have been extremely successful on YouTube, without their videos going viral.

"Companies can and should use YouTube to communicate their message to their target audience, and then work to build that audience by posting new content consistently. Using video, you can describe and showcase your products, for example, in an effort to reach new viewers. There is no need for a video to go viral for you to achieve these objectives. Even if you reach only a few thousand very targeted viewers with your message, that can be extremely valuable.

"I recommend that companies develop a very clear vision for the message that they want to communicate, and then figure out the best way to go out and share that message using video."

Is there a good or bad approach to take when filming videos for YouTube? For example, there's a consensus that an infomercial-style approach typically doesn't work.

"I think that it's important for every company that uses YouTube to find their own voice. Being able to explain your company, its products, and its services very clearly is really one of the most important things that a small business can do on YouTube. I don't believe that falls into the infomercial category.

"The most successful videos on YouTube tend to lead with quality content and not with a sales pitch. Create videos that you would want to watch."

How important is production quality when producing YouTube videos?

"I don't think having low-end video production equipment is a barrier to entry at all. We have seen businesses being really successful on YouTube after producing their videos with inferior video and audio equipment.

"Once again, I'd refer people to the 'Achieving Your Goals' help section of YouTube [www.youtube.com/yt/advertise/your-objectives.html], where we offer a ton of tips and tricks for producing videos on a low budget. What your video lacks in production quality, however, it needs to make up for in content."

…os that "engage the viewer" is a phrase you hear a lot when referring to producing …at are your thoughts on this?

creating content that you yourself would want to … second largest internet search engine in the world. …e searching for content, such as how-to videos, product …mos. If you put yourself in the shoes of your audience, the …for more information about the sort of products and services … can more easily create really engaging content that targets that

…ent is very important in a video. First, focus on getting your message out …ideo to get your hook in early. Then create content that will appeal directly …ence."

…easily avoidable mistakes that you've seen small-business owners make?

…hat it's really important to pay attention to your YouTube Channel and to think of it as your home on YouTube. The way that small businesses have traditionally engaged an audience with video is to put a paid, 30- or 60-second TV spot on local TV.

"You can do that on TV, or use that same commercial content online using YouTube's AdWords for Video [www.youtube.com/watch?v=jjJaNbMN6-g]. But the most effective way to utilize YouTube is to think of your channel page as the home for all of your content so that you can take advantage of the organic searches and the engages you'll get for your content. You can then use paid advertising and promotion to drive viewership to that channel page.

Do you have recommendations about a video's ideal length?

"I would say that you should target your video length to communicate your message, and don't go any further than that. On the videos that you promote using paid promotions via AdWords for Video, for example, I would say that shorter is almost always better.

"Think about the way you use YouTube yourself. You don't typically want to sit through a 10-minute-long video before you get to the content you're trying to watch. I strongly recommend that when planning and producing your videos, you find ways to generate interest very early in each video and then take only as long as you need to convey your message."

Most businesspeople publish videos on YouTube in hopes that it will go viral and be seen by millions of viewers. Is there a proven formula for producing a viral video?

"I don't believe that there is any one secret formula for producing a video that goes viral. If there were a formula, I would be out making those videos, along with everyone else. The viral videos all tend to be funny, interesting, and engaging, but that's a very broad description.

"Again, the small businesses that are the most successful on YouTube are not the ones that are swinging for the fences in hopes of creating a viral hit. Instead, they're the ones that speak to their audience using interesting and engaging content, and that have a lot of content on their channel page that's fresh, engaging, and that their audience can continue to consume."

Is there an approach to a YouTube video that is different from a TV commercial or infomercial that tends to work well for small businesses?

"I think there is a lot of great stuff that you can do with video on YouTube that is not possible using any other medium, including TV. For example, we give you super-detailed information about how your videos and related ads perform, and have great online-based tools for video editing, captioning, creating annotations, and embedding links within videos. You can be really, really scientific about the videos you ultimately create. I would recommend that as you get started using YouTube, you invest the time to learn how to utilize these tools and resources, which are available directly from YouTube. Once you know how to use the tools, utilize the heck out of them.

"Within the videos themselves, I think annotations are a feature that often go underutilized. You can also use your YouTube Analytics information to study the performance of each video and see where the engagement peaks, ebbs, and flows. As you study engagement, you can tweak your videos accordingly.

"There is no perfect formula, video format, or shooting style to follow. However, we do give you the right tools to make the perfect video for your audience and for the message that you're trying to convey."

For someone first learning to use YouTube, figuring out the specifics of YouTube Analytics can be a daunting task. What recommendations can you offer?

"YouTube offers a free advertiser playbook online [www.youtube.com/yt/advertise] that offers an introduction to YouTube Analytics and that discusses why these tools are useful. You'll also discover how to fully utilize these tools, based on your own needs and goals.

"For me, one of the most interesting features of YouTube Analytics is the ability to view the performance of each video, study your audience, and discover where interest within that video changes or drops off. You can actually see a histogram that shows viewership over time for a particular video, and discover exactly at what point in the video that people are losing interest. Knowing this information, you can tweak the video to continue engaging those viewers and improve the experience of people who are viewing your content."

NOW GO AND EXPLOIT THE POWER OF YOUTUBE

Now that you've got the tools you need to begin using YouTube, step back, think about your own business, its customers and clients and your core message, and then start developing creative videos that will convey that message to your audience.

Remember, your audience is already online and using YouTube from their desktop computers, notebook computers, tablets, smartphones, and internet-enabled TV sets. Now you need to find them and cater to their wants and needs with your video content.

Appendix

Appendix

Resources

CHROMA KEY (GREEN SCREEN) SOFTWARE

123 Video Magic—www.123videomagic.com

Magix—www.magix.com

NCH Software—www.nchsoftware.com

Pinnacle Studio—www.pinnaclesys.com

COPYRIGHT-RELATED WEBSITES

Library of Congress' Copyright website—www.copyright.gov

Take the Mystery out of Copyright—www.loc.gov/teachers/copyrightmystery

YouTube Community Guidelines—www.youtube.com/t/community_
guidelines

YouTube's Copyright Help Center—(www.youtube.com/t/howto_
copyright

YouTube Creative Commons Information—www.youtube.com/t/
creative_commons

MISCELLANEOUS RESOURCES

AOL—http://on.aol.com

Blinkx—www.blinkx.com

eLance.com—www.elance.com

Google Search Engine Optimization Starter Guide—http://static.googleusercontent.com/
external_content/untrusted_dlcp/www.google.com/en/us/webmasters/docs/search-
engine-optimization-starter-guide.pdf

Levenger Storyboard Paper—www.levenger.com/Special-Request-Storyboard--3-Ring-
Ltr-Core-8098.aspx

Moleskine Storyboard Pads—www.moleskine.com/us/collections/model/
product?id=59317#

Nextag.com—www.nextag.com

The UPS Store—www.theupsstore.com

TubeMogul—www.tubemogul.com/solutions/playtime/brandsights

U.S. Postal Service P.O. Boxes—www.usps.com/manage/get-a-po-box.htm

ONLINE ADVERTISING

Bing Ads—http://advertise.bingads.microsoft.com

Facebook Ads—www.facebook.com/ads/create

Google AdWords—www.google.com/adwords

Google AdWords Express—www.google.com/adwords/express

Yahoo! Search Advertising—http://advertising.yahoo.com/article/search-advertising.
html

ONLINE SERVICES

Google+ (Hangouts)—www.google.com/+

GoToMeeting—www.gotomeeting.com

LiveStream—www.livestream.com

Pixability (YouTube Research)—https://app.pixability.com/radar

TweetAdder Software—www.tweetadder.com

Viewbox—www.viewbox.com

Vimeo—www.vimeo.com

Virool—www.virool.com

YouNow—www.younow.com

YouTube—www.youtube.com

YouTube Buzz—www.youtubebuzz.com

PROMOTIONAL MERCHANDISE MANUFACTURERS

Bands on a Budget—www.bandsonabudget.com

Big Cartel—www.bigcartel.com

CafePress—www.cafepress.com

District Lines—www.districtlines.com

Topspin Media—www.topspinmedia.com

SCRIPT WRITING SOFTWARE

Celtx—www.celtx.com

Final Draft 8—www.finaldraft.com/products/final-draft

Movie Magic Screenwriter 6—www.screenplay.com

Script Writing Software Resources—http://en.wikipedia.org/wiki/List_of_
screenwriting_software

VIDEO EDITING SOFTWARE AND SERVICES

Adobe Premiere—www.adobe.com/products/premiere.html

Adobe's Creative Suite 6 Production Premium—www.adobe.com/products/
creativesuite/production.html

Apple Final Cut Pro X—www.apple.com/finalcutpro

Apple iMovie Software—www.apple.com/ilife/imovie

Avid—www.avid.com/US/categories/Professional-Video-Editing-Finishing

Camtasia—www.techsmith.com/camtasia.html

Ezvid Video Editor—www.ezvid.com

Microsoft Movie Maker—http://windows.microsoft.com/en-US/windows-live/movie-maker-get-started

Microsoft PowerPoint—http://office.microsoft.com/en-us/powerpoint

Movavi Screen Capture Studio for Business—www.movavi.com/screen-capture

OpenShot Video Editor—www.openshot.org

WeVideo.com—www.wevideo.com

Wondershare Video Editor—www.wondershare.net/ad/video-editor-win

YouTube Video Editor—www.youtube.com/editor

VIDEO PRODUCTION EQUIPMENT

Adorama—www.adorama.com

ATS Rentals—www.atsrentals.com

B&H Photo-Video—www.bhphotovideo.com

Borrow Lenses—www.borrowlenses.com/category/Video

Full Compass—www.fullcompass.com

Gekko Technology—www.gekkolite.com

Gitzo—www.gitzo.com

Glidecam Industries—www.glidecam.com

GoPro—www.gopro.com

HD Rental—www.hdrental.com

International Supplies—www.internationalsupplies.com

JAG35—www.jag35.com

Joby—www.joby.com

K 5600 Lighting—www.k5600.com

Kino Flo Lighting Systems—www.kinoflo.com

Libec—www.libecsales.com

Liquid Image—www.liquidimageco.com

Logitech—www.logitech.com

Lowel—www.lowel.com

Manfrotto—www.manfrotto.com; www.manfrotto.us

NewPro Video—http://newprovideo.com

OneQuality.com—www.onequality.com

PhotoBasics—http://fjwestcott.com/photobasics

PhotoLite—ww2.photolite.com

Radiant Images—www.radiantimages.com

Redrock Micro—http://store.redrockmicro.com

Rule—www.rule.com

Slik—www.thkphoto.com/products/slik

Splashcam—www.splashcam.com/underwater_video_cameras.htm

Studio 1 Productions—www.studio1productions.com

Sunpak—www.sunpak.jp/english/

Tiffen Company—www.tiffen.com

UsedAV.com—www.usedav.com

Vanguard—www.vanguardworld.com

VIDEO PRODUCTION MAGAZINES AND WEBSITES

HDVideoPro—www.hdvideopro.com

Reviewed.com—www.reviewed.com

Kelby Training—http://kelbytraining.com/online/courses/video

Studio Daily—www.studiodaily.com

The DV Show—www.thedvshow.com

Videography—www.creativeplanetnetwork.com/videography

VIDEO PRODUCTION MUSIC

Getty Images Music—www.gettyimages.com/music

Killer Tracks—www.killertracks.com

Music for Productions—www.musicforproductions.com

Premium Beat—www.premiumbeat.com/production-music

Reserve Music—www.reservemusic.com

StockMusic.net—www.stockmusic.net

VOICE-OVER ARTIST TALENT AGENCIES

Agent 99 Voice Talent—www.agent99voicetalent.com

Amazing Voice talent—http://amazingvoicetalent.com

Internet Jock—www.internetjock.com

Muzak—www.muzak.com/sprints/voice_over

Radio Voice Imaging—www.radiovoiceimaging.com

Voice Talent—www.voicetalent.com

Voice Talent Now—http://store.voicetalentnow.com

YOUTUBE-RELATED WEB LINKS

Video Online Complaint Form—http://support.google.com/youtube/bin/answer. py?hl=en&answer=140536

YouTube Analytics—www.youtube.com/yt/advertise/youtube-analytics.html

YouTube Captions—http://support.google.com/youtube/bin/answer. py?hl=en&answer=100079

YouTube Community Guidelines—www.youtube.com/t/community_guidelines

YouTube Creator Clubs—www.youtube.com/yt/creators/creator-clubs.html

YouTube Partners Support—http://support.google.com/youtube/bin/answer. py?hl=en&answer=72855#US

About the Author

Jason R. Rich (www.JasonRich.com) is the bestselling author of more than 55 books, covering a wide range of topics, including ecommerce, online marketing, digital photography, interactive entertainment, as well as the Apple iPhone and iPad.

He's also a frequent contributor to numerous national magazines, major daily newspapers, and popular websites, and serves as a marketing/public relations consultant to businesses.

Some of his recently published books include: *Blogging for Fame and Fortune* (Entrepreneur Press), *How To Do Everything with Digital Photography* (McGraw-Hill), *Your iPad At Work: 3rd Edition* (Que), *iPad and iPhone Tips and Tricks: 2nd Edition* (Que), and *How To Do Everything iPhone 5* (McGraw-Hill). You can follow Jason Rich on Twitter (@JasonRich7).

Index